IN SEARCH OF
GENGHIS KHAN

IN SEARCH OF GENGHIS KHAN

Tim Severin

Photography by
Paul Harris

ATHENEUM · NEW YORK · 1992

MAXWELL MACMILLAN INTERNATIONAL
NEW YORK · OXFORD · SINGAPORE · SYDNEY

Atheneum
Macmillan Publishing Company
866 Third Avenue
New York, NY 10022

Macmillan Publishing Company is part of the Maxwell Communication Group of Companies.

Library of Congress Cataloging-in-Publication Data
Severin, Timothy.
    In search of Genghis Khan / Tim Severin ; photography by Paul
Harris. — 1st American ed.
        p.   cm.
    ISBN 0-689-12134-2
    1. Mongolia—Description and travel.   2. Mongols—History.
3. Genghis Khan, 1162–1227.   I. Title.
DS798.2.S49   1992
951'.7—dc20   91-33870   CIP

Macmillan books are available at special discounts for bulk purchases for sales promotions, premiums, fund-raising, or educational use. For details. contact:

Special Sales Director
Macmillan Publishing Company
866 Third Avenue
New York, NY 10022

First American edition 1992

10 9 8 7 6 5 4 3 2 1

Printed in the United States of America

Contents

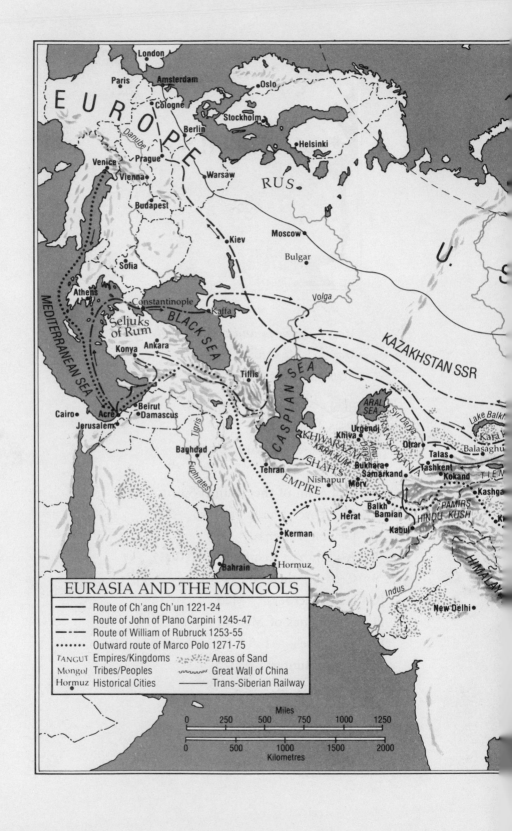

EURASIA AND THE MONGOLS

——————	Route of Ch'ang Ch'un 1221-24
– – – –	Route of John of Plano Carpini 1245-47
–·–·–·	Route of William of Rubruck 1253-55
··········	Outward route of Marco Polo 1271-75
TANGUT	Empires/Kingdoms
Mongol	Tribes/Peoples
Hormuz	Historical Cities

Areas of Sand

Great Wall of China

Trans-Siberian Railway

Miles

0   250   500   750   1000   1250

Kilometres

0   500   1000   1500   2000

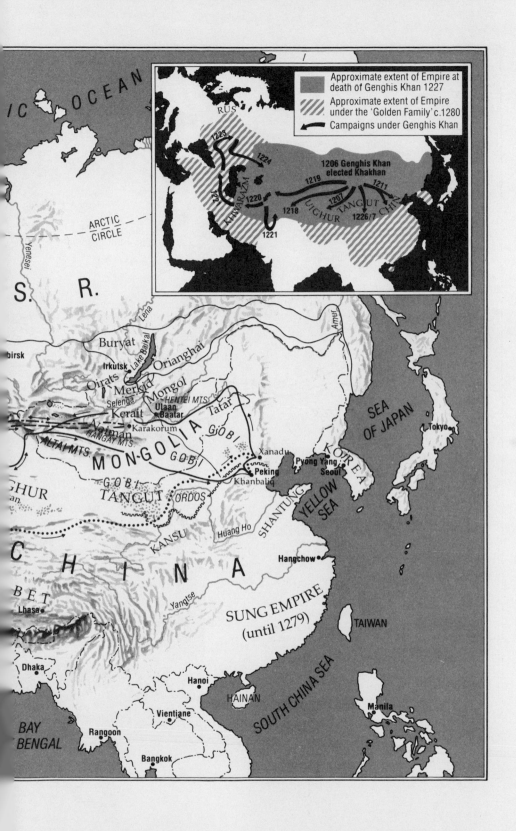

Approximate extent of Empire at death of Genghis Khan 1227

Approximate extent of Empire under the 'Golden Family' c.1280

Campaigns under Genghis Khan

RUS

1223

1224

1206 Genghis Khan elected Khakhan

1219

1211

1227

KHWARAZM

1220

1207

TANGUT

CHIN

1218

UIGHUR

1226/7

1221

ARCTIC OCEAN

ARCTIC CIRCLE

Yenesei

S. S. R.

Lena

Buryat

Irkutsk

Lake Baikal

Orianghai

Oirats

Merkid

Mongol

Selenga

HENTEI MTS.

Kerait

Ulaan Baatar

Tatar

Naiman

Karakorum

ALTAI MTS.

HANGAY MTS.

MONGOLIA

GOBI

GOBI

GOBI

Amur

Xanadu

KOREA

SEA OF JAPAN

Tokyo

Pyong Yang

Seoul

Peking

Khanbaliq

YELLOW SEA

UIGHUR

TANGUT

ORDOS

SHANTUNG

KANSU

Huang Ho

CHINA

Hangchow

TIBET

Lhasa

Yangtse

SUNG EMPIRE (until 1279)

TAIWAN

Dhaka

Hanoi

HAINAN

SOUTH CHINA SEA

Manila

BAY BENGAL

Rangoon

Vientiane

Bangkok

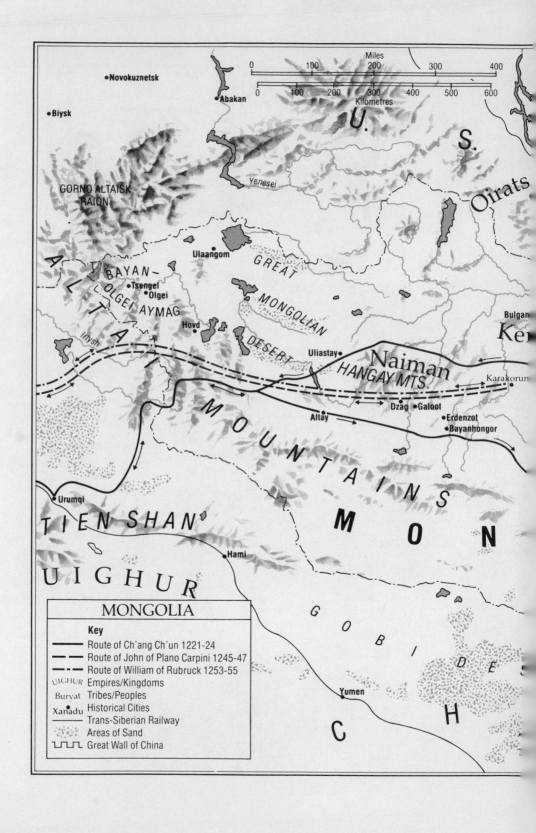

Novokuznetsk

Abakan

Biysk

U. S.

Oirats

Yenesei

GORNO ALTAISK RAION

ALTAI

Ulaangom

GREAT

BAYAN-

Tsengel

OLGEI

Olgei

AYMAG

Hovd

MONGOLIAN

DESERT

Irtysh

Uliastay

Bulgan

Ker

Naiman

HANGAY MTS.

Karakorun

MOUNTAINS

Dzag Galoot

Altay

Erdenzot

Bayanhongor

Urumqi

TIEN SHAN

M O N

UIGHUR

Hami

G O B I   D E

Yumen

C

H

MONGOLIA

Key

—— Route of Ch'ang Ch'un 1221–24

—·— Route of John of Plano Carpini 1245–47

—··— Route of William of Rubruck 1253–55

UIGHUR Empires/Kingdoms

Buryat Tribes/Peoples

Xanadu Historical Cities

—— Trans-Siberian Railway

Areas of Sand

Great Wall of China

Miles

0   100   200   300   400

0   100 200 300 400 500 600

Kilometres

Acknowledgments

would like to express my gratitude to those who made possible my travels in Mongolia. At the head of the list comes Deputy Foreign Minister H. Olzvoi (now Mongolian Ambassador in Beijing). As Chairman of the Mongolian National Committee for the Silk Roads Project he smoothed my path and offered help whenever it was needed. His colleague, Ambassador Ishetsogian Ochirbal and his staff at the London Embassy, set me on the right track, and from the UNESCO headquarters in Paris came the enthusiastic support of Doudou Diene, Eiji Hattori, and their office for the Integral Study of the Silk Roads.

Sirin Akiner of the School of African and Oriental Studies was generous in providing contacts throughout Central Asia. Nicolas Wolfers, Group Adviser to the International Department of the Midland Bank, thoughtfully put me in touch with another banker, Dugersurengiin Sukherdene, then with the Mongolian State Bank, who helped with my initial arrangements in Ulaan Baatar. His sister Ho'elun acted as interpreter. Hamish Hamilton of Buffalo gave me warm clothing and sleeping bags suitable for Mongolia in early May, and the firm of Timberland kindly provided boots and jackets.

In Moscow help came from the Mongolian Embassy, particularly from the jovial Cultural Counsellor Buandelgereen Borhondoi, and I could not have managed without the interpreting skills of Tanya Rachmanova.

The roll call of those who gave assistance in Mongolia includes: Academician Bira; Chulunny Ganbold of the Friendship Societies; Mr. Davaa of the Mongolian Horse Association; Mr. Chimidorj, Mr. Ganbat, and Mr. Gansukh from the Ministry of Foreign Affairs; Bumbyn Ganbaatar, Damdinsuren Yundendorj, sound recordist Tserendjav, and Mrs. Ishkhand all of Mongolian TV Film Studio who helped with the documentary filming. And then, of course, there were the dozens of *arats* who acted as guides and mentors during the ride. To them, in particular, I would like to say thank you very much indeed for revealing the *altan ov,* their "golden heritage."

The family of Doc Boshigt is owed a very special mention for the generous and open hospitality they extended to me and Paul Harris in Ulaan Baatar. And to David Allen of DHL I would like to say how very grateful I am for his imaginative and generous financial donation based on the link between the worldwide operations of the DHL company and the remarkable achievements of the medieval Mongol courier network.

Two of the leading Western authorities on Mongol imperial history, Dr. Peter Jackson and Dr. David Morgan, were kind enough to read through my text and alert me to the worst of my errors. Those mistakes which remain are my own fault, though it is reassuring to learn that I am not alone in proposing that the Mongols were responsible for bringing the Black Death to Europe.

TIM SEVERIN
COUNTY CORK, IRELAND

IN SEARCH OF
GENGHIS KHAN

1

In the Year
of the Horse

At the Hour of the Silver Horse, on the Day of the Black
Horse, in the Month of the Horse, and in the Year of the
White Horse we—six Mongols, Paul, and I—set out. A Westerner would have said that our departure took place between 2 and 3
o'clock in the afternoon, Central Mongolian Time, on 16 July 1990,
and it would have been reasonable to suppose that the starting date
had been scientifically calculated. Under normal circumstances it
should, for example, have taken into account whether we had given
ourselves enough lead time to select and train the horses and get them
fit, whether we had been able to field-test the different items of
equipment like the new tent and the special antique saddles, and
whether we would be setting out early enough so that we would
finish our trip before the winter snow.

But this was not how my Mongol companions had made their
choice. "When do we start?" I had asked six months earlier in Ulaan
Baatar, Mongolia's capital. Ariunbold, a Mongolian journalist whose
name means "True Steel," opened his diary. I noticed that it listed
both the Roman calendar and the Chinese year. He riffled through
the pages, then stuck his finger against a date, seemingly at random.
"Here," he announced. "This is a good day—July the sixteenth." I
did not venture to voice my doubts on his method of selection.

1

Ariunbold was supposed to be organizing the timetable for the venture, and at least I had a firm date to work to, or so I thought.

"Then it is settled," I said carefully via the interpreter, so that there should be no misunderstanding. "We begin the main journey on July the sixteenth. I will come back to Mongolia well before then so that I can help with the last-minute preparations." As the interpreter translated my words, I saw I had said something wrong. Ariunbold shifted uncomfortably in his seat. "Well," he replied in embarrassment. "Let us say that we will *probably* begin on July the sixteenth." He noticed the exasperated look on my face. "You see, Mongols believe that when you are intending to make a long journey by horse, it is very bad luck to fix the exact day of departure. If you are too precise, it can bring misfortune."

This expedition, I realized, was going to be different from anything I had undertaken before.

In previous journeys I had tracked the steps of Marco Polo by motorcycle, crossed the North Atlantic in the replica of a medieval leather boat to test if Irish monks like St. Brendan the Navigator might have reached the shores of North America 1000 years before Columbus, built the replica of an 8th-century Arab sailing ship and sailed her from Muscat to China to examine the origins of the stories of Sindbad the Sailor, and captained the reconstruction of a twenty-oar Bronze Age galley along the coasts of the Aegean and the Black Sea in search of the routes used by Jason and the Argonauts and by Ulysses. Most recently I had completed a horseback trek which did have some relevance to the new Mongolian adventure, at least at first sight. Two years earlier I had retraced the long march of the knights and commoners and women and children of the First Crusade from a castle in Belgium to the Holy Sepulcher in Jerusalem. That journey had taken eight months in the saddle and had covered over 2500 miles. But I had planned the Crusade trip and all the other voyages before them as meticulously as circumstances and my finances allowed. I had calculated daily distances and checked weather patterns, allowed for rest days and repairs, conducted trial runs and scouted the terrain wherever possible. Never before had I paid the least attention to the Lucky Days of the Chinese astrological calendar, least of all relied on it for my final choice of departure day.

But I made no comment to Ariunbold. If that was how the Mongols wanted to organize the start of their expedition, so be it. I just wondered if Ariunbold and his Mongol colleagues understood the complexities of running a successful long-distance project. In a stream of interviews and announcements over the past two months they had rushed ahead and proclaimed in the Mongolian newspapers and on television that they were going to celebrate the extraordinary feat of their ancestors who had established the fastest and most far-flung overland communications system the world was to know before the invention of the railways. It was an achievement well worth commemorating. In the Middle Ages Mongol riders on their wiry horses had carried dispatches and escorted foreign ambassadors along paths that spanned two-thirds of the known world. These leathery horsemen had traveled astonishing distances at high speed, using routes that extended from the banks of the Danube to the shores of the Yellow Sea. Even more notable was that they rode across lands that these same supreme horsemen had conquered while they established the largest continuous land empire the world has ever seen. Now Ariunbold and his friends had told the Mongolian public that they would emulate their forebears and ride from Mongolia to France in their tracks. The scheme was breathtakingly ambitious. It was the equivalent of riding from Hong Kong to London, and they had asked me to help.

It was an invitation I could not resist, because it fulfilled an ambition that I thought would never be realized. Twenty-five years earlier I had written a thesis for a graduate degree at Oxford University about the first Europeans to penetrate into the heart of Central Asia at the time of the great Mongol world empire in the 13th and 14th centuries. They had been courageous and astute men—usually friars from the mendicant orders—who had faced the unknown with the same sort of courage as Marco Polo or Columbus, and they deserve a measure of renown, although today their story is largely forgotten. Escorted by Mongol riders, these dauntless pioneers had been sent as ambassadors, missionaries, or spies to the courts of the great warlords of the steppe. It was, wrote one of them, "like entering another world."

They brought back eyewitness descriptions of a society so strange that Europeans found their tales hard to credit: barbarous assemblies of tribesmen under drunken princes who lived in splendid portable pavilions large enough to hold 2000 courtiers at a time; rough nomads who ate raw meat; heretic Christian priests who engaged in furious debate with witch doctors; and a professional horse army equipped and trained beyond the most ambitious ideas of any Western military leader. These fearsome riders dressed in armor of boiled leather, spoke in a grunting language which no one else understood, and, as the European visitors warned as soon as they got back home, posed a terrifying threat to civilization. Europe should cease her quarrels, arm and unite her forces, or risk being overrun by the Mongol Horde.

At the time I wrote my thesis in the 1960s, there was not the least possibility of going to see the homeland of these people for myself, although I had often wondered just how much still remained of the exotic lifestyle described by my medieval authors. But Mongolia was forbidden territory. As the world's second-oldest communist country, the Mongolian People's Republic then lay isolated between a suspicious Soviet Union and a wary China. For half a century Mongolia had fended off Westerners interested in her unique culture and historical achievements. Her rulers pursued a deliberate policy of inaccessibility. No one but socialist fellow-travelers and official delegations were given visas, and that was only after each application had been subjected to strict and tediously lengthy vetting. When these Western visitors did arrive, their program inside Mongolia was largely confined to seeing the country's only city—proclaimed on 26 November 1924 as the capital of the new socialist state—the dismayingly ugly modern creation of Ulaan Baatar, "Red Hero."

Travel in the countryside was discouraged. Even Mongols themselves had to obtain permits before they were allowed to leave the city zone, and the police maintained checkpoints on all roads leading in and out of town. This was not a difficult task, as the country possessed only two black-top roads. The communists of the Mongolian People's Revolutionary Party ran a severely Stalinist regime which from time to time behaved with bloodstained ferocity. Cabinet ministers had been denounced on trumped-up charges, hauled away from public meetings, and shot. The cliché of a "Show Trial" was given blunt and direct meaning when public cross-examinations were held on stage in the auditorium of the National Theater. One politician-cum-field marshal, too powerful for his own good, was fatally poisoned while eating his meal on the Trans-Siberian Express, the most reliable method of approaching Mongolia at that time, though the spur line to Ulaan Baatar was not opened until 1949, twelve years later. The alternative was a dreary seven-hour plane flight from Moscow with a final stopover at the Siberian city of Irkutsk near Lake Baikal before diverting down to the primitive airport at Ulaan Baatar. A shorter overland approach was through Beijing and across the Gobi Desert of Inner Mongolia, because Ulaan Baatar is on virtually the same longitude as Hanoi. But this route was open only sporadically. Nominally independent and with its own seat at the United Nations,* Mongolia was in fact a client state under tight Soviet control, and the Soviets openly used Mongolia as a buffer against the huge mass of China. When relations between the Soviets and the Chinese were good, Mongolia was allowed to open her border with China. When they were bad, the frontier was shut. Mostly it was shut.

Gradually the situation improved. In 1952 the Stalinist dictator Choybalsan died after a reign of thirteen years, and although his successor, Tsedenbal, was still very authoritarian, Mongolia very cautiously began to allow in more foreigners from the West. But the old habits and suspicions died hard. Thirty years later visits were still under official control. Tourists were obliged to come in groups and then were shepherded along preplanned tracks by nanny-guides. The main exception was small parties of wealthy foreign hunters who, for payment in much-needed hard currency, were taken into the mountains to shoot the wild animals in which Mongolia abounds— deer, elk, Asian bear, and Marco Polo sheep with their splendid spiral horns, the largest wild sheep in the world. Private free-ranging travel was still discouraged.

Then, in 1987, opened a window of opportunity. UNESCO, the world organization for culture and science, announced the launch of a huge multinational scheme to study the historic Silk Roads which linked East and West. The idea was that expeditions approved by UNESCO would crisscross the continent. A northerly branch of the Silk Roads had passed through Mongolia, so I researched a plan to follow the journey of a medieval Chinese sage, Ch'ang Ch'un, who in 1221 had been summoned from his home near Peking to meet Genghis Khan, the one Mongol whom all the world has heard about. Ch'ang Ch'un's journey by foot, horseback, and cart had taken him right across Mongolia and as far as Samarkand and the Hindu Kush.

*Paired on entry in October 1961 with Mauritania.

I presented my proposal to the UNESCO offices in Paris, obtained their approval, posted off the documents to Ulaan Baatar and Beijing to seek the permission of the Chinese and Mongol authorities . . . and heard absolutely nothing.

Months later, and totally unexpectedly, I was invited to be the guest lecturer for a small group of tourists traveling from London to Siberia, Mongolia, and North China on a cultural tour. The original lecturer had fallen ill, and the historical background from my Oxford thesis research qualified me as a last-minute replacement. More important, I did not need a special visa for Mongolia, because I would be included on the group visa. Promptly I cabled the national Mongolian committee of the UNESCO Silk Roads Project in Ulaan Baatar to say when I was arriving and that I would like to discuss my project with someone in authority. Once again, I heard nothing. So when on 11 September 1989 my tour group was collected at Ulaan Baatar airport by a bus of the national Tourist Company, I introduced myself to the young lady interpreter assigned to us and, without much hope, asked if by any chance there were any messages for me. "Yes," she answered, "at 10 a.m. tomorrow the bus will leave you at the main square and you will be met."

I was little the wiser. I had no idea whom I was going to meet, or where, or even whether the Mongols had received my Ch'ang Ch'un proposal. I did notice, however, that pasted to the dashboard of the bus was a garish postcard of Genghis Khan. He was shown mounted on a battle charger and leading his victorious army. Yet for the past thirty years, as I had been led to believe, no one in Mongolia had been allowed to mention Genghis Khan's name for fear of giving offense to the Soviets. It would have been tactless for the Mongols to remind their Russian mentors that the 13th-century Mongol armies of Genghis Khan and his successors had crushed the Russians on the battlefield, sacked Kiev, and imposed Mongol rule on large areas of Russia for nearly 300 years. I was aware that every Russian school-child was still being told again and again of the "Mongol Yoke"* which had held his country in thrall, and that some Soviet economists were even blaming the centuries of Mongol rule for their country's

---

*More often called the "Tartar Yoke" from the common use of Tartar (also Tatar) for Mongol. See Chapter 5.

economic woes. One rumor also claimed that the National Museum of Mongolia possessed only a single small room devoted to the most celebrated period in their history—the rise of Genghis Khan—and that no native Mongol was allowed in to see the display. Only foreigners were permitted past the door.

As with other rumors about Mongolia, I was to find that the truth was somewhat different, depending on whom you spoke to and how much was still concealed or half-veiled. I was to meet eminent Mongolian scholars who told me that even at the height of Soviet domination they had been quietly studying the history of Genghis Khan, writing and defending learned theses on the imperial era. The only danger, they explained, was to be too public about the topic of one's research. If you were discreet there was no real problem. But the authorities could lash out at anyone who had too high a profile and honored the memory of Genghis Khan at a time when Party theoreticians were looking for scapegoats who could be accused of backsliding and anti-socialism.

I was told about a notorious case in 1962 when a premature campaign had tried to rehabilitate Genghis Khan's memory. A particularly hideous monument, a 36-foot-high white slab set on end with a crude outline drawing of the world emperor, had been erected in the Mongolian countryside at the spot where Genghis Khan was believed to have been born 800 years earlier. A very senior Party member who was in the Politburo and was also Secretary of the Central Committee no less, by the name of Tomor-ochir, unwisely attended the unveiling ceremony. Shortly afterwards he was accused of wrong-thinking, bitterly attacked in the pages of *Pravda*, dismissed from the Politburo, disgraced by being given a minor post away from the capital, and finally expelled altogether from membership in the Mongolian Communist Party. A set of commemorative stamps issued for the 800th anniversary of Genghis Khan's birth was hastily withdrawn (a few examples did slip through the net and appeared for sale to collectors in the West). Now, twenty-eight years later, Tomor-ochir's so-called errors had been reassessed and he had been rehabilitated and readmitted to the Party. The only drawback was that his official exoneration had to be posthumous, because he had been murdered in mysterious circumstances in the early 1980s by an axeman who had broken into his apartment.

*   *   *

It was an overcast, rather chilly September morning when at precisely 10 a.m. the tour bus dropped me off in the monumental central square of Ulaan Baatar and went on its way, its tourist passengers deprived of their guest lecturer for the day. Waiting on the pavement to greet me was a smartly dressed, bespectacled man of about 45, fit-looking and with an unruly shock of iron-gray hair, who appeared to be exactly what he was: a well-placed, well-polished bureaucrat of the central administration. This was Ariunbold, who introduced himself, in faltering English that matched my hesitant Russian, as being the Secretary to the Mongolian National Committee for the UNESCO Silk Roads Project. Together we walked around the east side of the huge empty square with its central statue of Sukhebaatar, "Axe Hero," mounted on his prancing horse. Sukhebaatar had been instated as the new icon of Mongolia, communism's answer to Genghis Khan. He was the poor herdsman who in 1920 had smuggled to the Soviets the vital letter appealing for their help by hiding the document in the handle of his horsewhip. His reinterred remains now shared with the corpse of Choybalsan the grim marble mausoleum at the end of the square, which was a miniature and uninspired copy of Lenin's tomb in Red Square in Moscow.

Ariunbold led me around the back of what was, to judge by its pseudoclassical portico, the State Opera House and brought me to an office tower, the tallest building in central Ulaan Baatar, which housed the various international cultural associations. There, on the eighth floor, he had an office in the International Center for Mongolian Studies. On his desk lay a thin folder. This, he said, was the Mongolian proposal for an expedition along the Silk Roads in association with UNESCO. I glanced through the document. It was a faithful adaptation, paragraph by paragraph, of the exact same proposal for the Ch'ang Ch'un expedition that I had sent to Ulaan Baatar five months before. The names had been changed and now, instead of following the route of the Chinese sage from Beijing to the Hindu Kush, the text had been altered to propose that a team of Mongol horsemen should start from the center of Mongolia and retrace the medieval courier road to France.

The blatant plagiarism did not bother me unduly. It was much more important that there was a genuine local interest in launching

some sort of expedition on horses across Mongolia. I still did not
know who Ariunbold was working with, and I was skeptical about
anyone's capacity to ride over 6000 miles across Eurasia. The distance
was 40 percent longer even than my original scheme to follow Ch'ang
Ch'un. But all this did not matter. Here was the most wonderful
opportunity for me to travel freely inside Mongolia, not just as an
outsider following his own program, but in the company of Mongols
who were committed to rediscovering their own history. It was an
opening that no Westerner had ever been offered before.

Ariunbold explained that he and his friends were eager to organize
the venture and had been granted a small amount of official backing
by the local Silk Roads committee. But they lacked the necessary
foreign contacts to make their venture better known outside Mongolia, and if I would go along with them I could help smooth their
way—by obtaining permission from foreign countries to cross their
territories, by providing finance in hard currency, and by bringing in
extra equipment from the West that was impossible to obtain inside
Mongolia. I also sensed that, without saying it, he wanted the approval I had already obtained from UNESCO for the Ch'ang Ch'un
journey to be transferred to the new Mongol-centered venture. I
made a rapid reassessment of my position and decided that I was quite
ready to shelve the Ch'ang Ch'un journey if it meant that I could
participate in the traditional lifestyle of Mongol herdsmen and test
their age-old method of long-distance travel. After that, if Ariunbold
and his companions succeeded in demonstrating to me on their ride
inside Mongolia that they had the ability, diplomacy, and tenacity to
continue right through to France, then my advice might help them
to achieve that huge ambition. Meanwhile I would be happy to take
what would be for me a new role—not to organize or lead an expedition but to observe and record, and to supply the items of foreign kit
they asked for, such as sleeping bags and camera film, and let them
get on with the practical details of organizing a home-grown ride.

So eight months later, in May, I was to find myself back in Mongolia
on the first, local sector of that initial expedition intended as a trial
ride for the grand transcontinental venture to Europe to begin the
following year. Ariunbold and his colleagues had taken two weeks'
leave from their regular jobs, hired a couple of dozen half-wild ponies

from a commune's work brigade, and employed the local horseherds-
men to serve as guides to lead them into the wilderness northeast of
Ulaan Baatar. This was the region where Genghis Khan had lived as
a young outlaw and gathered around him the tribal heroes who would
one day set out to conquer the world. Thus I was enjoying the
situation of riding knee-to-knee beside a taciturn, hard-bitten Mongol
horseherdsman who must surely have been no different from the
original riders of Genghis Khan. Short and burly, Dampildorj had
the classic high cheekbones of the Mongol, and his close-cropped
head was so perfectly round that mentally I had nicknamed him
"Bullet Head." He seemed impervious to the hammering, jarring trot
of the small horses we rode and sat in the wooden saddle, or rather
stood in its short stirrups, for hour after hour as if on self-leveling
suspension. Taught to ride before he could walk properly, his legs
were like steel springs and he was much more at ease on a horse than
on the ground. Indeed when he dismounted he was so stiff and
bowlegged as he stumped forward on his thick-soled felt boots with
their turned-up toes that he looked like a wind-up toy, an unavoidable
impression enhanced by his thick wraparound gown known as a *del*
with its broad sash of orange silk, and his dainty hat like a doll's
headgear covered in blue silk and shaped like the dome of a mosque.
Dampildorj and the other herdsmen had promised to lead us to the
very spot which, according to legend, Genghis Khan had ordered all
Mongols to revere for eternity.

   Genghis Khan came from a people whose origins are still unclear.
Their language is sometimes placed in the same linguistic category as
Turkish and Manchu, but even that classification is hotly contested.
Some scholars claim that the Mongols were descendants of the ferocious warrior tribes the Chinese called the Hsiung-nu, and who,
according to other specialists, were the same as the Huns who invaded
Europe under Attila in the 5th century. But whatever the exact affilia-
tion, the cultural pattern of these steppe peoples was well established.
As early as 400 BC the Chinese were writing about the nomad tribes
who roamed their northwestern border, raised cattle, lived in felt
tents, and had no writing. The scanty archaeological record shows
that this lifestyle extended back at least as far as 1000 BC.

   But the shifting alliances of the tribes are never permanent or sta-
tionary for long enough to detect a definite heritage for the Mongols.

Central Asian kingdoms rose and fell under peoples with strange-sounding names, like the Juan-Juan, Toba, Uighurs, Jurchens, and the Khitans, who in turn spawned the Kara khitai or "Black khitai" and who gave Europeans their word for China as "Cathay." Some of these peoples spoke versions of Mongol; others used archaic forms of Turkish. A few were pure nomads, but most built themselves capitals in the well-favored valleys of the interior or at the foot of the great mountain ranges.

All this time the Mongols remained an obscure, half-glimpsed people on the edges of these civilizations. Indeed, as late as the 12th century the Mongols were, strictly speaking, only one tribe among a loose collection of tribes which the Chinese called indifferently the Meng Wu or Ta-ta, and were mistrusted acutely as they had a habit of raiding the Chinese frontier and carrying off children whom, it was rumored, they needed for breeding purposes. Nor did all the Mongols live by cattle-herding on the grasslands of the steppe, as is commonly thought. Some dwelt in the forests of southern Siberia as hunter-gatherers, and there the Orianghai, a part-Mongol, part-Turkic people, were said to attach the varnished bones of animals to their feet and skim across the frozen surface of ice and snow so fast that they could catch birds.

It was Genghis Khan who imposed unity on all this confusion. When he was powerful enough, he overrode the tribal distinctions and decreed that henceforth all the related peoples should think of themselves as Mongols. And when he began his rise to power, he had an even simpler definition of the people he intended to govern. He was, he said, "the ruler of all those who live in felt tents."

The horses we were riding would certainly have been familiar to Genghis Khan and his army quartermasters. No larger than a small cow pony,* each animal had a thick neck, a big, clumsy-looking head, and a gawky frame. No Western horse-dealer would have looked twice at them, yet they had the reputation of being the toughest horses in existence. It was said that they could survive hostile conditions that would kill any other breed. Legend had it that they managed to find food for themselves when other horses starved to

---

*By Western definition many Mongol horses are small enough to be classified as ponies. But Mongols strongly resent their horses being called ponies.

death, and that they thrived in subarctic temperatures where other horses perished of exposure. It was also the boast that they were closely related to the original Wild Horse of the steppes named after the Russian explorer Colonel Nicholas Prjevalski, who traveled in Mongolia in the 1870s and 1880s and discovered the Wild Horse in 1881. No one knows for sure if any Wild Horses exist nowadays outside zoos, and it seems extremely unlikely. But the last time a small herd of Prjevalski Horses was seen in the wild, they were running free in southwest Mongolia close to the Chinese border. Dampildorj had confidently told me that any horse that showed a black eel-stripe in the hair down the spine or had zebra-like bars on its legs was part Wild Horse. What is certain is that Mongolian horses similar to the ones we rode had carried Genghis Khan's mounted armies to victory in their blitzkrieg campaigns of conquest at the beginning of the 13th century, when the Mongol cavalry had over-turned the established world order. In battle after battle the Mongol flying column took their enemies by surprise, suddenly appearing, as if by magic, mounted on their sinewy animals after they had ridden across deserts or mountains that the enemy had thought to be impass-able, or had covered distances at such speed that their opponents were caught off-guard.

I was also learning that Genghis Khan himself, far from being a taboo subject in Mongolia, was now a national obsession. His name and image, after years of enforced obscurity, were everywhere—on hoardings, stamps, calendars, posters, as the name of a brand of Mongolian vodka. Some of the herdsmen riding with me wore little cap buttons with his portrait, and when a Mongolian newspaper had asked its readers to suggest a name for the glossy new hotel being built in Ulaan Baatar, the overwhelming response was that it should be called, in its Mongolian spelling, the Chinggis Khan Hotel. *

By any standards the Great Mongol was one of the most extraordi-

---

*Mongol names, ancient as well as modern, have confusingly different spellings in both their traditional and their modernized versions, even in Mongolia itself. To muddy the water still further, outside Mongolia the name of the Great Mongol is sometimes spelled according to how his name was first reported. The accepted English version, which I use throughout as it is so well known, is derived from the early French transliteration of his name in the Persian sources which were studied by the pioneer Western historians of the Mongol empire. Presumably Chinggis Khan will become the eventual international spelling.

nary men who ever lived. He was an untutored orphan who came
from a tribal society that lived in utter obscurity, and yet he conquered far more territory than Alexander the Great. Illiterate, alleged
to be subject to fits, probably an alcoholic, his main imperial heritage
was to endure under his immediate family for more than a century,
while minor fragments were to survive very much longer. The last
ruler in Europe still claiming to be descended from Genghis Khan
was a khan of the Crimea deposed by the Russians in 1783, and in
Central Asia the ruler of Khiva was making the same boast when the
Russians forced him to abdicate in 1920. Elsewhere Genghis Khan's
legacy can still be seen and felt. The Great Wall of China was modified
and rebuilt from the 15th century onwards, into the form we see now,
chiefly as a reflex to the terrifying Mongol invasions he unleashed. In
Central Asia there are once-fabled cities like Bukhara still in compara-
tive decline because they never recovered from the Mongol attack he
directed at them so brilliantly and so devastatingly. Yet while the
outside world has grown accustomed to using Genghis Khan's name
as a synonym for destruction, war, and cruelty, inside Mongolia I
was beginning to find that Genghis Khan was being accorded the
status of a national hero, even a god.

I suspected that I was at a crucial moment in modern Mongol
history. The forbidden land of the past half-century had suddenly
been thrown open to foreign view, and simultaneously the Mongols
themselves were being given unparalleled freedom. The Soviet army
was withdrawing its divisions from Mongol soil, the ruling Mongolian
People's Revolutionary Party had decided to imitate Soviet perestroika and glasnost by relaxing the iron grip of central government,
and ordinary Mongols were responding by trying to find their true
national identity. A huge upwelling of nostalgia for Mongolian origins
and traditions was taking place, and my own quest for the survival
of the nomad world described by the medieval European travelers
could scarcely have been better timed.

I was not the only seeker after Mongolia's medieval traditions.
Genghis Khan and his era represented a source of pride to all Mongols, and they had a very real justification, because if one looks at the
record from their point of view there is an astonishing fact. The entire
Mongol nation led by Genghis Khan had numbered no more than
2 million people, and his army is calculated to have been 130,000

strong. Yet this insignificant collection of clansmen, living in one of the most isolated and difficult environments in the world, suddenly rose under his leadership to become acknowledged overlords to more than half the known world.

How did this happen? Was Genghis Khan himself entirely responsible, or did the abilities and character of his people play the major role? By riding with their descendants I was hoping to find an answer, just as Dampildorj and the ordinary Mongol *arats* or herdsmen on their horses around me wished to celebrate their greatest ancestor and make him a symbol for their own hopes for the future. We were, all of us, searching for Genghis Khan.

2

Heartland

With 5000 miles of sensitive frontier, and landlocked between the People's Republic of China and the Soviet Union, Mongolia is the fifth-largest country in Asia by area. At more than 604,000 square miles the country is more than twice the size of Turkey, four times that of Japan. Yet it is so overshadowed in its international location that it is a common misconception that Mongolia is simply another Soviet republic, or perhaps just another part of China. Indeed, in the 19th century, when Mongolia was little more than a neglected Chinese dependency, Europeans took to using the same dismissive distinction used by the Chinese themselves between "Outer" or Distant Mongolia—which is modern Mongolia—and "Inner" or Nearer Mongolia, which was at least closer to the Celestial Throne as far as the Chinese were concerned, though they still considered it shudderingly uncouth and remote.

Geographers were scarcely more complimentary when they placed Mongolia at the center of what they called "the Dead Heart of Asia." In their classification Mongolia is a cold desert. Bleak, harsh, and empty, it is a land so distant from the ocean's moderating effect on climate that all life is dominated by extreme continental influences. The growing season is barely four months long, and across more than half the country the bedrock is permanently congealed. In winter the temperatures fall to minus 35 degrees centigrade and remain below freezing point until March. In consequence some species of rodents and hooved animals add a month to their normal gestation period,

while the furry marmot (of whom we shall hear more later) does not
shed its winter coat until July and promptly begins growing a new
winter coat. In December the smaller rivers have become solid ice,
right to the bottom, and the heavy masses of very cold air in the
lowlands mean that it is often warmer on the high mountain ranges
than in the valleys, where temperatures have been recorded at minus
55 degrees. Statistically Ulaan Baatar on the banks of the Tula River
in the central north of Mongolia finishes up with an *average* annual
temperature of 3 degrees below zero.

Summer can be just as intimidating, with its wild swings of day-
to-day weather. Charles Bawden, who as recently as 1968 became the
first writer in English to publish a history of modern Mongolia,* cites
a Russian geographer's description of a fifteen-hour period in the
capital in June 1942. A calm, warm, sunny evening was suddenly
interrupted by a 60-mile-an-hour gale that brought dust, fog, and
nine-tenths cloud cover. This tempest lasted just one hour. Then the
sky cleared, the wind ceased, and the stars came out. Between 1 and
2 a.m. there were heavy showers of rain, and the following morning
the sky was once again clouded over. By 9 a.m. there was fog, driving
snow, and a temperature of 1 degree.

Seven hundred years earlier the first of the European pioneers to
write about Mongolia, a Franciscan friar named John of Plano Carpini, experienced the harshness of the Mongolian summer at first
hand as his Mongol guides made forced marches across the steppe in
order to get to Mongolia in time for Carpini to observe the coronation
of Genghis Khan's grandson as Khakhan or Great Khan. Carpini was
not cut out to be a long-distance rider. He was 60 years old and
overweight, fell ill on the first leg of the transcontinental journey,
and suffered agonies as he was jolted about on the uncomfortable
Mongol ponies, complaining that he was frequently given the worst
of the remounts. Carpini had set out on Easter Day 1245 on the
instructions of Pope Innocent IV, ostensibly to carry a message to
the Mongol emperor. In fact his real task was to spy and to gather
intelligence about Mongol political and military intentions. He got
back safely two years later and made what amounted to a lecture tour

*In *The Modern History of Mongolia* he writes that "there can be fewer blanker
pages in the history of the civilised world than the story of Mongolia in the 19th
century."

across northern Europe, warning of the dangers of a Mongol invasion. His observations were very acute. "The weather there is astonishingly irregular," Carpini reported in his *Description of the Mongols Whom We Call Tartars*:

> In the middle of summer when other places are normally enjoying very great heat, there is fierce thunder and lightning which cause the death of many men, and at the same time there are very heavy falls of snow. There are also hurricanes of bitterly cold wind so violent that at times men can ride on horseback only with great effort.*

When at last they reached the imperial camp, he and his companions had to crouch on the ground and lie "prostrate on account of the force of the wind, and we could scarcely see owing to the great clouds of dust." Between the election of the Khakhan and his actual coronation ceremony, a massive hailstorm raged. The sudden melting of the immense quantities of hail produced a flash flood which drowned 160 men as well as washing away many dwellings and destroying much property. "To conclude briefly about this country," he informed his readers, "it is large but otherwise—as we saw it with our own eyes during the five and a half months we travelled about it—it is more wretched than I can possibly say."

Mongolia's distance from the sea also means there is very little air humidity. So although the winters are intensely cold, there is comparatively little snow, usually less than three feet. The native horses, as foreign visitors as far back as Carpini have been fascinated to note, have learned how to scrape away the snow with their hooves to get at their pasture. The pickings are very meager—a few mouthfuls of dead and deep-frozen vegetation—but this is enough to sustain them. Natural selection means that only the fittest animals survive, and no Mongol herdsman would think of bringing his horse-herd into shelter just to escape the rigors of a normal sub-zero winter. His main fear is that a late blizzard in spring will bring a thick snowfall at a time when the horses are at their weakest after months of semi-starvation and unable to clear the snow with their hooves. With that catastrophe the animals die by the thousands.

*In *The Mongol Mission: Narratives and Letters of the Franciscan Missionaries in Mongolia and China in the Thirteenth and Fourteenth Centuries*, edited by Christopher Dawson, Sheed and Ward, 1955.

With so little air humidity to produce clouds, Mongolia's otherwise hostile climate is partly improved by an unusual amount of sunshine. Mongolia enjoys as much as 500 hours more sunny weather every year than other regions on a similar latitude, such as Switzerland or the mountain states of the United States. This abundance of sunshine and the bright clear skies had a profound effect on the psychology of the Mongols of Genghis Khan's era. To them the immense blue vault of their sky was Tengri, the Supreme God, whom the tribal medicine men, the shamans, worshiped. Tengri was the unification of all the hundreds of lesser gods and spirits who inhabited the earth, waters, winds, and mountains, and to this day sky blue is still the Mongols' good-luck color. More ominous, it was almighty Tengri who author-ized Genghis Khan to go out and conquer all the world.

The combination of Mongolia's crystal air, the huge vistas, and the unrelenting distances has also influenced the way country Mongols think. Genghis Khan's given title seems to have meant "Oceanic Ruler," and in their broad horizon-to-horizon landscape the Mongol herdsmen are still prone to use images more suited to the sea. Trying to point out to eager Mongol herdsmen the obstacles to riding all the way to Europe, it dawned on me that some of them imagined that their rolling grasslands must surely extend forever, right to the shores of the Atlantic. They had no concept of the barriers of huge rivers like the Volga, great cities, or modern motorways. To them a Mongol could ride anywhere and do anything, provided his horses were well cared for. And at the end of his ride, the herdsmen assured me with total sincerity, even if a Mongol had reached the farthest point of Europe, he could turn loose his horses and, unaided, they would find their way back to Mongolia. Like homing pigeons they would seek their path back to the pasturelands of their own country, because a Mongol horse would be happy only in Mongolia. Had not this hap-pened recently, they asked, when a number of Mongol horses were sent to North Vietnam? They had run away from their new masters and walked back home.

Such confident naïveté is understandable. With an area larger than the British Isles, France, Germany, and Italy combined,* the Mongol homeland is not only huge but is physically isolated behind massive

*Slightly larger (3 percent) in area than Alaska, Mongolia has the same population density as Nevada.

barriers. Across the north extend the trackless taiga forests of Siberia. To the west and south rise the mountain ranges of the Altai, and in a great arc along the southern and eastern flank lies the Gobi, not a single broad desert so much as a series of barren basins, surfaced variously with gravel, stones, dust, or sand. The basins are believed to have been scoured out over the aeons by the action of the wind, which in the spring season can still raise a dust storm that lasts for one or two weeks and has been known to continue for fifty-seven days without interruption. At other times, after the rains, parts of the Gobi become a sprinkling of shallow alkaline marshes. Here time itself seems to be in a warp. As if this were the boneyard of the Lost World, scores of dinosaur skeletons have been found lying on the surface of the ground just where they fell, including two—one a meat-eater, the other a herbivore—still locked together in their death struggle. Here have been found the recognizable remains of monsters as terrifying as Deinocheirus, the "Terrible Handed," with its 24-inch claws, or as bizarre as Aviraptor, a proto-bird that flew and had a massive beak like a parrot and a crested head like a cassowary. In the Mesozoic era all these grotesques bred, lived, and died in what is now the wilderness of the Gobi, and their nests fossilized and survived. Some contain clutches of petrified dinosaur eggs, surprisingly small to produce such giant offspring. Others were the final resting place for broods of hatchlings that died in a pathetic huddle, eight or ten at a time.

Waiting for the ride to begin, I made a reconnaissance into the Mongolian Gobi and quickly appreciated that the Mongols were not just the horse-breeding people that their historical image projects. In what must be one of the bleakest, least hospitable places on earth, a single Mongol family of a Gobi *aymag* or district was tending 400 camels, a constantly bawling, groaning, squealing, defecating troop. Here life was stripped to the bone. The father was almost black, his skin darkened by the constant sun and wind. A big, taciturn man, he seemed old at first sight, stooped and bowlegged, but he was probably still in his mid-40s. He had a round, impassive face battered by wind and driving dust and was dressed in a faded, padded coat of khaki, the right shoulder smeared with a fresh streak of bright-green camel excrement. His three sons, aged between 6 and 14, ran back and forth yelping and chivvying the camels, which were being separated into nursing mothers and barren females. The high-pitched screams of anxiety from the forlorn offspring as they saw their mothers driven away must make the cry of the baby camel one of the most distressing and pitiful sounds in creation.

The children held long poles with short strings that they used as cattle switches. Occasionally a boy would scramble onto the back of a pony to go chasing after some straying camel. The women of the household were equally careworn and stoic—the wife in a shapeless gown of blue silk, her hair tied in a scarf to keep out the dust and sand, and a wizened grandmother who occasionally appeared from the tent, moving with tortoise slowness, her dark brown face so wrinkled by age and exposure that even her skeleton seemed to be collapsing inside the shriveled skin. Everything in view was muted and weatherbeaten. The stony plain of tiny gravel fragments, sharp and angular, merged imperceptibly into sand hummocks interspersed with clumps of grass and occasional bushes of dusty gray-green. The camels had shed their winter fur and, incongruously, their skins had the texture and color of elephant or water buffalo hide.

His beasts, the camel-herder explained, traveled best in late autumn or early winter. Then, with their humps fattened by the summer pasture, they could go for thirty-three days without food, and nine days without water. Each could carry 550 pounds of baggage and cover thirty-two miles a day. In short, they matched the speed and exceeded the carrying capacity of a horse, and I realized that the Gobi, which was seen by the outside world as a barrier, had been to the Mongols nothing of the sort. The Chinese might have hoped that the Gobi was an immense natural dry moat lying along the foot of the Great Wall, helping to shield them from the steppe barbarians. And on Mongolia's opposite border the great oasis civilizations of Bukhara and Samarkand may have felt secure behind their surrounding waste-lands. But they were deluded. No desert could have hindered the ambitions of these tough, resilient people. Colonel Prjevalski traveled with them in the Gobi and witnessed their ability to endure the daily hardship of crossing the barrens on their regular trips between Mongolia and the Chinese trading cities:

In the depth of winter, for a month at a time, they accompany the tea caravans. Day by day the thermometer registers upwards of −20 degrees of Fahrenheit, with a constant wind from the north-west, intensifying the cold until it is almost unendurable. But in spite of it they keep their seat on their camels for fifteen hours at a stretch, with a keen wind blowing in their teeth. A man must be of iron to stand this; but a Mongol performs the journey backwards and forwards four times during the winter, making upwards of 3000 miles.*

From his nation's camel-herders Genghis Khan formed the supply train of the medieval Mongol war machine.

Beyond the camelman's tent was a wonderful contrast. For another four miles the Gobi continued flat, then came a mountain wall. There were no real foothills, just a few deeply eroded slopes before the bare rock began. Then the land reared steeply upward across a front that extended as far as the eye could see in either direction. It was the northern face of the Gobi Altai Mountains, a small sector of a rampart 1000 miles long. On the far side lay China. Standing on shifting desert sand among noisy camels, I found it odd to look up and see on the main crest of the nearest ridge a white line—permanent snow. As if to accentuate the contrast, a line of eight crescent sand dunes lay against the foot of the rock wall. They were glowing butter-yellow in the evening sunlight. Hundreds of similar dunes would merge farther southeast to form a sea of sand with ridges 250 feet high. When the gale sweeps across these sand hills, the sands shift and moan with musical notes. Marco Polo believed the sound to be the wailing of demons trying to lure caravan travelers to their death.

As if that combination of mountain, desert, and snow were not arresting enough, I could see a lake shimmering beside the dunes. But it was a mirage. The light was reflecting off a white expanse of salty mud, dried hard as cement and cracked into crazy paving with a web of fissures. Thirty-five years earlier there had indeed been a lake here, with fish and gulls and reed-beds. After the rainy season it spread outwards for ten miles from the foot of the mountains. Then came an earthquake. The local inhabitants said that the earth's crust must have split, because the water drained away downwards, leaving the fish to die in a desert. I recalled the story of the first American expedition to examine the Gobi scientifically, in the 1920s. They had camped overnight on the shore of a similar shallow lake. In the night

---

* *Mongolia, the Tangut Country, and the Solitudes of Northern Tibet*, translated by E. M. Morgan, 1876.

the wind, which had been heaping up the water on one side of the lake, changed direction and, blowing from another quarter, drove the water away so quickly that hundreds upon hundreds of small silver fish lay stranded on the damp ground. In the moonlight the scientists watched as the fish lay and flapped in their death throes. The noise of the doomed shoal was like the sound of a crowd softly applauding.

If the West has been allowed only a distorted picture of Mongolia in the past 100 years, that half-knowledge was nothing compared to the total ignorance which held sway at the time of Genghis Khan immediately before pioneers like Carpini ventured into the steppes. No one in Europe had even heard of Mongolia or knew anything whatever about its inhabitants until the advance guard of Genghis Khan's mounted army burst upon them. It was a complete mystery where these ferocious cavalrymen had come from. There was a theory that, like the vanishing lake in reverse, the earth had split open and the Mongols had ridden up from Hades. Nor did Europe find itself dealing with talentless savages. Leading that first raid was Sübodei, a Mongol tribesman turned general whom Genghis Khan had selected to command a probe in depth. Liddell Hart, the military historian, judges that the strategic ability of this humble tribesman and his master was matched only by Napoleon.* Sübodei's raiding force operated unsupported in the field for two years, made a great 5000-mile circuit of the Caspian Sea, defeated twenty nations including an army put together by the Russian princes, and withdrew in good order as mysteriously as it had appeared. It left behind the black legend of the Mongol Horde. Traumatized by the shock of the invasion, the victims claimed that the Mongols were cannibals who ate raw flesh and rode giant steeds.

Nearly eight centuries later something of the same dread lingers on. Superficial reactions to the mention of Mongols and Mongolia can evoke a hint of the Yellow Peril, of brutal barbarians, even a momentary confusion between Mongol and mongolism, the congenital condition now known to result from the presence of an extra chromosome which retards normal human development. Typically, the Victorian doctor who first recognized the condition named it because the victims reminded him of caricatures of the Mongol face.

*Great Captains Unveiled, 1927.

Reports from the few Western travelers who ventured into Mongolia in the late 19th and early 20th centuries did little to dispel these
misgivings. On the whole they describe the Mongols as degenerate
and dirty. They complain of the appalling squalor and lassitude, the
poverty, and the enormous numbers of priest-lamas who wandered
about the countryside begging and spreading syphilis until 90 percent
of the population was infected. The visitors pronounced the Mongols
to be incapable of hard work. Prjevalski, in whose honor the Wild
Horse was named, roundly declared that "the most striking trait in
their character is sloth":

> Their whole lives are passed in holiday making which harmonises with
> their pastoral pursuits. Their cattle are their only care, and even they
> do not cause them much trouble. The camels and horses graze on the
> steppe without any watch, only requiring to be watered once a day in
> the summer at the neighbouring well. The women and children tend
> the flocks and herds. The rich hire shepherds who are mostly poor
> homeless vagrants. Milking the cows, churning butter, preparing the
> meals and other domestic work falls to the lot of the women. The men
> as a rule do nothing but gallop about all day long from yurt to yurt
> [felt tent to felt tent], drinking tea or kumiss, and gossiping with their
> neighbours.

Just before the First World War a formidable Englishwoman, Beatrix Bulstrode, had much the same impression. "The Mongols have
never worked, and it is highly improbable that they ever will," she
stated in her book *A Tour in Mongolia*, after she had made two
forays into Mongolia out of China, where she had already traveled
extensively.* The first trip was by oxcart and pony and took her into
Inner Mongolia, and the second went through Siberia and down to
the capital, then called Urga. Mongolia's reputation for lawlessness
and civil strife can be judged from the fact that setting out for the
second expedition she carried no fewer than four firearms: a hunting
gun taken to pieces and hidden in her trunk among her underwear, a
Mauser pistol and a large Colt revolver under her Burberry, and "a
smaller weapon I carried in my pocket." This walking arsenal per

---

*Some idea of her forthright character can be gleaned from the fact that on her first
trip she traveled alone and on her second her companion was a Mr. Edward Gull of
the Chinese Maritime Customs, whom she described as "a peppery little man." She
married him.

suaded *The Times* correspondent in Peking, David Fraser, to contribute a foreword to her book in which he wholeheartedly endorsed her
view of the Mongols. She was "particularly instructive in her analysis
of Mongol character. The Mongol is simple, happy, good-natured,
intensely lazy, and apparently entirely lacking in practical qualities.
His very disposition is the cause of his past and present troubles. He
is, in short, not fitted to compete with the outside world."*

The Times correspondent, Beatrix Bulstrode, and other critics did
not grasp that by their culture the Mongols abhorred laborious routine. The only fit occupation, in their opinion, was to raise sheep and
cattle and camels and horses on the grasslands, and move freely,
obeying only the change of seasons. The notion of cultivating the
land was anathema. To the Mongols a plowman was the picture of a
man in bondage, pitifully stooping over the dirt like a slave. When
arable farming was introduced as an experiment in the early 1920s,
the Mongol *arats* had the absentminded habit of planting a field of
crops, then moving away and not coming back for the harvest.

Seen from the air, the first impression of modern Mongolia is still
one of a vast emptiness. In a country that extends across three time-
zones there is only one full-sized city, and just 500 settlements can
claim to have more than 500 inhabitants. Ridges of bare bleak hills
extend below the wings of the aircraft without a trace of human
habitation except for an occasional cluster of tiny dots that are sheep
flocks grazing the stony slopes. Every thirty or forty miles a neat
white round blob like a tiny field mushroom marks the home of the
herdsman. It is his *ger*, the circular felt tent that has been the Mongolian dwelling since long before the time of Genghis Khan and is better
known in the West as a yurt, the name Colonel Prjevalski preferred.
In Ulaan Baatar, where there is a chronic housing shortage, hundreds
of *gers* are laid out in streets and blocks to form suburbs. Each is
wired for electricity but lacks drainage or plumbing, and at night the
interiors are lit by the luminous white light of television screens. In
the modern city, the apparently anachronistic *ger* is still more suitable
in some ways than the grim Soviet-style apartment blocks, their
shabby exteriors disfigured by rust streaks from the decaying iron
balconies, ugly festoons of external wiring, and graffiti-scrawled

---

*A Tour in Mongolia, Methuen, 1920.

doorways to filthy communal stairwells. The concrete apartments may have central heating and running water, but when the winter comes the city *ger* dwellers, like their country cousins, add extra layers of felt to the roofs and walls of their tents to keep out the aching cold. The drab apartment blocks are one of the more unsightly legacies of the austere communist rule which has remorselessly pressured the ordinary Mongols to change their way of life for the past seventy years.

The communists took power in 1921 just when Mongolia was experiencing a brief period of independence after centuries of Chinese rule had left the country totally undeveloped and in an arrested state of feudalism. Mongolia's independent identity was too shallow-rooted to withstand the aftershock of the Russian Revolution, which rippled across the whole of Central Asia. Roving bands of desperadoes from the breakup of the old Imperial Russian Empire in Siberia entered the country from the north.

No intruder was more bizarre or more destructive than the "Mad Baron" whose escapade would only have been possible in such an out-of-the-way corner of the world. A Balt and renegade junior officer in the White Army, Baron von Unger-Sternberg crossed into Mongolia and seized power with the help of an irregular tsarist force he grandly dubbed The Asian Cavalry Division. His portrait shows a haunted-looking man about forty years old with a high forehead, receding hairline, and pale eyes which have a psychotic stare. He wears a traditional Mongolian robe, its high collar closed with the usual braid fastenings. He has added epaulettes to the shoulders of the gown, and he wears the Star of the Saint George's Cross pinned to his chest. The odd mixture of West and East in his costume reflects the Baron's crossbred plans. He proposed to march back into Siberia at the head of a Mongol army, drive out the Reds, and establish an eastern Asiatic kingdom loyal to the tsar. His brief regime in Urga unleashed a wave of executions, looting, and arson. His ruffians went around murdering every suspected Bolshevik they could lay their hands on. They made themselves so detested that when a detachment of the Red Army began to advance on the Mongolian capital, the Mad Baron and his followers had to evacuate the city with a few additional recruits to the imperial cause and withdraw pell-mell. On 21 August 1921 he was captured by Red soldiers and taken away to Novosibirsk where he was shot the following month. It is said that at his trial the judge offered him his freedom if he would sing the first verse of the Internationale. He retorted that the judge would have to sing the Russian National Anthem first. By then the Red Army, using Mongol-speaking agents from Siberia, was firmly in control of Urga, which was to be renamed Ulaan Baatar. With the Red Army watching from the wings Mongolia's fledgling communist party announced the new regime, and Mongolia became the world's second-oldest communist state.

From that moment forward Mongolia's history has shadowed that of the Soviet Union. The communists of the Mongolian People's Revolutionary Party faithfully copied every change in Moscow policy, from Stalinism through Brezhnev to the most recent clamor for reform. In theory Mongolia was modernized, industrialized, and sovietized. It was a newborn, forward-thinking nation rejecting its feudal past and marching toward the bright new socialist dawn. Yet in the spring of 1990 the first demonstration calling for democracy in Ulaan Baatar, as it was reported in the Western press, included a member of the Mongolian crowd carrying a placard that read: "Men and Women of Mongolia! Mount Your Horses!!!"

3

The Secret History

At my first meeting with Ariunbold in Ulaan Baatar, he had introduced me to his partner, Gerel, who walked into the room halfway through our rather halting discussions. Gerel looked much more the popular image of a descendant of the Horde. He was tall for a Mongol, at least six feet, and had an intense, untamed air. His fierce-looking face was framed by jet-black hair which was rather long and greasy, and his menacing appearance was accentuated by a wisp of a Fu Manchu beard and mustache. He had an abrupt way of speaking, which gave the impression that he was bottling up his anger and about to explode with rage at any moment.

Gerel was a sculptor by profession, and his long slim fingers and delicate hands contrasted with his intimidating manner. He was pure macho. His all-consuming passion was hunting, and his sculptures were images of deer and bear and big-horn sheep. He liked to work with bone and antlers and set his pieces on backgrounds of natural rock, felt, and leather. A huge bearskin, the pelt of one of the many dozens he had shot, was spread across the floor of his tiny apartment. He kept hunting rifles tucked behind the sofa, and he proudly leafed through his collection of grainy black-and-white photos with scene after scene of hunting camps and hunting parties, and dead animals with hunters standing proudly over them.

Gerel and Ariunbold were both romantics, but whereas Ariunbold was an officeworker with dreams, Gerel had worked as a hunter-guide and could cook over a camp fire, break in a horse, and tie a pack saddle. He carried himself with a swagger, and there was no doubt that he was a powerful, if rather volatile, personality. Despite his forbidding appearance I was to find that he was very genuine and helpful and committed to making the expedition a success, though at the initial encounter he said very little and only looked rather forbidding, his face set in a frown.

Ariunbold and I agreed that I would inform UNESCO about the new direction the project was taking, and Ariunbold began to find horses and recruit suitable Mongolian members for a riding team.

After my first visit as a tour guide I went back twice to Ulaan Baatar, in October 1989 and then in April the following year. Each time, I tried to pin down a firm commitment for the expedition schedule, hoping to give some definite shape to Ariunbold's wishful but rather vague ideas. Eager to get at least part of the project underway as soon as possible, I proposed that in the summer he and his team should ride across Mongolia as far as the Soviet border where they could leave their horses. This would provide the practical experience on which to base plans for the transcontinental ride later on and would enable me to judge whether the Mongol scheme for the immense journey to France was practicable. But Ariunbold was in favor of delaying the expedition for at least a year and setting out on a single nonstop ride all the way to Europe. He failed to explain why he wanted this delay, and I never discovered the reason, so it took considerable patience to wait for him to accept that nothing would be lost by a step-by-step approach.

Meanwhile each visit to Ulaan Baatar revealed that my Mongol acquaintances were increasingly convinced that this expedition was to be a Mongol venture and had to be done in a Mongol way. Rather unexpectedly, I found myself enjoying my new role as an observer and counselor. It was a luxury to watch and advise and not have to worry about the practical details. Even if my advice was ignored, I realized that as long as the expedition was on Mongol soil, it was a genuinely Mongol affair and I would have a most unusual insight on how modern Mongols ran their projects. Also, I told myself, the team of Ariunbold and Gerel was promising. The one was the bureaucrat who could look after the administration; the other was the field man who could organize the practical aspects of the ambitious scheme. I had the impression—wrongly as it turned out—that they had a long experience of working together. In fact they had shared only a few short hunting trips.

Eventually Ariunbold did decide that we should undertake the first sector across Mongolia in the summer, setting out in July. Gerel improved the plan by suggesting that in May we make a trial ride into the wilderness of Hentei, the area most closely associated with the early career of Genghis Khan. This trial ride seemed an excellent idea. It would give me a chance to field-test my own equipment, particularly the miniature film camera I would carry, and it would provide my companions with an assessment of the Mongol volunteers who had put their names forward for the main expedition.

Once again no one was able to provide a clear picture of where or how far we would ride. There were no proper maps available, either because they were restricted for security purposes or, more likely, were simply not printed for public circulation. But I understood we would be in the field for a week or more and would climb a special mountain to the northeast of Ulaan Baatar in a region called Hentei. Gerel had prepared two oval plaques in bronze, each about twelve inches across, that he wanted to place there. One plaque showed Genghis Khan as a handsome man in his late twenties at the time he was first acknowledged as the leader of his own war band. The other was based on a famous portrait of Genghis Khan that is held in the Imperial Museum in Taiwan. Drawn by a Chinese court artist a generation after Genghis Khan's death, it shows the man who had become the founder of a new imperial Chinese dynasty, the Yuan. By this time Genghis Khan was a much older man, and the Mongol armies had overrun North China and had taken Peking. The Chinese artist had no model to work from, so he had instinctively turned Genghis into a Chinese monarch, giving him almond eyes, a soft mouth, smooth face, and a long, wispy beard. As a result he looks more like a model Confucian prince than a self-made warlord from the steppes.

Both plaques were lying flat on a stained, tattered tarpaulin, with Gerel crouching over them, as we assembled for the trial expedition in May, seven months after my first visit to Ulaan Baatar. Gerel was carefully gluing the bronzes to marble slabs shaped like small gravestones which would be erected at the selected sites. Each slab had been carved with a suitable inscription in the vertical lines of the elegant Mongol script and picked out in red ink. The writing itself was a direct legacy of the genius of Genghis Khan, and a sign of the changing times in modern Mongolia. The Mongols have had a mania for trying out different scripts, perhaps a sign of their position on a cultural crossroads, and at various times the country has known ten different scripts based on Tibetan, Near Eastern, and Russian originals. But until the rise of Genghis Khan the Mongols either did not possess a written language or had no real use for one. So Genghis Khan ordered his bureaucrats to work with an ancient script used by a Central Asian people called the Uighurs, and it was this lettering that became the official script for administrating his huge empire. It survived in general use in Mongolia for more than 700 years until, in 1941, it came under official Communist Party displeasure. A Party committee decided that it was archaic and backward. So a law was passed that it was to be phased out and replaced by the "modern" Cyrillic writing used by their Russian advisers.

All Mongols were to be trained in the use of Cyrillic writing, and schools would no longer teach Mongol script. The Second World War delayed the implementation of this short-sighted reform until 1945, when it soon had the unforeseen result of damaging the Mongol language. Many sounds and nuances in spoken Mongol could not be properly represented in Cyrillic, so spoken Mongol began to be stilted and simplified in order to fit the straitjacket of the new writing. Mongols who were proud of their traditions began to look wistfully across the border to the Chinese province of Inner Mongolia where, ironically, the Mongol script had been retained among the native Mongol population.

Now, forty-five years later, that misguided policy had been reversed. The authorities in Ulaan Baatar had just announced that the Mongol script was to be revived as part of the new liberalization program. There were plans, as yet unclear, to make it once again the official national script, though no one knew how much it would cost to restore. By one estimate the price of replacing all the government typewriters would exceed the total civil service budget for two years. On Gerel's Genghis Khan plaques, of course, the alien Cyrillic script would have been unthinkable.

The quotations Gerel had selected for his inscriptions were taken from what is the Bible for all those who study the life story of Genghis Khan. No one knows exactly who composed the original text, or why, but *The Secret History of the Mongols* ranks as one of the most remarkable documents in Central Asian literature and is perhaps the most unusual written chronicle ever produced by nomads.

The splendidly named Archimandrite Palladius, a scholar-priest attached to the Russian religious mission in Peking, caused a sensation when he announced in 1866 that he had come across a hitherto un-known work in the Chinese archives which described the career of Genghis Khan through the eyes of a Mongol. Palladius' discovery sent shock waves through the serene world of Oriental scholarship. Until then everyone had accepted that the limitation of studying nomad cultures is that nomads do not leave any written records. Moreover, the nature of their shifting lifestyle means that they rarely build up much in the way of an archaeological legacy. Yet the saga that Palladius now published was nothing less than an account, composed shortly after Genghis Khan's lifetime, which purported to describe the origins of the Mongols and gave an account of the birth, rise, and incredible career of the greatest Mongol of them all.

Palladius' news was just the start. Over the next decade other versions and fragments of *The Secret History* began to surface in China, in both private libraries and official archives. It seemed that for centuries Chinese scholars had known of the existence of this unique document but had paid it little attention. It was, after all, a saga about the barbarian Mongols and not about China, the center of civilization. *The Secret History* itself posed exquisite riddles that still have not been solved to everyone's satisfaction. They mainly spring from the fact that although the original version was composed in the Mongol language, the surviving examples were written by Chinese scribes who did not use Mongol script. Instead they tried to match the Mongol sounds by using Chinese characters phonetically. They did their best, and even provided a glossary of the meanings of some of the more abstruse Mongol words, for it seems that the text was used as a training manual for Chinese interpreters and translators trying to learn Mongol. But inevitably the Chinese intermediaries clouded the saga with obscurities, and the original Mongol version has never been found. At least one of the priceless Chinese copies disappeared in the upheaval of the Chinese Civil War, and it has taken

Orientalists more than a century to try to reconstruct the original Mongol version, though there are still many ambiguities.

It is generally agreed that *The Secret History of the Mongols* was meant to provide Genghis Khan's descendants with an official account of the origins of their illustrious forebear, and there is a theory that it came to be called "secret" because only members of the imperial line were allowed to read it. Others claim it was "secret" simply because it was so little circulated. Whatever the truth, *The Secret History* has the echo of a tribal bard speaking over the campfire as he tells the creation legends of his people and the rise of the man whom all Mongols still consider the Father of the Nation.

Gerel and Ariunbold had arranged our rendezvous at a place they said was mentioned in *The Secret History*, on the bank of a small lake, Blue Lake, some 190 miles to the northeast of Ulaan Baatar. Although it was late May, the long Mongolian winter had not yet relaxed its grip. The sedge down by the shore crackled with frost, flocks of crows cawed in bare trees, and the surface of the little lake, no more than half a mile across, was three-quarters covered by a sheet of melting ice. Patches of frozen snow lay in the shaded hollows, and the grass on the slope of the steep hill that rose on the far side of the lake was seared brown. The slope of the hill was disfigured by an ugly slogan, laid out in stones, which praised the victory of the Soviet October Revolution. This was ironic, as we were there to celebrate the very reverse of that Soviet victory: it was at this spot that we would leave the first of Gerel's plaques. This commemorated the momentous day when a handful of insignificant Mongol tribesmen gathered together some 800 years ago to swear allegiance to a 28-year-old Mongol named Temujin. The pledge of fealty was both allegorical and homespun. One man promised to be his new leader's cook, another to be his archer, a third would be his chief shepherd and look after his flocks, a fourth would work as his cowherd, a fifth would maintain his carts. Several were sworn in as personal bodyguards. One man vowed, in the archaic poetry of *The Secret History*, that:

> Becoming a rat,
> I shall gather with others
> Becoming a black crow

Whatever is outside
I would like to scoop up with the others
Becoming a covering of felt,
I will try to cover over [you] with the others,
Becoming a wind break of felt,
I will try to cover over [you] with the others.*

Within twenty years the names of that rag-tag little gang would terrify most of Asia. Temujin had changed his name to Genghis Khan, and his loyal "rat" had become the cavalry general Sübodei, whom Liddell Hart so admired, and who would eventually leave as his epitaph that he had "conquered 32 nations and won 65 pitched battles."

In May 1990, however, a dozen Mongols were standing around, watching Gerel's efforts with his bronze plaques, and it took me a little time to realize that our trial ride was to be accompanied by a group of professional artists as well as two expedition volunteers. The latter were recognizable by the fact that they were dressed up in a sort of expedition uniform of brand-new dark maroon dels and heavy felt boots with unsullied embroidery down the side. They were hoping to be selected for the ride to France, and—with Ariunbold still copying my original expedition proposal—they were a doctor and a veterinary surgeon.

The doctor was a rather shy young man who, surprisingly for a Mongol, sported a trendy pony-tail hairstyle. His companion, the middle-aged vet, looked positively like Samson. He was barrel-chested and had a splendid craggy face. Also, he affected a wide leather body-belt like that worn by weightlifters and on his head wore a traditional Mongol pointed hat that he covered, disconcertingly, with a plastic shopping bag whenever it rained. As it turned out, he was a sham. He loved to preen himself, and his girth was the result of gluttony. Over the next few days he spent most of his time hovering by the campfire, waiting to snap up second and third helpings of food. As for his veterinary skills, it turned out that the local horse-herders knew more about the care and management of livestock than he did. He was not to be selected.

---

*The History and the Life of Chinggis Khan, translated by Urgunge Onon, E. J. Brill, 1990.

Nor did the young doctor prove to be any more suitable, though he was quiet and likeable and made every effort to help out whenever he could. His incurable disadvantage was that he was one of the few Mongols I ever saw who was actually ungainly in the saddle, and he never learned to ride with any degree of self-confidence. He either joggled along in acute discomfort or, if his horse shied, fell off. Everyone felt sorry for him, including the artists, who were oil-painters, sculptors, water-colorists and included several very competent riders.

They all belonged to the Mongolian Artists' Union, and my guess was that they had been invited by Gerel to join the trial ride because their presence gave it a semiofficial status as a "union project" and, equally important, because they would share the cost of hiring the horses and guides we required to enter the mountains. Obviously nothing like this expedition had been attempted before in Mongolia, and we needed to comply with the administrative mind-set of the country.

I noted at once that decision-making among Mongols was a group activity. The day's program, the number of horses, the route, the fit of the saddles, every single subject was being argued backward and forward by everyone, whether or not they had any expertise. Contributors wandered up to deliver their opinions and then left the discussion to go back to their other activity—the contemporary Mongol preoccupation with mending worn tires.

We had arrived at the rendezvous after a six-hour drive from Ulaan Baatar, crossing an undulating landscape of low hills. Our transport was a motley collection of jeeps and cross-country vehicles which had been begged and borrowed from various state organizations and cooperatives. The vehicles were kept running by a process cheerfully called "Mongolization," which described the salvage and modification of any spare part from whatever source. Thus a jeep was likely to have the cracked windshield taken from a similar vehicle which had been destroyed in a wreck, the back axle from a different casualty which was probably a different model, and the gearbox salvaged from a small car. Minor items like lights and mirrors, if they were there at all, were attached with lengths of string or wire. Inevitably these hybrid vehicles could be kept running only with frequent halts for repairs, and their tires were in a permanent state of decay.

The dilapidated state of the vehicles underscored just how difficult it was to organize an expedition in a society where no one had any access to reliable equipment. It was all too apparent that Mongolia lay at the very farthest end of a long line of supply which originated somewhere in the USSR. Any equipment which was imported was, as often as not, a Soviet cast-off. Nor was the life expectancy of the vehicles helped by the fact that Mongolia still had virtually no paved roads. Vehicles traveled from one place to the next simply by following the wheel ruts of previous travelers across the open steppe, through the passes, or into the river fords. There were no bridges. When the wheel ruts became too deep, a driver was free to veer off and pick out a new line over the terrain. The result was a severe rattling for every vehicle and its occupants, and an ecological eyesore. A braided network of road-scars multiplied in all directions, and the surface of the land was cut to shreds.

Ariunbold had located an interpreter, Dr. Boshigt, who was precisely the sort of unlikely contrast I was to encounter again and again in modern Mongolia. He had been trained as a cardiac specialist but did not practice medicine in a country desperately short of doctors. As a freethinker he lived in a totalitarian state, and as a man who dreamed of becoming a successful politician he went off fishing during the crucial run-up to the first free elections. Like all educated Mongols, "Doc" spoke fluent Russian—a compulsory school subject and the medium for all further education—but he also had a very good command of English and had taught himself French and German as well. Because he had done his medical training in Budapest he spoke fluent Hungarian, and after a spell at a Stockholm hospital could manage a little Swedish. He liked horses but loathed riding, and he suffered acutely from hay fever, a major affliction in a country where the summer pollen count must be among the highest in the world. Yet Doc never gave up. His name meant "Fundamental" and he was to accompany all my travels and prove indispensable. He was kindhearted, determined, loved animals, and was exceedingly well informed. As he never went anywhere without his collapsible fishing rod, he was also to provide the best chance of improving what turned out to be a very limited diet.

Two other members made up the core of our trial-ride team. Paul Harris had come with me to take the still photos of our travels. An

Englishman in his early 30s, Paul was working as a professional photographer in London and had come on a photo assignment to my home village in Ireland where I met him. Later, when I wrote to ask if he knew anyone who might like to go on an expedition to Mongolia, he promptly took up the invitation himself, since his main interest was in outdoor photography and he had wanderlust. I had no doubts that Paul would prove to be a good companion. He had been on climbing expeditions in South America and Nepal and was enthusiastic and adaptable. Above all, he was dedicated to doing the best job possible even when it meant getting up well before dawn to be in the best position and catch the best light for his photographs.

Bayar, on the other hand, had been assigned to help me make the documentary film of our journey in the role of second cameraman. Bayar was an employee of the Mongolian TV Film Studio, a very ambitiously named organization that operated from a shabby building in the shadow of Ulaan Baatar's enormous television mast. At some time in the past the Mongolian TV Film Studio must have been an important organization, churning out the sort of newsreels and short documentaries favored by the Eastern bloc. As elsewhere, news film had been surpassed by video, and the Film Studio was very much in eclipse, leaving a few veteran camera operators and sound-recordists to struggle with their antique equipment while all the funds and glamour had passed to their colleagues equipped with video cameras. Bayar was rooted firmly in the old tradition of cameramen. The son of a herdsman, he had been sent to the Moscow Film School to attend the shortened form of film course designed to train cameramen from "friendly socialist countries" and, on his return, had been assigned to the Mongolian TV Film Studio where he had labored for twenty years. He was small, neat, and lively, and had an impish sense of humour. Paul and I found it almost incredible when we discovered that he was a grandfather. It did not seem possible for someone so boyish.

Bayar arrived at our rendezvous burdened with a battered film camera that must have been at least thirty years old and made a low grumbling sound as it ran. He mounted this antique on a stout wooden tripod of equal vintage, and swiveled his peaked leather cap back-to-front before he peered through the viewfinder. As he wore breeches and long black leather boots, he looked like a refugee from a 1920s Hollywood film set. His camerawork left something to be desired—the film-changing bag he used was full of dust and hair, and he casually wrapped the exposed reels in tattered black paper bags instead of storing them in tins—but his vivacious approach to our work was a terrific bonus. He had grown up in the countryside, so he could handle horses and run a camp as well as anyone in the group, and on the trial ride he impressed me hugely by slinging his bulky camera, all knobs and metal corners, in a thin canvas sack on his back. It was not the recommended method, but in Mongolia a padded camera case was not available. With every step of the horse the awkward camera bumped and banged against his ribs and must have been excruciating. Yet, whenever you caught his eye, Bayar invariably responded with a cheeky wink and a broad grin. It was singularly appropriate that his name meant "Happy."

Gerel had made advance arrangements to hire horses and guides from the local agricultural commune or collective. The countryside of Mongolia had been divided by the Party theorists and bureaucrats first into provinces called *aymags* and then into smaller subdivisions known as *somons*. To all intents and purposes the smaller unit, the *somon*, was the territory covered by a single large collective or commune which organized the labor of all the inhabitants living within it. It had its own administrative base, the so-called *somon* center, which might be no more than two dozen buildings and a small dirt airstrip. Here in the classic central-command economy, the *somon* committee directed the lives of the herdsmen and their families, distributed the communal herds to be looked after, issued supplies, and in turn received back the production to be sent on to the central government. Each herdsman was, however, allowed to keep a number of animals privately, and the proportion of private to public livestock varied according to the policy in favor at the time and the nature of the terrain, with private cattle and horses adding up to perhaps 15 percent of the herds.

So next morning, May 17, half a dozen herdsmen rode into camp, each leading three or four spare horses, some of them privately owned, others hired out by the collective. It was difficult to know which were more motley—the riders or their animals.

The animals were a typical mixture of angular, small, unkempt, unshod beasts with heads too big for their bodies, unprepossessing lines, and a hotchpotch of colors. They were all geldings, because the Mongols keep the mares for milk and breeding purposes and retain only a few stallions, which are often allowed to grow immense manes which hang down to the ground so that they seem about to trip on them. The standard working geldings which showed up that morning were scruffy, ill-favored, tough-as-leather creatures, with no trace of breeding or any hint of grace. These were the animals that had just survived the usual Mongolian winter, standing with their tails to the wind in the howling blizzard when the wind roared out of Siberia and fending for themselves when every living plant was nipped dead by the appalling temperatures. It was horses like these that Captain Scott chose to take to the Antarctic to pull his sledges to the South Pole—an experiment that failed—and that enabled Genghis Khan's armies to move 80 miles a day on forced marches. Now Paul and I were to try riding them ourselves.

The herdsmen were an equally indestructible-looking lot, all wearing their standard clothing of tall black boots, shabby working *dels*, and either a woolly hat topped with a bobble, or a weathered trilby, which gave them a startling resemblance to South American gauchos. Quietly they rode up to the edge of the camp and tied their half-wild horses to outlying trees so they would not be scared by the strangers, and then walked forward to be offered tea and cigarettes. They glanced curiously at Paul and me, and politely turned their attention back to our Mongol colleagues and the endless discussion of plans. The conversation was impossible to follow. For one thing I was finding the Mongol face particularly difficult to read. It is so impassive that it makes the Chinese countenance seem positively open. For another, the Mongol language offered no linguistic handles. Although it is often said to be of the Altaic group of languages and related to Turkish, it is so far removed from modern Turkish that, even after months of living with Turkish villagers on my Crusade ride, I could not pick out a single word in the harsh, rapid Mongol conversation. When the argument grew really fierce the sounds increased in tone and pitch until the exchange sounded like two cats coughing and spitting at each other until one finally threw up.

Doc stood aloof, clearly unimpressed by the lack of planning. He translated for us that the herdsmen had not brought enough animals. We would have to wait another day for extra horses to arrive. In the meantime the "nearby" village—"nearby" being several hours' ride away—had donated a sheep for a feast. The evening drew in, and still no sheep appeared. The temperature fell below freezing. There were four little wooden cabins on the edge of the lake, presumably for fishermen or holiday campers. Paul and I retreated into one of them, swept aside the mouse- and bird-droppings and spread our sleeping bags on the wooden floor. At midnight the grinding noise of a Russian-built truck could be heard. Peering out of my sleeping bag, I witnessed a terrified and scraggy sheep being hauled out of the back of the truck, taken around to the light from the headlamps, and slaughtered. The cooking took another two hours, and at 3 a.m. I was awakened by Doc. He thrust a scalding hot metal bowl under my nose. "I brought this over for you. It will keep you warm," he said in a kindly voice. I did not have the heart to reject his generosity and drank the scorching liquid. It was thin and greasy, and slimy morsels of boiled sheep heart and lungs slithered down my throat.

By mid-morning next day the local Party Secretary had turned up, accompanied by a dozen or so functionaries who looked very out of place dressed in their utilitarian dark suits. The Secretary was a young man who could not have been more than 30 and was just as eager as anyone else to celebrate the local link with Genghis Khan. He even sported a lapel button with Genghis Khan's portrait, something that would have been unthinkable for a Party member three years before. The theme of the morning was to be a ceremony typical of the communist world: everyone was to receive commemorative medals, though we had not done anything yet to earn them. Gerel had created chunky medallions which depicted on one side a Mongol dispatch rider, his horse trotting westward. On the other side was a picture of a *paiza*, the famous passport of the medieval Mongol couriers. The *paiza* was the tablet issued by the Mongol overlords to ambassadors and important officials. Made in materials ranging from wood to copper to gold according to the rank and importance of the bearer, a *paiza* entitled a traveler to special privileges in the imperial realms— armed escorts, free use of guides and lodging, and unhindered passage.*

---

*Two Venetians, Nicolo and Maffeo Polo, who traveled overland to the court of Kubilai Khan, Genghis's grandson, were issued a gold *paiza* to help them get back home. When they made a second trip to see Kubilai, still using the passport, they took along with them Nicolo's son—Marco.

Gerel's medallions dangled from ribbons of lucky sky-blue silk, and everyone was to be given one. First, however, Ariunbold honored the two herdsmen, who had decided that they wanted to give, not hire, horses to the expedition. They were so enthusiastic about the idea of the ride to France that they said they wished to donate an animal apiece to make the journey. Everyone gathered in a circle and Ariunbold walked solemnly forward in his plum-colored *del* and heavy felt boots. He carried a long blue scarf across his outstretched arms and a small silver and wood bowl brimming with mare's milk. The scarf, or *khata* as it was known to the Chinese, was an essential in traditional Mongolian etiquette as it signified honor and esteem between giver and recipient. Ariunbold presented the scarf to the first herdsman, who looked awkward and embarrassed, then together they approached the gift horse. In theory the traditional Mongol ceremony called for the gift to be sealed with a splash of milk poured into the nearside stirrup to bring good luck and a safe journey. But naturally the half-wild horse was terrified to be approached by a stranger holding a fluttering blue scarf and clutching a shiny silver bowl, and promptly reared up and tried to bolt. With a certain skepticism I noted that although the herdsmen rode some fine animals, the horses they had produced for our use were not of the best, and the two animals being given to the expedition were positively elderly and infirm. I quietly enjoyed knowing at last what was meant by the old adage about not looking a gift horse in the mouth.

So the second day passed, still in camp, and Paul and I adapted to a more lackadaisical Mongol pace. Everyone was very attentive and kind, and the *arats* in particular seemed impressed that we were interested enough to have come all the way to the remote Hentei. They could see how our Mongol colleagues from the city might be interested in the legacy of Genghis Khan, but it was a source of pride that two foreigners should be making the effort not only to get to the Hentei but to want to try riding their horses and living in the Mongol way.

So Paul and I were fed the better parts of the slaughtered sheep and were shown how to tie the lead rein of a horse around its front feet as a hobble. This meant squatting down beside the animal, shifting its forefeet so that it stood with its two front legs close together, then taking the free end of the rawhide lead rope and wrapping it twice around the forelegs to shackle them about four inches apart, finishing off with a special quick-release knot. Like sailors with their fancy knots, each herdsman had his own idiosyncratic way of hobbling his horse. One after another each came up and insisted that his was the best method, and laughed at our fumbling efforts as we got more and more confused by the conflicting styles. On the steppe, we were told, we would not find a convenient bush or tree where we could attach the animals when we halted. If a horse did run away, there were no fences to deter it. In theory, I calculated, a bolting horse in Mongolia can run the distance from London to Rome without encountering an obstacle to stop it.

Paul had not ridden since childhood, and although I had given him prior warning he was visibly taken aback when he was introduced to a Mongol saddle. It was an excruciating-looking design, upswept at back and front, very narrow and tall, and made of wood. It resembled saddles found in the tombs of the Chinese emperors. The herdsmen were very proud of their personal saddles, which were works of art. They covered them in red velvet, painted the woodwork—bright orange was the favorite color—and paid large sums for silver edging and massive silver studs of intricate workmanship. These studs, a good two inches across and an inch tall, were positioned just about where the rider's thighs would touch the saddle, and must have been agonizing for anyone but a Mongol herdsman, whose backside has been inured to pain by a lifetime of riding. Of course such prize saddles were not available for the novice team members and artists from the city. They were to use standard government saddles, two hoops of steel on wooden panels covered with thin leather cushions. They were no more comfortable than the traditional version.

Cannily, I had brought with me the same saddle in which I had ridden the Crusade route, and this now caused a sensation. I might as well have brought a two-headed cat. The herdsmen had never seen a saddle like it and, when I was not looking, took it away to try fitting it to a compliant horse. European girth, straps, and stirrup leathers were all arranged so differently from their Mongol saddles that they stripped down the foreign saddle and tried to rig it in their own way. In five minutes it was strapped in place by one stirrup leather, and the second stirrup leather had been cinched around the animal's stomach as a second girthband in the Mongol style. When I showed how the saddle was really meant to work, all the herdsmen took it in turns to ride up and down the campsite, grinning with pleasure, to test the fit.

Finally, when there was still enough daylight, everyone—horse-herders, Party officials, expedition applicants, artists—lined up to have Paul take their photo like some memento of a football team. In the center of the group, instead of a soccer ball, was Gerel's first bronze plaque propped up on the spot where, in future, it would stand in memory of Genghis Khan's first step on the path to becoming the "Oceanic Ruler."

4

Arat

The first task next morning was the selection and loading of a pack-horse to carry the expedition's tents, our reserve camera equipment, and a collapsible stove with its metal chimney in three sections, the entire load topped off with the remaining bloody chunks of the dead sheep. The herdsmen had brought in a further draft of half a dozen horses, so there were plenty of animals to pick from, and logically enough they selected the sturdiest horse in the group to carry our gear.

Unfortunately the creature was also thoroughly bad-tempered and obstinate and had never been used as a pack-horse before. The herdsmen managed to slip the standard crude metal bit between its teeth and get a bridle on its head, but the horse then objected violently to having the saddle put on its back. It reared and plunged. Unperturbed, Dampildorj, the senior herdsman, looped the thin lead rein of rawhide around the horse's upper lip and pulled it extremely tight. The lip stretched out and out until the horse had a long snout like a tapir, the rope squeezing the nerves of the lip in the same way that a Western blacksmith applies a nose-twitch to control an awkward horse while it is being shod. But the sinewy, half-wild Mongol horse still had plenty of fight left in him and thrashed from side to side trying to shake his head free.

So the herdsmen put on a full hobble. Two rawhide loops cuffed the two forelegs close together and a third loop was tied back to the nearside hind leg. Even then the trussed-up horse refused to be quelled, and it bucked and lunged in fury. So a Mongol crept up on each side and, suddenly snatching out, like someone trying to seize a fly in midair, each man grabbed an ear. Then they pulled the ears downward and twisted, further anesthetizing the wretched victim, which now stood with its head and feet trapped and motionless enough for a saddle to be cinched in place. In double quick time the packs were loaded and roped firmly.

All was now ready. The ear-pullers and the twitch-holder released their victim and skipped clear. The furious, frightened horse gave a great leap to escape. Of course it had forgotten the hobbles. The first huge bound was checked in midair and the horse nose-dived into the ground with a tremendous crash which made me wince both for the fragile items in the packs and for the unfortunate animal. To my amazement the horse bounced back on its feet, even under packs and in hobbles, and tried again to gallop forward. Once more there was a tremendous pratfall. After this the horse scrambled upright and stood sullenly. A herdsman reached cautiously down and untied the rear hobble. The horse was led forward, found it could bunny-hop, and again tried to shake off the packs, this time deliberately flinging itself on the ground and rolling. A herdsman prodded it back on its feet, and the animal stood in a semi-daze. Dampildorj tugged on the lead rope and the half-defeated horse hopped forward. Ten yards farther on the front hobbles were removed, and we had a very grumpy pack-horse.

We set out soon afterwards in an untidy straggle of about fifteen men and perhaps twice as many horses, with the extra mounts being brought along on lead ropes. The air temperature was only just above freezing. If we had been starting a cross-country ride in Europe we might have begun gently in order to loosen up the muscles of the horses on such a chilly morning, and then during the day followed with an alternating rhythm of walk, trot, and canter to vary the pace. The Mongols did nothing of the sort. Their system of cross-country travel was extremely straightforward. In the first half-dozen steps they urged their horses into a fast, pattering run and then kept up the same blistering pace with no variation whatsoever for the next two hours. Then they halted for a five-minute break. They would dismount, have a smoke and a chat, and on a word from the senior herdsman would swing back onto their horses and repeat the fast run all over again. They could keep this up all day if necessary. It was a no-nonsense way of covering the ground and was remarkably effective. A walk would have been too slow with the short legs of their mounts, a canter too exhausting. The flat, hammering run of the Mongol horse was the only option. There was nothing graceful or elegant about the gait. It was the pace of completely unschooled horses, without any concessions for the rider's comfort.

Within ten minutes of starting I knew that Beatrix Bulstrode had been right when she commented that "riding, I soon found, was not much fun," and from his groans I knew that Paul was in agony. The runty little horses gave a thoroughly uncomfortable ride. If you sat down firmly in the saddle, you were jolted and rattled. If you tried the rhythmic rise and fall of a trot in European style, the motion was made awkward and tiring by the short steps of the animal, which also became puzzled and nervous about what the rider was doing. The solution was to do what the Mongol herdsmen did, but that required a lifetime of training. The horse-herders either rose in the stirrups and just stood there, for 20 or 30 or 50 miles a day, apparently on legs of pure sinew and swaying with the motion of the horse. Or they sat down in their wooden saddles and relaxed, letting themselves go limp and be shaken up and down like peas on a drum. A line of Mongol herdsmen proceeding in this fashion made a remarkable sight, with their heads wobbling back and forth like demented puppets.

We rode at first through a thin forest of immature pine trees. There was not a cloud in the sky, and a slight tang of wood smoke and a bluish tinge hung in the air. A forest fire had started on the far side of the slogan-defaced hill behind the lake, and the smoke was drifting in our direction. Forest fires must have been common, because much of the forest was already scorched and black. It was unlikely that the fires had been started by man, because that part of the Hentei was uninhabited. When we emerged from the trees and entered the first of a succession of broad valleys, the overwhelming visual impact was the complete emptiness of the land. The valley stretched away into the distance. There was not a trace of human activity, not a fence, a telegraph pole, a track, or any form of domestic animal. It was com-pletely deserted, just mile after mile of partridge-brown grassland sloping up on each side to the hills. On the upper slopes were more trees, widely spaced and bare. A few rocks broke through the thin soil, but otherwise there was nothing to catch the eye except the distant shapes of large birds of prey, falcons and eagles, wheeling and hovering over the steppe. I understood why the ordinary *arats* did not consider space or time in the same terms that most Westerners would judge it. Their country was so vast and their means of transport so limited that they would think nothing of riding five or six hours across country simply to pass the time of day with a neighbor in the next felt tent perhaps 20 miles away and then riding back home.

An hour later the pack-horse got its revenge by running away. It chose its moment well, waiting until the rider holding its lead rein had crossed a small stream and was on the far bank. Then the pack-horse flung backwards, snatched the lead rein free, and whirling in its tracks galloped off in a bid for freedom. Our ragged line of riders halted and watched the pack-horse dwindle in the distance, chased back and forth by the most junior horse-herder, who was obviously enjoying himself in a private gallop. It seemed a good time to take a break, and Paul and I got down from our horses, as did Bayar, who was riding with us. Our colleagues had stopped a little distance up ahead, and in two or three small groups we waited. There was the stump of an old tree nearby so Paul, Bayar, and I tied up our horses and sat down on the ground to stretch out our aching legs.

After a few moments I decided that it was a good opportunity to make some notes and walked over to take my notebook from the saddlebag. Our three horses were standing close together and, un-thinking, I pushed between them. The herdsmen had picked our horses for being calm and well behaved by Mongol standards, but I promptly learned just how untamed they really were. A Mongol horse taken from the open range is completely one-sided. If a stranger approaches it confidently and slowly from the nearside, it may stand quietly, though it still regards with acute suspicion a foreigner who dresses and smells differently from a normal Mongol horse-herder. But any movement or touch from the offside produces hysteria.

As I approached my horse, I brushed against the offside of Bayar's mount. It reared up in panic, throwing itself back on the lead rein. The thin strip of rawhide snapped and the horse ran off. Fortunately it went only a couple of hundred yards and joined the next group of waiting horses, where it was caught by one of the artists. Bayar got to his feet and walked off to retrieve it, but the pony-tailed doctor, who was still on horseback, had already begun to lead it back. On the way the doctor's horse tripped, the doctor tumbled out of the saddle, and his horse as well as Bayar's were so badly spooked that they both ran off, this time heading into the nearby hills. Observing the commotion, Paul leaned forward to pick up his camera to photograph the scene, and the sudden movement alarmed his horse as well. It too snapped its lead rein and careered off in fright. In the space of a few moments we had a total of three escapees galloping energetically off into the distance, each making the others even more scared than before. It was a mini-stampede and our herder-guides went tearing off to catch the runaways, weaving and dodging between the trees and rocks until they too had vanished.

Half an hour later they reappeared, leading the horses but looking solemn. They said something to Bayar and his face fell. They were telling him that his precious tripod, which had been dangling from the saddle, was lost. Galloping between the trees his horse must have brushed it off, and it could not be found. Bayar was despondent. The tripod was the property of the Mongolian TV Film Studio, and in a country where even the smallest item is irreplaceable the loss would get him into trouble. When the errant pack-pony was led in, we rode onward with a glum Bayar no longer wearing his cheery smile. Two hours later, after a tobacco break, as Bayar remounted his horse he found his tripod dangling in its usual place. The herders were grinning broadly. They had been hiding the tripod as a practical joke. Obviously country Mongols, however taciturn and straightfaced, had a sense of humor.

The appearance of the average *arat* or herdsman was as Prjevalski had described: "a broad flat face with high cheek bones, wide nostrils, small narrow eyes, large prominent ears, coarse black hair, scanty whiskers and beard, a dark sunburnt complexion, and lastly a stout thickset figure, rather above the average height." They were unaffected and friendly people whom it was very easy to get to like. They were decent and obliging, and they respected competence and experience. In our little traveling group it was clear that they took their lead from Dampildorj, the close-cropped veteran. He was recognized as the ablest horse-handler and the man who knew the wild Hentei terrain best. It was Dampildorj who set the pace. It was he who decided when and where we would halt for the rest breaks, and it was he who, at the end of each halt, gave a brief grunt to signify that we should mount up and ride on.

Each halt was identical. Without a word Dampildorj would turn his horse aside from the path, pull up, and dismount. Behind him the other *arats* did the same and walked forward toward Dampildorj, who by then had sunk down to sit on one heel with the other leg stuck straight forward, already searching for his pack of cigarettes. The other herdsmen would join him, each man sinking down into exactly the same posture, to form a tight, intimate circle. Cigarettes were offered and accepted, a box of matches handed round, and very often a small bottle of snuff appeared as well.

The herdsmen carried these small items tucked in the front fold of the wraparound *del*, which made a single large pocket, and there was a definite formality about the giving and taking. When the snuff bottle was offered, politeness demanded that it was held out in the right hand, with the right arm outstretched and the elbow cupped by the left hand. The recipient took the bottle with exactly the same gesture, turned the snuff bottle over in his hand to admire the workmanship, uncapped the bottle's ornate top with its slim spatula, and spooned out a tiny helping of snuff. With slow, deliberate movements the snuff was taken, the stopper replaced, and the bottle passed back, again right-handed, to the donor, with exactly the same ritual gestures. The first man then offered his snuff bottle to the next herdsman in the circle, and so on. All the while the horses looked on. Instead of tying or hobbling his horse, each herdsman usually kept the animal on its lead rein, standing close behind him like a dog on a leash. So an outer circle of horses looked inward over the heads of their riders.

I was struck by how the herdsmen derived real pleasure from traditional style and craftsmanship. Besides the silver ornaments on their saddles, they valued anything that was old and of good workmanship. One of our guides was something of a dandy. He wore a short overjacket of striking emerald-green silk with a high collar picked out with red patterns and edged with gold braid. From his belt hung a matching green silk tobacco pouch, and he carried a long slender Chinese pipe with a tiny bowl which he lit up during our rest breaks. His knife was not the workaday penknife of the other riders, but a beautiful antique dagger, an heirloom, long and slim and held in a silver-mounted sheath which he tucked into an orange cummerbund behind his back. The sheath had an additional double socket which contained two ivory chopsticks, also silver mounted, and from it a heavy silver chain led to an antique half-moon steel once used for striking sparks against flint. This steel too was in a massive silver mounting. Time and time again these trinkets were fingered and admired by his colleagues, and each time they warmly complimented their friend on possessing articles of such workmanship and long history. It was an interesting contradiction to official Mongolian policy where, in theory, such values should long ago have faded away as they represented Mongolia's feudal past.

Toward their horses the herdsmen were neither cruel nor particularly affectionate. They regarded their animals as working tools which had to be maintained properly or else herding life was impossible. The *arats* had no vehicles, and with the huge distances involved they were utterly dependent on having fit and reliable horses for transport and work. They never walked, even twenty paces, if they could ride, and a horse was always kept saddled and ready outside their *ger*. Naturally they needed plenty of remounts, and each man had access to so many spare horses that with rare exceptions they did not bother to name their animals. That is not to say they could not recognize each animal individually. Many herdsmen carried a battered pair of binoculars or a small telescope inside the front fold of their *dels*, and when they saw a distant group of horses grazing they would whip out the spy glass and at five or six miles be able to identify each one of their own horses in the group by its color, conformation, and movement. They had raised the animals themselves and knew them intimately, literally picking up the tiny foals and carrying them to their mothers in the first weeks of life. When it came to treating sick horses they had little use for modern veterinary medicines or techniques but relied on time-honored cures. If a horse developed an abscess in the hoof, they stood the injured foot in the hot ashes of the campfire. A sore back was swabbed with a simple solution of salt and water.

Bloodletting was the cure-all. At the end of our first day's travel Dampildorj decided that most of the horses were in poor condition after their long winter semi-starvation and should be bled. He and three other herdsmen stalked the animals, which had been hobbled and turned loose to graze. It was a gruesome business. Each animal as it was caught was again treated to the nose-twitch. But this time a second loop of rawhide was slipped over the lower jaw and pulled downward to open wide the animal's mouth. Dampildorj produced a small penknife and tied a scrap of cloth around its blade, leaving bare a centimeter of the sharp metal tip. Peering inside the horse's mouth, he carefully picked his spot and then jabbed crisply upward into the gum behind the upper teeth. A thin stream of blood dribbled down, filled the horse's mouth, and began to drip to the ground. The animal appeared to feel no pain and began to slobber and lick the blood. The blood was supposed to flow until it stopped naturally, so the mouth had to be held open until this happened, either with the leather thongs or with a billet of firewood thrust into the animal's mouth to make a crude wooden gag.

After some five hours' riding, we came to a campsite in a gully where a small stream oozed from under a patch of snow on the hillside and provided water for the horses and their riders. There was no special treatment for the horses, other than a brisk currying with a thin wooden blade like a croupier's spatula which scraped away the dried sweat. The animals were simply turned loose to graze in their hobbles. If a particular horse was a known wanderer, it was first hobbled and then tied head to head to another horse to act as a drag. The agility of the little Mongol horses was phenomenal. Even when closely lashed in pairs, one horse would get down on the ground and roll, then wriggle back up on to its feet without throttling its companion. Then they would bunny-hop side by side as they grazed, like contestants in a three-legged race. Never did I see the herdsmen give their animals any hay or grain or extra feed. Even with the pasture completely dead and frozen, the horses were expected to forage for themselves, finding enough sustenance in the early morning and at the end of the day's ride, and getting enough rest, to enable them to run eight hours next day.

Bayar had set up the camp stove, a metal cube of sheet iron which could be folded flat and had been carried in a sack on the pack-pony. With its three-piece tin chimney, the entire contraption was extremely efficient. Firewood was loaded into it and set ablaze. A large bowl of water was fitted into the hole on top of the stove and in ten minutes was simmering away briskly. Bayar was brewing tea, the first meal of the day. The tea he produced from a cloth bag like a large tobacco

The Great Birthday Party celebrating the eight hundredth birthday of Genghis Khan, held in the main square of Ulaan Baatar by popular acclaim.

Riding to the summit of Burkhan Khaldun, the mountain which Genghis Khan promised to revere all of his life; he told his people to remember his vow.

Herdsman Dampildorj chatting with fellow *arat* (Mongolian herdsman) on the day of the expedition's trial ride from Blue Lake, the place where Genghis Khan was chosen as leader of his clan.

Herdsman's proudest possessions: silver-mounted steel for striking fire.

Delger Saihan, the expedition's groom.

Ariunbold and Tim Severin (in peaked cap) ride out of the main gate of Erdenzu on the start of the expedition.

Lama outside the newly reopened lamasery of Erdenzu.

The nine-yak-tail banner on display—the symbol of the medieval Mongol army and the emblem of the Golden Family, the descendants of Genghis Khan.

A guide smoke-drying meat inside the expedition tent.

Fording a river. Summer is Mongolia's brief rainy season, and in a country largely without roads or bridges, travel is only by four-wheel-drive vehicle or horse.

Dampildorj loading a difficult pack-pony.

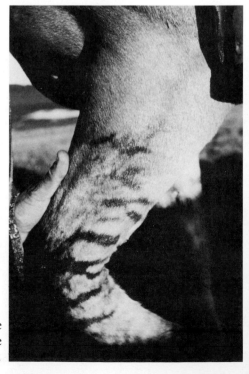

Zebra stripes on the leg of a Mongol horse
are said by the herdsman to show they are
related to the Wild Horses of Mongolia.

Riding to the summit of Burkhan Khaldun, the heartland of Mongolia. According to tribal legend, the first Mongol was born within sight of this mountain.

Ariunbold placing Gerel's second plaque in honor of Genghis Khan on the stone cairn, the "Seat of Genghis Khan" on the summit of Burkhan Khaldun.

Two herdsmen galloping over the prairie.

Adding an offering to an *obo*, or
sacred shrine, at the foot of the
Mountain of the Shaman Spirit.

pouch was of the worst possible quality. It was brick tea imported from China at the cheapest price. Knowing the disdain in which the Chinese hold the Mongols, still regarding them as uncouth barbarians beyond the Great Wall, it was not surprising that they sent rubbish to Mongolia, nor were the impoverished Mongols able to afford anything better. The tea bricks they received were compressed from twigs and dust and sweepings from the factory floor, and there was very little genuine leaf. The tea brick, the texture and color of a lump of dried peat, had to be battered with a hammer to break off what was needed for the brew.

The Mongol herdsmen did not care. They endured one of the most rudimentary cuisines in the world, a fact lamented since earliest times by travelers to the Mongol empire. "They have neither bread nor herbs nor vegetables nor anything else, nothing but meat, of which, however, they eat so little that other people would scarcely be able to exist on it," complained Carpini, who, as a friar, must have been accustomed to plain fare and occasional fasting but who found the Mongol food as inadequate as it was unhygienic:

> They do not use table cloths or knapkins. . . . They make their hands very dirty with the grease of the meat, but when they eat they wipe them on their leggings or the grass or some other such thing. . . . They do not wash their dishes and, if occasionally they rinse them with the meat broth, they put it back with the meat in the pot. Pots also or spoons or other articles intended for this use, if they are cleaned at all, are washed in the same manner.

Prjevalski had been equally scathing about the way the Mongols made tea. "The mode of preparation is disgusting," he wrote:

> the vessel in which the tea is boiled is never cleansed, and is occasionally scrubbed with *argols*, ie dried horse or cow dung. Salt water is generally used but, if unobtainable, salt is added. The tea is then pared off with a knife or pounded in a mortar and a handful of it thrown into the boiling water to which a few cups of milk are added. To soften the brick tea which is sometimes as hard as a rock, it is placed for a few moments among hot *argols* which impart a flavour and aroma to the beverage. This is the first process, and in this form answers the same purpose as chocolate or coffee with us. For a more substantial meal

the Mongol mixes dry roasted millet in his cup and as a final relish adds a lump of butter or raw sheep tail fat. The reader may now imagine what a revolting compound of nastiness is produced, and yet they consume any quantity of it!

Twenty to thirty cups of tea each day was normal, said Prjevalski. Rich Mongols drank from ornate bowls of solid silver while the lama priests used cups made of human skulls cut in half and mounted in silver.

Paul and I had been issued small copper bowls of traditional shape but modern manufacture and were glad to note that camp hygiene had greatly improved since Prjevalski's time. Also we were very hungry, not having eaten all day, and quite prepared to wolf down whatever food was put in front of us. But we soon found that one feature of Mongol cuisine had not changed since Prjevalski's journey: a Mongol cooked his food by putting it into boiling water, and that was that. Over the next few months very rarely did I see anyone bother to roast, to barbecue, or—if fat was available—even to fry a camp meal. The excuse I heard in Mongolia was that the busy herdsman normally had no time to prepare or eat a more demanding meal, even when he came home to his *ger*. But palpably that was untrue of the long evenings. The answer seemed to be that a Mongol liked his food boiled, and nothing else interested him. When Doc, our dedicated fisherman, caught half a dozen splendid trout-like fish the following evening, the treatment was the same. The fish were gutted, chopped up, and then the lumps thrown into boiling water, and the taste boiled out of them.

Doc's fish were regarded with suspicion by several of our companions; what they preferred—when they could get it—was mutton. No other flesh had quite the same appeal, though Carpini claimed that the Mongols of his time would happily eat dogs, wolves, foxes, horses, and even body lice, saying, "Why should I not eat them since they eat the flesh of my son and drink his blood?" Carpini grimly added, "I have even seen them eat mice."

Our Mongol companions told us that they would eat beef willingly, camel if necessary, horseflesh under duress. But sheep was easily their favorite, and they were eager to demonstrate the correct way of slaughtering and cooking, though it required a strong stomach to watch them at work. To slaughter the animal, the herdsman threw the sheep on its back and knelt across it like a wrestler holding down his opponent. He then deftly slit the bellyskin with a very sharp knife and, with the animal still alive, slid his hand inside the guts as far as the aorta and squeezed, stopping the heart. In a few moments the sheep's head flopped over to one side and the animal was dead with scarcely a drop of blood spilled. Briskly the carcass was flayed, and only the half-digested contents of the stomach were thrown away. The rest of the animal—tripes, head, meat, bones—was considered fit to eat and would sooner or later be boiled in the cauldron. In the harsh and demanding world of the nomads nothing—except perhaps the ears—was wasted if it was remotely edible. As Carpini put it, "They consider it a great sin if any food or drink is allowed to be wasted in any way; consequently they do not allow bones to be given to dogs until the marrow has been extracted." Carpini was understating the case. On one occasion a few weeks later our little team of riders sat inside a tent and consumed most of the half-boiled intestines of a sheep spread on the earth floor. When they decided they had eaten their fill, they picked up the rest of the meal and threw it out of the tent door to a pair of circling dogs. The dogs, I noted, refused to eat the offal.

Even if one could skirt around the worst of the sheep guts, it was difficult to escape the monotony of the menu. The regular diet of the herdsmen in late spring consisted of just two items: mutton and tea. Either you started with lumps of boiled sheep and finished with tea, or you began with tea and finished with bits of the sheep. The only substitution occurred at breakfast when Dampildorj dumped the head of the sheep into the embers of the fire. I thought we might have roast sheep's head for breakfast. But no, he merely wanted to singe off the hair. The charred head was pulled out of the fire with a twig, the tiniest scraps of meat and marrow picked out with the point of a knife . . . and dropped into the lukewarm tea.

At every meal there was salt, but no pepper, and packets of flat, tasteless Chinese flour noodles were added to the boiling pot. Much to Paul's dismay, for he was a vegetarian, there were no vegetables. But this was just as Carpini had warned, and the official government handbook about Mongolia was being disingenuous when it boasted that "the country is self-sufficient in vegetables." It was not a difficult claim to make. In the countryside the *arats* ate no fresh vegetables whatsoever. The climate was too short to grow most types of green stuff and the *gers* were moved too frequently to make it worth starting a garden. Besides, the herders detested any form of agriculture.

Theoretically they should have been ill from such an unbalanced diet and the lack of vitamins, but they were not. On the contrary, they seemed to be outstandingly healthy, and it was not uncommon to meet countrymen and women in their 90s still looking remarkably fit. As with Bayar, it was difficult to judge real age among the Mongols. Men in particular looked at least ten or fifteen years younger than they really were. What was even more puzzling, as I was to learn later, was that in the easy days of summer they thrived on an intake of alcohol and high cholesterol that should have been lethal. The only explanation for their robust good health was that a herdsman's life was incredibly active and, like their horses, only the fittest survived.

Their hardiness was awe-inspiring. On that first day's ride the weather was so cold that Paul rode wearing an Andean wool hat, and I had an ex-army fleece-lined cap pulled as low as possible. Nevertheless my earlobes began to bleed from chilblains caused by a scything wind. By contrast the Mongol herdsmen considered the day to have brought reasonably mild spring weather. Their *dels* had extra-long sleeves which they could unfold six inches beyond the tips of their fingers as ready-made gloves, but they did not bother to do so, and their headgear of wool hats or traditional steeled caps left their necks and ears exposed. That evening when we set up camp, Paul and I erected our small mountain tent and unrolled double sleeping bags. Gerel, Ariunbold, and the contingent of Mongol artists and volunteers had a tattered canvas tent. But the *arats* merely picked a spot where a tangle of low leafless willow bushes offered a little shelter from the constant wind. There they placed their saddles side by side in a line on the ground to make a token windbreak, spread their saddle blankets and lay down in the open, close together for further warmth. The temperature dropped to minus 12 degrees in the night and the wind-chill factor must have made conditions even worse. Yet the herders slept soundly in conditions that would have risked hypothermia for anyone less hardened.

A quarter of a mile from where we had camped was a so-called

"Tomb of Genghis Khan." On a low grassy knoll stood a stone sarcophagus made of four great panels of rock set up on edge to form the sides of what had once been a massive coffin. The lid, the fifth panel, was missing, and the sides of the box had fallen askew. It could not possibly have been the real tomb of Genghis Khan, because the sarcophagus was far too modest and the style of the patterns carved into the stone panels was of a later period. It was the burial place of a more recent and less important Mongol chieftain, but nevertheless it was clear why his people had chosen that particular spot. The dead chieftain's last resting place had been selected with an eye to all that would have been most important in his life. The tomb was placed a little to one side of the broad valley where the south-facing slope gave a commanding view. The grave looked out toward the warmth of the sun, the rich grassland, the nearby source of water, and a great sheltered sweep of open valley where his tribe could safely graze their horses. It was a magnificent and timeless setting, and I could imagine no finer site for a nomad grave.

5

Mountain of the Shaman Spirit

Gerel's aim was that we should ride to the summit of Burkhan Khaldun, "Mountain of the Shaman Spirit." Here in the Hentei, according to *The Secret History of the Mongols*, was the very fountainhead of the Mongol nation, for it was in sight of this mountain that the ultimate forebears of the Great Mongol had started the ancestral line that led to Genghis Khan himself. It is not clear whether these forebears were seen as ancestral totem animals similar to the creature ancestors claimed by many North American Indian tribes, or whether they were real people who merely carried the names of animals. *The Secret History* calls them the Wolf and the Beautiful Doe, and tells how they arrived from across the sea and settled at the source of the river Onon close by Burkhan Khaldun. There Qo'ai-marael, the Beautiful Doe, gave birth to a son, Batachi-khan. His descendants pastured their herds in the meadows of the Hentei and hunted the abundant wild game of the forest-clad slopes of Burkhan Khaldun until in the twenty-first generation a young male child was born. In his right fist the baby held a clot of blood the size of a knuckle bone. It was a magic omen: the infant was the future Genghis Khan.

The early Mongols lived in a manner so strikingly similar to the much better-known Plains Indians of North America that one has the feeling that the extraordinary achievement of Genghis Khan was the equivalent of the Sioux Indians or the Pawnee producing a military genius who went on to conquer every nation from Alaska to Cape Horn, including the Mayans and the Incas, had they been contemporary. In Mongolia, as in the American Great Plains, the indigenous tribes lived in tented camps which they shifted from place to place while they indulged in wife-snatching, belief in dreams, skirmishes between rival groups, shamanism to ecstatic dances, horse-stealing, hunting, and clan feuds.

Genghis Khan's father was a clan-chief, Yesugei the Brave, whose reputation—the Plains Indians would have considered it a coup—included the abduction of Genghis Khan's mother Ho'elun just after she had married a man of the Merkid tribe. Yesugei was out hunting with his tame falcon along the banks of the Onon River when he saw Ho'elun being taken in a cart to her new home, escorted by her husband. Yesugei was so attracted by her beauty that he hastily rode back to his felt tent to summon his two brothers, and all three chased away the unlucky Merkid, who had to gallop off for his life. Ho'elun was left weeping so bitterly that, as *The Secret History* put it, "the river Onon churned and the forest echoed to the sound of her loud crying." Unmoved, one of Yesugei's brothers roughly told her to cease her wailing and forget her fugitive husband. In the saga's blunt stanzas:

> The one you embraced
> Has crossed many ridges
> The one you cry for
> Has crossed many waters
> Even if you cry out
> Looking from afar, he will not see you.
> Even if you search for him,
> You will not find his path.
> Calm down.

Despite this unpromising start Ho'elun adapted well enough to life with Yesugei the Brave, and at regular two-yearly intervals gave him five children—four sons and a daughter. She announced her first pregnancy to Yesugei soon after he had returned from yet another plundering raid on a neighboring tribal chief, and to commemorate his prowess he decided to give the child the same name as the man he had just despoiled. So the first-born boy child was called Temujin, "the Ironsmith," and when he was 9 years old his father took him to find a future bride among his mother's clan. On the way, however, Yesugei met a man of the Onggirat, a tribe noted for the loveliness of its women. The Onggirat remarked on the intelligent look of the boy and told Yesugei that he had recently dreamed a strange dream in which a white gyrfalcon had brought him the sun and moon in its claws. It was an omen, he said, that Yesugei would come to him with his son. The Onggirat had a 10-year-old daughter, Borte, and he asked if Yesugei would come to his tent to meet her. When Yesugei saw the girl, he agreed that she would make a fine daughter-in-law and that she and Temujin should be betrothed.

Yesugei then left Temujin with his fiancée's family so that they could get to know one another better, and rode back toward his own camp. Tired and hungry, he unwisely stopped to share a meal with a rival tribe, the Tatars. They recognized him as an old enemy and, according to *The Secret History*, mixed poison in his food. Three days later Yesugei struggled back to his own tent, mortally sick. He died after he had identified his killers, and it was a murder that would cost the Tatars their existence. When Temujin was powerful enough, he would launch a campaign to exterminate the Tatars, though by a twist of fate their name would cling to his memory for ever. Carpini and the other European visitors confused the Tatars with the similar-sounding classical name of Tartarus for a region of Hell, and because the Mongols appeared to be devils incarnate transferred the name so that the Mongols came to be known in the West as Tartars while, to add to the irony, the Chinese also sometimes used Ta-ta as a description of the Mongols.

Yesugei's death was a catastrophe for his family. Temujin was too young to succeed his father as clan-leader, and the senior women of the clan rejected Ho'elun. When the time came for the spring migration the little band moved off, deliberately leaving Ho'elun behind with her children. A tribal elder who protested at this harsh treatment was speared in the back by one of the new clan-chiefs and left to die. It was the beginning of the darkest days for Ho'elun and her young family. How she survived is part of the Genghis Khan legend. According to *The Secret History* the mother and her orphaned children lived like wild creatures along the banks of the Onon. She gathered wild fruit and dug up edible roots to feed them. The children helped by fishing with needles bent into fishhooks and knotting homemade nets to sweep the river for sprats. All the time, they nurtured a terrible bitterness against the clan, the Tayichigud, that had abandoned them.

Reared in the wild, Ho'elun's children grew up no less savage than their foes. They were joined by two of Yesugei's sons by a second wife, and the gnawing shortage of food in the little group led to bitter quarrels that culminated in a particularly cold-blooded murder. Temujin and his brother Qasar were furious when their half-brothers snatched away the fish and small birds that they caught, and they eventually decided to do away with their half-brother Bekter. They crept up on him as he was sitting on top of a hill watching over the family's few remaining horses. Seeing that he was trapped, Bekter coolly dared them to follow up on their threats. They riddled him with arrows as he sat on the ground.

Such ruthlessness in the young Temujin must have caught the attention of the Tayichigud. Fearing that he was reaching an age when he might lay claim to his father's title, they sent some men to capture him. While his brothers put up a fierce resistance, Temujin ran away and hid in the thick forests of Burkhan Khaldun. But the Tayichigud were patient. They waited for nine days until hunger forced him to emerge, caught him, and took him back to their camp.

There Temujin was forced to wear the *cangue*, or portable stocks, a heavy wooden board that is clamped around the neck like a yoke and has two holes for the hands. It is difficult for the wearer to sit, near-impossible to lie down and sleep. As a prisoner Temujin was passed from tent to tent, forced to spend one night in each, until eventually he got his chance to escape during a feast. Catching his guard by surprise, Temujin swung the *cangue* so that it hit him in the head, then ran for the river and slipped into the water, using the wooden board as a float to hold his face just above the surface of the stream. The alarm was raised and the Tayichigud hunted high and low for their captive. Luckily the man who spotted Temujin in the river was a sympathizer and, instead of leading the hunt to him, warned Temujin to lie still. Three times the searchers passed by, and each time the sympathizer warned Temujin. Finally, as darkness fell, the search was suspended and in the night Temujin crept into the tent of his new-found friend, who removed the *cangue* and gave him a horse and food so he could escape.

Once more Temujin fled back to the sheltering wilderness of Burkhan Khaldun, where for a time he and his family lived like outlaws, eating marmots and field mice that they trapped. He managed to contact Borte's family and his fiancée came to live with him. As the months passed the young chieftain began to build up a small group of loyal followers as kinsmen and local supporters drifted in to join him. But the Tayichigud had not forgotten him. With the help of the Merkid, still resentful about the abduction of Ho'elun, they launched a surprise raid, hoping to catch Temujin in his camp. Only the warning of an old woman, his mother's servant, saved him. She dreamed that the earth was shaking, and that this meant soldiers were riding to attack. She alerted Temujin so that he and most of his followers once again fled into the forests. In their haste they were obliged to leave Borte behind. The raiders found her hiding in a cartload of wool and carried her off. Borte was recaptured later, but there was a lingering suspicion that her first son, Jochi, had been conceived while she was a captive and was therefore not Genghis Khan's child.

However, the Tayichigud failed to take Temujin himself, though three Merkid warriors followed his tracks through the grass as far as Burkhan Khaldun and circled the mountain three times trying to flush him out of the dense undergrowth. Finally the hunters gave up and withdrew. This time Temujin was more cautious about leaving his refuge. He remembered his previous mistake in emerging from the safety of the mountain too soon and sent men to trail the raiders until they were safely three days clear on their homeward route. Only then did he leave the forest and bring the rest of his family down from Burkhan Khaldun, which he announced had saved his life. He vowed that in future he would offer a sacrifice every morning to Burkhan Khaldun and each day pray to the mountain, and that his descendants would remember the pledge. He sealed his oath formally by facing the sun, removing his hat, and unwinding his sash and draping it over his neck. Then he knelt nine times to the sun and, striking his breast with his hand, prayed and gave offerings to the mountain.

The bald smooth summit of Burkhan Khaldun came in sight on the fourth day of our ride. We had been making erratic progress. The first day had proved to be a running-in period, while the second was

a helter-skelter attempt to catch up to our original schedule, delayed
by the late arrival of the horses at the rendezvous. So on Day Two
we tore along at a great pace for seven hours, still without seeing a
living soul, and ended with an hour-long gallop that sorted the riding
team into novices and professionals. When we halted, the herdsmen
got off their horses as if they had just ridden in from a half-hour
jaunt. The rest of us—Mongol artists, expedition hopefuls, Ariunbold, Paul, and myself—slumped to the ground in total exhaustion,
grateful to be finished with the pounding agony of the ride.

We had reached the only permanent buildings we were to see during
the entire ride into the Hentei. It was a winter cattle station built to
a Soviet design which had been developed for use in Siberia, though
the place could equally have been an authentic set for a film about
the American West. Five small log cabins sheltered behind a wooden
stockade. Peering out over the top, all one could see was the surrounding expanse of the broad valley, a line of distant willow bushes
that marked a river, and the nearby mountains. A single small gate,
which was shut and padlocked at night, led into the compound where
a dog on a chain barked angrily at any strangers. One log house was
a meeting hall, two were empty storehouses, another was a small
bunkhouse, and the fifth was the home of the cattle station's only
occupant, a toothless old caretaker who was delighted to see us. The
cattle had calved earlier in the month and the herds had been driven
off to pasture, so he had not expected to see any new faces for a long
while. He had nothing to break the long monotony of his existence.
He listened to an ancient radio, lived off tea and flat unleavened
pancakes made of sugar and flour, and every second day laboriously
trundled a dented metal churn in a rickety wheelbarrow for half a
mile over the bare ground to fetch water from the river. His life was
desolate and isolated and desperately lonely.

We stayed overnight, leaving our saddles in the meeting hall under
display boards that exhorted the local work team to greater efforts.
The wooden boards had the crudely drawn outlines of the five animals
essential to the Mongolian pastoral economy—camels, horses, cows,
goats, and sheep. Alongside each picture was a number showing the
present quantity of adult animals, then a number for the target quota,
and finally a third number to show how many foals, calves, kids, and
lambs had been born. We were so far to the north, I noted that there
were only ten camels in the whole collective.

The forward planning that had characterized the campaigns of Genghis Khan was painfully lacking in our little expedition. When the Mongol army set out, it had a baggage train that carried stores and equipment for the duration of operations. Months earlier, the army's route would have been reconnoiterd by mounted scouts. Hostile cities had been surveyed by spies disguised as merchants, and paid agents had been sent ahead to infiltrate the enemy camp, spread discontent, and suborn the foreign troops into deserting. By contrast our meager ration of food ran out while we were in the little stockade, and there were no stores to be found except in the caretaker's tiny larder.

Next, our herder-guides announced that we had ridden the horses too hard on the previous day. We would have to rest them. So all the extra time we had managed to catch up in our whirlwind ride was now discarded. We spent the whole of the third day idling around the stockade while the horses recuperated, and we periodically gazed into the distance, hungrily hoping that we heard the engine of a supply truck arriving. The Mongols were unperturbed. Some of them went off to the river; others just lay indoors and dozed. Only the two doctors found something useful to do. Doc went off to the river with his fishing rod and came back with five fish, each about three pounds, with rainbow flanks and bright red flashes. His pony-tailed colleague spent the afternoon treating the aged caretaker with acupuncture, and the old man passed the rest of the day lying in his bunk in semidarkness, the only points of light being the sharp gleam of silver needles thrust into his face, ear, and hand.

Our badly needed stores finally arrived by lorry the next morning, and it was evident that word had got out among the local *arats* that we were heading for Burkhan Khaldun to do honor to Genghis Khan. As we rode on, our little column of riders began to lengthen. We were joined by men who had come four or five hours in the saddle and were leading extra horses which they offered to us as remounts. Other *arats* emerged from the *gers* we saw along our route, asked where we were going, and promptly abandoned their normal chores to ride along with us. At midday we overtook a very dashing-looking man riding along the track with his two young sons. The father was wearing a scarlet *del*, a broad-brimmed black hat like a sombrero, and had a polished rifle slung across his back. His sons, aged about 7 and 9, wore purple and green. All three promptly swung in with us, adding a burst of color to the long file of riders as we trotted purposefully along the valley with the dust kicking up around the horses' hooves.

Our scarlet-clad herdsman knew the perfect campsite, on a low bluff over the river where we could find many dead willow trees to use as firewood. We must have been about thirty strong when we arrived to find the lorry there ahead of us, and a couple of very threadbare canvas tents already set up. Space inside the tents was very limited, so Paul and I insisted on erecting our own two-man mountain tent. We woke after another very cold night to find the inside lined with ice crystals which showered down on us as we got up. The Mongols laughed and pointed out that their system was better. They had piled the floors of their tents two or three inches deep with saddle blankets and rugs, and then had lain down in a great huddle to keep warm as they slept.

We needed to make an early start, for this was the day we were scheduled to ascend to the 7680-foot-high summit of Burkhan Khaldun. In the dawn the leafless bushes of the scrub in the valley floor were white with rime, and a dense mist made ghostly figures of the herdsmen as they went about their early morning tasks of watering and currying the horses. We swallowed the usual unappetizing breakfast of watery tea and soggy mutton and rode off along the narrow bridle path as the sun began to disperse the mist. The track crossed and recrossed the river, and each time we splashed through a ford and then squelched through bogland followed by more heath. Heavy cross-country vehicles had been before us, for we could see the tire tracks sunk deep into the mud. The occasional patches of forest had been so badly burned in forest fires that they looked like old photographs of no man's land in the First World War, with the broken limbs and shattered trunks of the trees stark against the bare hillside. Eventually we crossed a ridge and found ourselves looking down into the final valley before the foot of Burkhan Khaldun. The scrub-covered hillside fell away in a steep slope and then came a level expanse of snow and ice still covering the river flats. On the far bank, a little more than two miles away, was a remarkable sight.

In the middle of the wilderness stood a little tented town. There were a number of large tents of military khaki, with high ridge poles and stove pipes sticking out of their roofs and with smoke curling out of the chimneys. Even more striking was a higgledy-piggledy cluster of bright yellow and white ultra-modern nylon tents shaped like igloos, and beyond them half a dozen brand new cross-country vehicles stood parked in a neat line as if in a garage showroom. The vehicles had been polished until they sparkled. The effect of all this modern equipment set down in the middle of the Hentei badlands was that visitors had landed from another planet. We had come across the Gurvan Gol or Three Rivers Expedition, a joint Japanese-Mongol project which was searching for a prize that would shake the world if ever found: the tomb of Genghis Khan.

Unlikely though it may have been, Genghis Khan had died peacefully. He succumbed to old age, fever, and the effects of a heavy fall from his horse while he was out hunting. Although he knew he was very sick, he had insisted on continuing with a military campaign in western China. It was there on 25 August 1227 that he died while directing his army's operations. Legend recounts that his death was kept a state secret. Business continued to be conducted as usual. Ambassadors and foreign envoys who had come to negotiate with him were made to wait outside the imperial tent, while go-betweens hurried back and forth, pretending to carry messages and answers from the Ruler of the World. And when the visitors had gone and the cortège set out for Mongolia, carrying the corpse of a man his people revered as a god, the journey was made under conditions of absolute secrecy. It is said that Mongol troopers killed every living creature they met so that news should not leak out that the Great Khan was dead.

The Secret History of the Mongols glosses over the details of the death and says nothing about the burial. But a Persian account relates that Genghis Khan had decreed that no matter where he died his body was to be taken back to the homeland. There, on the slopes of Burkhan Khaldun, his guardian mountain, he was to be buried at a favorite spot he had known in the days of his youth. No precise details are given about the site, nor is there any description of how the most powerful and wealthiest monarch of his era was laid to rest. According to Carpini, the Mongols preferred to hide the tombs of their great chiefs. They carefully removed the turf, roots and all, before excavating an underground chamber where the dead man was placed, perhaps with a favorite slave. Then the pit was filled in and the turf put back so that no one would be able to detect the site.

Sometimes trees were planted to conceal the exact spot and leave a sacred grove in the dead chief's memory. In the open steppe, teams of horses were driven over the grave to wipe out any trace of the burial. Carpini said that the burials included "a great deal of gold and silver." According to a Persian source, Genghis Khan's son and heir to the Great Khan Ögodei ordered food to be offered for three days in succession to the departed soul of his father, and that forty maidens decked out in jewels and fine robes be sacrificed at the site together with choice horses to join the spirit of his ancestor. But all this is hearsay, and the tomb itself has never been found.

Naturally the mystery of Genghis Khan's burial place has fueled intense speculation as to where it might be hidden, and whether it would be stuffed with treasure looted by the most successful plunderer in history. Theories abound. For several centuries Genghis Khan's body was believed to be buried, not in the Hentei, but in Inner Mongolia in the Ordos region. Prjevalski had heard that there was a shrine where the body lay "in two coffins, one of silver, the other of wood, placed in a yellow silken tent in the centre of the temple. Here, too, beside the coffin lie the arms of Genghis Khan." This tomb has a murky political history. Several times the "relics" have been removed and then returned as symbols of Mongol nationhood. When the Japanese invaded Manchuria they tried to capture the relics. They had prepared a plan to create a puppet Mongol state centred on the Genghis Khan shrine, and they even drew up architectural drawings for a new mausoleum to house the relics. These plans were never fulfilled, but when the Chinese communist government opened the present memorial building in 1955, observers commented that it bore an uncanny likeness to the Japanese design. And when the celebration of Genghis Khan's 800th anniversary was being muted in Mongolia, the Chinese communists cleverly gained popular credit with the Mongols by permitting a special pilgrimage to the Ordos shrine. Thirty thousand Mongols went there to pay homage to their great ancestor.

Today most scholars believe that the Ordos shrine contains, at best, Genghis Khan's weapons. There does not seem to have been an inventory of the contents of the shrine, and after all the comings and goings, and the multiple shiftings of the supposed relics, it is doubtful how many of the original items would still remain. What is more, there may have been a very early misconception about the location of the shrine itself. A possible reason for the mistake is that when

Genghis Khan was buried on the slopes of Burkhan Khaldun, a Mongol tribe was charged with guarding his sepulcher. But the forest grew over the tomb, all trace was lost, and the tribe eventually migrated to the Ordos where they continued to claim to be the guardians of the tomb of Genghis Khan but in a totally different location.

To try to get at the truth, the Japanese–Mongol Three Rivers Expedition, funded by a major Japanese newspaper, was in the Hentei enthusiastically attacking the problem at enormous expense and with every available gadget of state-of-the-art technology. They had begun their search by scrutinizing satellite photographs of all the area around Burkhan Khaldun. Then they had flown a mosaic of aerial surveys and were now engaged in a painstaking field survey using theodolites and range finders. But they pinned their main hopes on a massive remote-sensing program, checking the vegetation, soils, rocks, and magnetic electrical fields. Teams of Japanese and Mongols were scouring the area with instruments that looked like mine-detectors, or with black boxes of equipment hung round their necks as they peered at dials and listened to headphones clamped on their ears and fiddled with knobs and switches. If the tomb of Genghis Khan was there, ran the argument, it was large enough to have disturbed the normal surface pattern. Traditionalists and skeptics countered with the ancient tale that Genghis Khan's tomb had been buried in the valley floor, and that a river had been diverted to cover it, or even that the site had been flooded to create a lake over the spot. Not to be bamboozled, the Japanese technicians were making precise maps of the lakes and riverbeds and searching for anomalies in the drainage pattern. The Mongolian authorities had allowed the expedition three years for the search; when we found them, they were only just completing the first season.

What the Japanese researchers thought of a troop of very rough-looking Mongols suddenly appearing on the hillcrest and riding down through the camp like a band of brigands, rifles on their shoulders and mounted on shaggy horses, can only be guessed. But our Mongol companions certainly enjoyed the sensation they created. They pulled up their skittish horses, called out loud greetings to Mongol friends who were working with the Japanese, and generally promoted the feeling of being swashbuckling and much too dashing to indulge in the earthbound routine of the humdrum archaeologists. Then, after a glass of hot tea, we were on our way, riding among the yellow and

white igloos and leaving behind a crowd of astonished Japanese,
among whom I detected a definite envy for the happy-go-lucky way
of their brief visitors.

We rode for another hour until we had reached the foot of the
mountain. There in a glade among the pine trees we came across what
at first sight looked exactly like an Indian tepee.

It was a lean-to of dead branches stacked together to form a tall
cone. From the uppermost twigs of the branches fluttered dozens of
streamers of cloth, faded from long exposure to wind and rain. Other
ribbons and cotton swatches dangled from the branches of several
small pine trees which formed a semicircle around the central wigwam. In front of the semicircle, about five paces from the wigwam,
a low boulder served as some sort of altar. On it lay offerings of
matchboxes, lumps of sugar, brass cartridge cases, coins, and even
one or two bank notes. We had come to an *obo*, or shrine, linked to
the sanctity of the mountain. When we arrived, the entire column of
riders circled clockwise around the *obo* to do it reverence. Then we
dismounted, tied our horses to the nearby trees, and added our own
offerings at the *obo*. This was done without the slightest trace of self-
consciousness. Artists, herdsmen, and doctors all found scraps of
cloth to tie to the branches of the *obo*, or searched in their pockets
to find small items to place on the altar stone. Observing a historic
Mongol tradition, Ariunbold plucked a white hair from the tail of his
horse and tied it to the branches. The vet knelt before the rough stone
altar and lit a small pile of incense. Others laid down offerings of bread
or money. While all this was going on, Dampildorj had produced the
lid of a tobacco tin, filled it with smoldering incense, and was quietly
walking round all the tethered horses. He stopped before each horse
and passed the smoking incense beneath its nostrils. "It will bring
them good fortune and make them healthy," he explained. Then, with
the same total absence of self-consciousness, all the riders gathered in
a group before the *obo*, stood or sat in two ranks, and had their
photograph taken by Paul as if they were a coachload of trippers who
had just toured a foreign cathedral.

It took us three very strenuous hours to climb to the summit of
Burkhan Khaldun. The primeval forest of Genghis Khan's day, with
its dense undergrowth where he had hidden from his searching enemies, had been replaced by a much thinner forest of pines which had
been burned to skeletons by forest fires. Many lay jumbled on the

ground, blocking our climb with bone-white tree trunks and sharp broken stubs of branches. To make our progress more difficult, the side of the mountain rose very steeply, and the ground was often loose with sliding rocks and earth. The Mongols did not dismount but urged their little horses up these steep and treacherous slopes. The horses panted and gasped as they scrabbled with their unshod hooves and heaved themselves upwards, the shale clattering down behind them. It was an impressive and athletic performance and I had no doubt that Mongol cavalry had well earned the reputation of being able to surmount any obstacle.

We scrambled out of the zone of burned forest and emerged on the shoulder of the mountain above the tree line. From there we looked across a vista of ridge after ridge of brown rock extending away to south and west. Every mountain top had been worn smooth by ancient glaciers and planed off so that they were all at much the same height. This gave the illusion that the horizon was impossibly distant. Nearer at hand, along the flank of the mountain, a recent landslide had made a natural dam and was holding back a small lake. The frozen surface of the lake was a patch of dazzling whiteness in the general drab colors of the frigid countryside.

We rode the final mile over bare rocks and lichens. I could feel even my toughened Mongol horse flinch as its bare hooves struck the raw rock-face riven with deep cracks where the steady alternation of frost and thaw had split the stone into a hexagonal pattern like a great stone honeycomb. We were exposed to the wind, only a mild breeze by Mongolian standards, but bitterly cold. The last 100 feet of the ascent was made on steep shale where the summit of the Holy Mountain rose to its final bald dome. On the crest of the dome we found a strange lunar landscape where small jagged rocks had been set on edge or heaped up in little piles. They were small *obos*. Dozens and dozens of them covered the head of the mountain where devotees had simply stacked up the loose rocks to form the sacred cairns. On the edge farthest from where we arrived rose an *obo* much larger and more substantial than the rest. Dead branches had been thrust into crevices of the rocks which formed the cairn, and their twigs stuck out like withered claws. Lodged around the base of the *obo* were the same offerings we had seen at the wigwam *obo*—matches, money, cast-off clothing, even a block of Chinese tea. This cairn was locally called "Genghis Khan's Seat" and here, according to legend, he came as the young clan-chief to survey his first domain around Burkhan Khaldun.

We now installed Gerel's second bronze plaque. Certainly the stone slab with its metal portrait of Genghis Khan as the mature Ruler of the World was more imposing and spectacular than any previous offering. Ariunbold propped it against the summit of the *obo*. Then, spontaneously, the entire party—*arats*, artists, and the expedition volunteers—lined up beside the *obo*. Every man extended his arms stiffly in front of him, facing the plaque. There was no lama-priest to lead the orison, so, haltingly at first but then with increasing certainty and self-confidence, our Mongol companions began to call out "Hoooooray! Hooooooray! Hooooooray!" It was a strange sound to hear on a bleak mountain top in a wilderness in the uttermost heart of Asia. I was to hear the exact same call some weeks later in the National Stadium of Mongolia, where the chant was to express respect and loyalty to the state. But on the summit of Burkhan Khaldun when I heard it called out against the thin cold wind and in homage to the memory of Genghis Khan, I realized that our journey, which was an exploration for Paul and myself, was something much more to our Mongol companions—it was a pilgrimage.

Before we left the summit, the scarlet-coated herdsman produced a conch shell from his saddlebag. The shell was decorated with a streamer and two bright red feathers and must have come from a Buddhist lama temple. But precisely where he had obtained it was a mystery, because the Mongolian lamaseries outside the capital had been destroyed or abandoned for nearly half a century. If official Communist Party propaganda was to be believed, there was no longer any popular religion in the countryside, and the possession of religious relics was frowned on. The herdsman handed the conch shell to his youngest son, the one in purple, and the lad walked in turn to the four corners of the *obo*, faced outwards, and each time blew the long haunting blasts of the conch call over the distant valleys. In a lamasery it would have been the sound to call the faithful to prayer. On the windswept summit of the Mountain of the Shaman Spirit I knew that we were witnessing a return to the ancestor worship of Genghis Khan. Then we remounted our horses and rode down off the crest.

6

The Three
Manly Sports

It was now late in the afternoon, and exuberantly the entire cavalcade clattered downhill to try to reach the camp on the river
bluff before dark. As we hurried along the shoulder of the mountain on open ground, Paul's horse stepped in a hole and stumbled,
dislodging Paul in a spectacular flying fall. Half an hour later, as we
were plunging recklessly down the steep slope of the burned-out
forest zone, with the horses almost standing on their heads, I noticed
that the ears of my horse seemed to be coming closer to my knees.
A moment later my saddle slid up the animal's neck and came to a
halt just behind its head. I continued onward over its ears and into a
bush.

When we all assembled at the foot of the mountain, the horse-
herders were chuckling and grinning. They had noted our mishaps,
and they raised gales of laughter by gleefully miming our individual
spills. I promised myself that the next time I rode a Mongol horse up
and down the mountains I would bring a crupper strap to hold my
saddle firmly in place. The Mongol saddles are fitted with two girths,
fore and aft. The girths are no more than thin straps of plaited horse-
hair, and the herdsmen tighten them so severely that the rear girth
almost disappears into a fold of the animal's gut. Western purists
would say that the horses would be injured or at least made uncom-

fortable, but the chunky Mongol horses do not seem to object and their riders know what is required for the rugged terrain they have to negotiate.

At the foot of Burkhan Khaldun Paul, Bayar, and I stayed overnight at the camp of the Three Rivers expedition, while Gerel and the others continued on to our earlier camp on the bluff. We managed to film and photograph members of the Japanese-Mongolian team at work, but it was difficult to judge what progress they were making. The mass of data they were so painstakingly accumulating would be largely unintelligible, I was told, until it was collated and assessed in Japan the following winter. Meanwhile the field force labored on, strangely reminiscent, despite their hi-tech gadgetry, of the large-scale archaeological expeditions that earlier in the century had searched assiduously for the tombs of the Egyptian pharaohs. With forty Mongols and thirty Japanese making up the field team, plus a host of interpreters, handymen, drivers, and cooks, there was no spare accommodation for us in the main tents. So Paul and I were invited to share a tent with the Mongol assistants. We passed what was the most comfortable evening of the entire Hentei trip, for we lay like tinned sardines in a row of Mongols and were kept warm by body heat.

By riding hard next morning we managed to catch up with the main party before they had left camp and reached them just as they were loading their saddles and equipment into the supply truck. It seemed that the majority of the Mongol artistic contingent had had their fill of riding. They were going back to Ulaan Baatar in the truck and suggested that we join them. Paul and I declined, preferring to carry on with the *arats*, who would be taking all our horses back to their communes. We were rewarded with the best riding of the entire trip.

Our falls from horseback as we were coming down the mountain seemed to have been rites of passage as far as our herdsmen companions were concerned, and now they were uninhibited about the way we should ride with them. Freed of the larger group, they set off with us across country at a tear-away stride. Each man led three, four, or even five spare mounts. The rawhide lead rein from the bridle of each animal was loosely knotted around the throat of the horse on its left, and the last animal in line was led right-handed by the rider. In line abreast, he and his group of horses then swept across the scrubland at full speed, swerving around obstacles, swooping through ditches, overtaking one another and being overtaken in a whirlwind of good spirits. We pounded along at this hectic pace for mile after mile, stopping only for the obligatory five-minute tobacco breaks, and then for an hour at midday at the *ger* of the scarlet-coated herdsman, who said goodbye.

The reputation of Mongol horses is that they are so tough that no rider can possibly tire them out. This may still be true for the finest horses, well rested and fit from summer feeding. With such animals Genghis Khan's cavalry could make forced marches of 70 or 80 miles a day. But in spring, when still in poor condition after the winter, our mounts reached their limit around 30 miles at their maximum speed. First Dampildorj was forced to stop and change his horse, and then my own mount abruptly slowed to a leaden walk as if someone had unplugged its battery. We pulled up at once, the saddles were removed and placed on remounts, and the tired horse was briskly curried with the long wooden spatulas. Then it was turned loose to follow at its own pace, trotting along like a tired dog following its master home.

We had covered between 35 and 40 miles in five hours by the time we reached our evening camp. As we were making our way the last few miles across an open valley, a herd of horses came trotting toward us, curious to see the strangers. They came from a line of *gers*, which glistened against the distant hillside in the late afternoon sunlight like the white cocoons of silkworms. The herd took us by surprise as they emerged from a dip in the ground led by four or five pure-white animals. With the sunlight behind them they seemed from another world, their hooves barely touching the ground, and their tossing manes making iridescent plumes around their heads like the breaking crests of ocean waves backlit by the sun. Riding at a gallop behind them appeared a Mongol girl, the first I had seen working among the horse-herders. She could have been no more than 10 years old. Her pigtails were tied up in a pink chiffon scarf, and she rode like a demure angel rounding up the herd to bring them back to her parents.

After we had made camp, Paul and I rode over to visit the line of *gers* as the sun was setting. There were six of the felt tents and a seventh was dismantled for repairs. The thick gray blankets of felt for its roof lay folded up on a nearby cart, and what I first mistook for a spare wooden cartwheel was in fact the central domed wheel of the tent roof, an essential part of the *ger's* structure.

The owner, a leathery herdsman in his 50s, was busy checking over the latticework side wall of his home. The lattice was made of thin strips of wood fastened together where they crossed by tiny thongs of rawhide, so that the whole lattice could be moved in and out like an accordion. The size of the *ger* depended on the number of sections of latticework that were joined together end to end to form the circular lower wall. When this lattice wall was ready and its painted wooden door in place, the owner set up the two slender roof pillars in the middle of the circle and balanced on top of them the central roof wheel. While he held it steady, his family and friends gathered round to insert the long slender roof poles into slots on the central wheel so they radiated out like the spokes of a giant umbrella. The lower ends of the spokes were slipped into leather loops attached to the upper edge of the lattice wall. Next, the *ger* received its cover. A single layer of canvas was stretched tightly across the roof, followed by thickly padded side curtains which were hung around the lattice sides to make an insulated side wall. Then layer upon layer of shaped felt was spread on the roof, the number and thickness of the layers depending on the season of the year and the need for extra insulation. Finally a covering of white canvas was stretched taut over the top to keep off the rain. All that was left was a small triangle of canvas, controlled by cords from the ground, which could be adjusted to open or close the smoke hole at the top of the *ger* and let in light and air according to the weather and the wind direction.

Today most Mongols find it more convenient to order their new *gers* as ready-made kits from teams of *ger* makers who work in the collectives. They will make up a *ger* according to the size that is wanted, using local materials except for the canvas for the rain cover, which is imported from the Soviet Union. Traditionally, the nomads prepared the felt blankets for themselves by beating wool into felt and trimming willow saplings to make the latticework. The only foreign material was the canvas, which was imported from China.

It takes a family less than two hours to assemble and erect their home. In Prjevalski's opinion:

> this habitation is indispensable to the wild life of the nomad. It is quickly taken to pieces and removed from place to place, whilst it is an effectual protection against cold and bad weather. In the severest frost the temperature around the hearth is comfortable. At night the

fire is put out, the felt covering drawn over the chimney, and even then, although not warm, the felt yurt [ger] is far more snug than an ordinary tent. In summer the felt is a good non-conductor of heat, and proof against the heaviest rain.

As with all Mongol gers, the half-erected structure Paul and I inspected had been set with its door facing south, the lucky direction. Dangling from the latticework was another invocation of good luck— the paws of a freshly killed bear. Mongols are avid hunters. The official estimate is that 50,000 out of a population of just over 2 million go hunting, and their official bag is in excess of 3 million head of game every year, but that is probably an underestimate. Animals are hunted for food, but also because the Mongols believe in the sympathetic transfer of characteristics from animal to man. Eating the flesh of a bear, or keeping its paws as a trophy, will bring courage and good fortune. Some folk-medicine beliefs, as Doc explained them, left little to the imagination. Impotence can be cured by eating the sex organs of deer. Swollen livers, toothache, and stomach complaints can be alleviated by eating the gall bladder of the tarbagan, or steppe woodchuck. Chronic indigestion can be treated by eating the intestines of a wolf, on the reasoning that the wolf eats all sorts of carrion yet never suffers from a bad stomach. The most extreme fancy is that hemorrhoids can be cured by sprinkling food with powdered wolf's rectum, for the omnivorous wolf is spared that affliction as well.

Belief in these folk cures is not restricted to the country people. In keeping with his macho hunting spirit, Gerel was keenly hoping we would meet bears on our Hentei ride. It did not matter that the hunting season for bear was over and that the animals were emerging from hibernation with their cubs. Gerel, like many other Mongols, was firmly convinced that the bear's spleen and liver were cures for many ills, including stomach cancer. The rifles that had been carried to the top of Burkhan Khaldun were not just for show, and two days later while Gerel was returning to Ulaan Baatar with our gift horses, he and Bayar shot two bears for their medicinal value, an act which by any standards was wasteful as the animals would soon have been ready to breed again.

This contrast between the cheerful good nature of our colleagues and their occasional lapses into neo-barbarism was matched by similar clashes of old manners and new technology which sometimes looked very incongruous. Next day another gift-receiving ceremony was arranged at short notice when two of our herder-guides announced they too would like to donate two gift horses to the expedition. Again a fresh batch of local party dignitaries arrived to witness the event. The Party chief of the commune wore a gray office suit and light city shoes, while his deputy, in full Mongolian regalia of *del*, silk sash, and long boots, looked much more at ease. On the other hand both men were displaying large enamel badges showing them to be members in good standing of the Mongolian People's Revolutionary Party, and the badge looked much better on a suit lapel than pinned to the front of a Mongol *del*.

Most of the participants arrived on horseback, but one family of six—father, mother, and four children—all bumped up on a large Czech-made motorcycle painted a vivid yellow. However strange the machine looked on the open grassland, one had to admit that it was a very sensible form of transport for those huge open spaces. The family posed beside their machine with just as much pride as the herdsmen alongside their favorite horses.

An even more anachronistic moment came when Gerel again issued his bronze medals with their blue silk ribbons after the horse-giving ceremony. These medals were much admired, but the real flurry of excitement came when Gerel produced a Polaroid camera and took pictures of the medallists. The crush that had been admiring the medals was nothing compared to the number of people who clustered around to see how the photographs had turned out and then showed the pictures to all their friends and relations.

I appreciated why Gerel had asked me to bring in a large supply of Polaroid film from abroad to supply his camera, which he had managed to obtain through a friend in Moscow. Normally I would have been embarrassed by such a cliché of foreign travel—impressing the natives with instant pictures of themselves—but here it was a Mongol dealing with Mongols and they were unaffected in the pleasure of adding new photos to the collection on display in every felt tent.

Next day Paul, Doc, and I hurried back by jeep to Ulaan Baatar, for the *arats* had told us a rumor of a unique birthday party that was to be held that weekend. It was to celebrate the birthday of Genghis Khan, the very first time such a festival had been permitted in the capital of communist Mongolia. What was even more extraordinary was that the organizers of the festival were a private group with no official government connections, though presumably they must have received permission to hold such a public celebration. The Genghis Khan Society was a very recent creation. It had been founded by a veteran Mongolian journalist, Dojoodorj, a well-known television figure who hosted a weekly travel and interview show. His program was normally rather bland and safe, but a few weeks previously he had caused a furor by conducting a hostile interview with a retiring cabinet minister of the Communist Party. Now the Society proposed to celebrate the birth of Genghis Khan by calling a public assembly in the main square of Ulaan Baatar. It did not matter that no one knows for certain the precise day of Genghis Khan's birth nor, for that matter, the year in which he was born. One source says he was born in the Year of the Pig, but that could variously have been 1155 or 1167, while other scholars prefer 1162. Such academic precision did not deter the members of the Genghis Khan Society. They arranged for a temporary wooden stage to be erected at one end of the main square. An antiquated public-address system was wired up, and banners depicting the Father of the Nation were hung from the lampposts. To give the occasion a touch of glamour an actor from the Mongolian Artists Union was persuaded to come along dressed in medieval stage costume. He had the appropriate long silk cloak and fur-lined hat, because an epic film was already being made about Genghis Khan.

There was no official publicity or advertising for the Great Birthday Party. People heard about it only by word of mouth, and the event was set for a Sunday afternoon, 27 May, immediately following a sports meeting in the National Stadium, which was sure to attract a large number of spectators, as there was very little other entertainment in Ulaan Baatar on a weekend. To everyone's astonishment the popular response to the Birthday Party was phenomenal. A crowd estimated at 40,000 people filled almost half of the main square, a feat which the Party machine was able to organize only on the most important official occasions. Also the behavior of the crowd was like nothing Ulaan Baatar had witnessed before. Instead of being subdued and serious as they were at Party rallies, the onlookers were good-humored and nonpolitical. It was much more like a holiday. They came of their own accord, partly out of curiosity, partly to join in if they approved. So they began by listening politely to the formal speeches in praise of Genghis Khan. Then they clapped for the succession of Mongol poets who read out their poems in honor of the great hero. Finally they were cheering the artists who entertained them with traditional Mongol song and dance.

The afternoon turned into the largest popular carnival central Ulaan Baatar had ever witnessed. It did not matter that the public-address system was a disaster and ruined the star turn of the live entertainment. The lead singer of Mongolia's foremost pop group appeared on stage. His long hair hung to his shoulders and he wore a long flowing satin dressing gown, high-heeled cowboy boots with white embroidery, and a huge medallion the size of a dinner plate around his neck. The figure on the medallion was, of course, Genghis Khan, and the refrain of his song was a loud yell of "Genghis Khan! Genghis Khan!" to the accompaniment of pounding guitars and clashing timpani usually heard on pop shows. The crowd loved it, even though the singer was only miming to the music and a technical failure meant that the recording played at half-speed and produced an appalling flutter. The audience was too good-humored to let such errors detract from the fun. They had already tested their mettle. A couple of the early speakers had completely misread the mood of the throng and, behaving in Party style, had tried to harangue the crowd on politics. They were jeered off the stage, an unheard-of act of *lèse-majesté*. By the end of the afternoon the success of the event had literally brought tears to the eyes of the hardened journalist who had organized it.

Perhaps heeding the lesson of the Great Birthday Party, the committee for Naadam, Mongolia's National Day celebration, which was held six weeks later, revamped their usual arrangements. They dropped or cut short the customary displays of massed children's gymnastics, the military parade, and the tedious speeches by Party luminaries. The Red Flag was abandoned, quite literally. On previous Naadams the Red Flag had flown from a flagstaff in the center of the national stadium. When I attended the celebrations as a guest of Bayar's organization, the Mongolian TV Film Studio, I noticed that on precisely the same spot rose a tall cluster of poles bearing the banner with nine white yak tails which had been the rallying symbol of Genghis Khan's army and which symbolized the presence of the "Golden Family," as his descendants came to be known. And when the contingent of troops from the modern Mongolian army put in their obligatory appearance, it was not in marching ranks of khaki but clattering along on horseback, every soldier dressed up in costume as a trooper of Genghis Khan. This cavalcade trotted rather shakily round the stadium's running track, several troopers looking decidedly apprehensive, while the crowd in the terraces roared their approval. It was quite unnecessary to swell the din by playing back, as was done, additional recorded cheering through the public-address system, the same "Hoooooray! Hoooooray! Hoooooray!" that we had heard on the peak of Burkhan Khaldun. But some Party habits die hard.

In fact the Mongolian People's Revolutionary Party had hijacked a long-established Mongolian festival. Traditionally Mongol tribesmen marked the highpoint of their brief summer by riding hundreds of miles across country to converge on a meeting ground where they could gossip and feast and compete in the three "manly sports" of archery, wrestling, and horse-racing. In a country where the population is so thinly spread, this annual assembly is still very dear to the heart of every Mongol. The medieval get-togethers, or *quriltais*, of the Mongol chieftains which travelers like Carpini witnessed had evolved from tribal councils when clan-leaders congregated to discuss grievances, pass laws and, if necessary, elect a supreme leader. By the time Genghis Khan and his heirs had established Mongol rule over most of Asia, their grand *quriltai* was the nearest equivalent to a world ruling council. One imperial *quriltai* even saved Western Europe from a holocaust. In December 1241, when the apparently unstoppable Mongol armies were poised to invade the West and Mongol patrols had probed as far as the forward defenses of Vienna, a grand *quriltai* was unexpectedly summoned 5600 miles away in central Mongolia. The Great Khan Ögodei, Genghis Khan's son, had died and his successor had to be elected from the senior members of the Golden Family. The Mongol generals shelved their war plans, turned their horses, and headed back to Mongolia to take part in the political infighting and intrigue which followed.

A modern Naadam is a faint echo of those extraordinary medieval gatherings, but it is still an impressive sight. Naadam assemblies are held all over Mongolia, but they are dwarfed by the great central

Naadam which takes place on the open plain on the outskirts of Ulaan Baatar. Most participants arrive on horseback and may have ridden for weeks to get there. Others show up in battered trucks, and a few bring their camels hauling crude wooden carts loaded with their food and chattels for a week of entertaining. To accommodate each new contingent the camp expands in every direction. Day after day more and more *gers* and tents are set up. In front of each one is a tethering cord like a clothesline stretched between two poles. Tied to each line are a dozen or so horses of the visitors. Plumes of smoke rise from the stove pipes, dust is kicked up by hooves, and soon a pale brown fog hangs over the usually deserted plain while pedestrians and horsemen crisscross between the lines of tents, hail friends, exercise, and show off their mounts, or simply wander around to see who has arrived and what is new.

Despite the name, women participate in two of the three "manly sports" which are the core of Naadam festivities. There are women archers and women riders in the horse races. Only wrestling is an all-male preserve, though this was not always the case. Marco Polo records one formidable Mongol lady, daughter of a khan, who amassed a fortune and an enduring reputation by daring all comers to wrestle. Many men accepted the challenge, but none succeeded in flooring the steppe Amazon, who continued to reign supreme. Every time she won, her opponent forfeited a portion of his flocks and herds, and in this way she is estimated to have won over 10,000 horses. Even when a highly eligible suitor came to claim her hand, and her father begged her to throw the wrestling match, she refused and up-ended her opponent who departed "in grief and shame," leaving behind another 1000 horses. In the end the khan himself gave up, and took his daughter whenever he went to battle. "In every affray," says Marco Polo, "there was never a knight more doughty than she. For many a time it happened that she plunged in among the enemy and seized a knight by force and carried him off into her own ranks."

The wrestling finals of a modern Naadam are the climax to a long and dedicated professional business. Mongol boys begin to be coached in the techniques of traditional Mongolian wrestling at an age when boys in other cultures might spend their weekend afternoons training for football or tennis. They learn the classic moves and throws, as well as the correct wrestler's stance, which is supposed to combine the body posture of a lion with the outstretched wings of the mythical gharial bird in flight, and the slow-motion "eagle dance," arms held high, which the victor performs to celebrate his triumph when he has obliged his opponent to kneel or to touch the ground with an elbow. The best young wrestlers are talent-spotted for special training and turn semiprofessional with their own training camps and workout schedules. The ultimate goal is to be good enough to compete at Naadam in the National Stadium in the knock-out competition which starts with an awesome drove of 512 beefy contestants lumbering into the ring dressed in heavy Mongol boots, tight body trunks, and short embroidered jackets. It ends with just one champion left on his feet. To the uninitiated it may be tedious to watch the grappling monsters locked in slow-motion combat. But the finer points are appreciated by the Mongol spectators. They groan, cheer, or growl according to the bad luck, the clever twist, or an unsporting move. At the end of the contest the victor is carried shoulder-high around the stadium by his adoring fans despite his considerable bulk. If he has won the competition several times before, he receives the title of Titan.

The archers are much more sedate. Men and women compete in separate classes, but both use exactly the same equipment and technique—the classic double-curved bow of the steppe nomad, the string drawn back with the aid of the Mongol thumb ring. Nowadays a pad of leather, the thumb ring was traditionally carved of stone, and it enables an archer to release the bowstring with a crisp snap more effectively than using the bare fingers. The Naadam targets are wickerwork discs set in a row at the far end of the archery field. Each contestant tries to drop his or her arrow precisely on the center disc, which is marked with a bright red rag. Success requires strength and skill, and the target is far enough away that the impact point of each arrow is signaled by watching attendants who raise their arms and sing out to indicate the direction of the shot. Today the range is between 180 and 300 paces, the same distance from which a good archer was once expected to land his arrow on the head of a marmot peering out of its hole, killing the animal stone-dead. But a stone tablet erected in Genghis Khan's time records a tremendous shot by a certain Isuke who hit the mark at 360 paces' distance. When Genghis

Khan learned of this remarkable stroke, he decreed the tablet should be erected in its honor.

The Naadam archers are the last survivors of the deadly Mongol mounted bowmen who revolutionized the medieval battlefield just as English longbowmen were to overturn the dominance of the heavily armored Western knight. Where the English long bow had a range of 250 yards, the double-curved Mongol war-bow of sinew and wood sent its arrows even further, and in battle the Mongol horse-archer opened fire at a range that shocked his opponents. In Liddell Hart's opinion, the Mongols added to their advantage by inventing the technique of "rolling fire," softening up the opposition with a forward barrage of arrows and, later, adding mobile catapults and artillery to their onslaught. Under this hail of projectiles their enemies fell "like the leaves in autumn" without even coming to grips with the Mongol army, according to one awed European chronicler. Every trooper had two bows, one for long-range and one for short-range work, and was sent into battle with a minimum of sixty arrows, including a fearsome range of special arrows—armor-piercing arrows, fire arrows which laid down smokescreens, even whistling arrows whose tones, combined with signals from black and white flags, were used to control the maneuvers of the squadrons. This more than anything else terrified the opposition. The Mongol cavalry wheeled and turned, fell back, and advanced in perfect unison and total silence until the heavily armed strike force of lancers on their leather-plated chargers delivered the crushing blow.

But the most obvious reason for the military success of the Mongols under Genghis Khan was their superior horsemanship. Even now no other nation on earth is so dependent on the horse, nor so accustomed to its management. Herdsmen still teach their children to ride at the same time as they learn to walk, and although the horse races at Naadams were previously ridden by *arats* on unbroken horses, now the jockeys are children seldom more than 12 years old. The Mongols take it for granted that every Mongol child can ride, and so the purpose of a race must be to test the horse, not the jockey. I went out into the grassland south of Ulaan Baatar to watch the extraordinary sight of at least 200 children, girls as well as boys, many wearing gaily colored cloth hats like the paper hats from Christmas crackers, assemble at the start of one of the Naadam races. The army had been called in to help. A long line of soldiers held the bridles until the signal sounded, and then the entire mob of excited horses suddenly surged forward in an uncontrolled charge with the rumble of unshod hooves underscoring the high-pitched yelps of excited children screaming their mounts onward. By Western standards the races are marathons. They can vary from 9 miles for 2-year-old horses, to over 17 miles for adult animals. During my visit a 4-year-old jockey riding bareback won a major race.

7

Leaving Erdenzu

On the whole, our trial ride in the Hentei had been very
promising. Paul and I agreed that it had been a spectacular
experience to ride with *arats* like Dampildorj and see for
ourselves the stunning scenery of the Hentei wilderness as it emerged
from six months of winter refrigeration. The lifestyle of the flamboy-
antly dressed herdsmen, the *obos*, the unaffected and sincere ceremony in honor of Genghis Khan on the summit of Burkhan Khaldun,
even the off-putting diet, all had been exotic and memorable. On a
technical level I could see the excuses for the lack of expedition
organization and the slack planning which had meant that we proceeded in fits and starts, ran out of food, and never seemed quite sure
what would happen in the next twenty-four hours. In Mongolia it
was difficult, if not impossible, to lay in extra stores or find good-
quality tents and equipment, and the system of central state organization was so cumbersome that everything you tried to arrange in
advance happened in slow motion. Yet in the long run these deficien-
cies did not matter. Certainly they had not deterred the Hentei trial
ride, and we had achieved our objective with some panache. Gerel,
who had been in charge, had proved himself to be every bit as good
a field man as I had hoped, and Bayar, cheerful and competent, was
a real gem. The vet and the pony-tailed doctor, as Ariunbold and
Gerel had seen for themselves, were not suitable team members and
would be let go. But it was Ariunbold himself, as far as I was concerned, who was still the enigma. He was a leader in the highly

ambitious project to ride to France, which he and Gerel had set their hearts on, yet he had seemed always to be slightly out of step with the other members of the group as we rode to Burkhan Khaldun. He was immediately to the fore when it came to officiating at horse-giving ceremonies or making speeches to the local commune officials. But he was not a leader when it came to making practical decisions. Gerel had done that unhesitatingly, while Ariunbold remained detached yet trying to make it clear that he too was in authority. I was uneasy about Ariunbold's behavior.

One lesson from the trial ride did worry me: neither Gerel nor Ariunbold showed any real appreciation of the variety of conditions they would encounter if their proposed expedition left Mongolia. This was partly the result of inexperience, as they had not traveled widely in foreign countries outside the main cities, but also it was a result of their increasing chauvinism. They were unshakably convinced that what was the right thing to do inside Mongolia was also the correct method when they left the country, whatever the circumstances. I found it an ominous mixture of inflexibility and self-esteem. Sometimes their obstinacy showed up in relatively minor practical matters.

For example, I advised that the expedition horses would need to wear shoes if they were to travel really long distances. But neither Gerel nor Ariunbold would hear of it. Mongol horses did not have to wear shoes, they told me flatly. In fact I was later to observe that this was not the case—cattle drovers in the west of Mongolia, whom Gerel and Ariunbold had never seen, did shoe their horses when they rode three or four hundred miles on cattle drives, taking steers to be sold to meat packers in the Soviet Union. But this was not how Gerel and Ariunbold approached the question. They knew what was best because this was—or so they thought—the traditional Mongol way.

By extension, their intransigence spilled over into a tendency to see their proposed expedition as a Mongol venture which would somehow bestow a privilege on the people they encountered. Several times I tried to explain to them that they would need to rely on the help of a whole array of different nationalities and cultures—Kazakhs, Russians, Ukrainians, and so forth—as they rode toward Europe. The only way to succeed was to welcome local peoples fully to the expedition, integrate as much as possible, and make the ride truly international. But once again I encountered an adverse current. This was to be a Mongol expedition celebrating historic Mongol achievements, and the people they encountered should appreciate the unique contact offered to them. In short, they did not seem willing to share with other nationalities the common heritage of the great transcontinental courier roads, and I began to feel that my own role was little more than a convenient contact with the West to enable them to obtain materials, drum up publicity, and extract personal benefit from the venture. Gerel was sure that art galleries in the West would want to buy his sculptures; Ariunbold was confident that journals and magazines would queue up asking him to write about his experiences; and Bayar had visions of making an award-winning documentary film. It was fruitless to warn them that the world outside Mongolia might not place the same high value on their efforts. Looking ahead, I saw the danger of their falling victim to their feeling of self-importance.

The main part of our trans-Mongolian ride was due to begin six weeks after the Hentei journey. Paul and I used the interval by making a brief trip back to London to process and check the quality of our photographs and film, and to pick up a few items such as more Polaroid film and half a dozen ex-army sleeping bags which I could give to the Mongol riding team. Then we returned to Ulaan Baatar to stay with Doc and his family in his three-bedroom flat on the top floor of one of the scruffy apartment blocks. Previously the government had forbidden private citizens to take in foreign guests. All visitors from the West had been obliged to stay in what amounted to semi-quarantine in one or the other of Ulaan Baatar's two cheerless hotels. This meant that a closer eye could be kept on them, considerable profit could be reaped from exorbitant hotel charges, and the local citizens were spared the temptation of receiving payment in foreign currency, which they were forbidden to hold. Doc would not accept any rent, and instead we contributed gifts of whisky and fishing tackle, which were just as welcome. In fact we spent most of our six-week wait in the company of Bayar and a jovial team from the Mongolian Film Studio, bumping around the Mongolian countryside in another Soviet-reject jeep tracking down local horse festivals and *arat* families, and making a trip to the Gobi Desert to look at camel-herders.

During these days I also gleaned a little more about Ariunbold's background. By Mongolian standards Ariunbold had been born with a silver spoon in his mouth. He had been a child during the last years of Choybalsan's dictatorship and had lived most of his life under the regime of Choybalsan's hard-line successor, Tsedenbal, who had a Russian wife and fostered a personality cult. Ariunbold was rumored to be part-Russian himself, and certainly his family was very well regarded in Party circles. In a rigidly communist society this meant that as a boy he had received every advantage. After secondary school Ariunbold had been selected for a coveted place at the training center for bright young stars from the Soviet satellite countries—the Higher Party School in Leningrad. There he studied Party theory and government, acquired his very polished and professional style, and perfected a command of Russian which he spoke virtually without any trace of a foreign accent. On his return to Ulaan Baatar he had been rewarded with the most coveted position for a young man in the Mongolian official hierarchy—he was appointed secretary to the Chairman of the Presidium, Tsedenbal himself. Young, good-looking, and with impeccable credentials, Ariunbold was poised to climb to the very highest rungs of the Party apparatus.

Yet something had gone wrong, and there were rumors: that he was lazy and shallow, and a womanizer. His subsequent career, as much of it as came out in casual conversation, seemed to confirm these reports. He had never fulfilled his early potential. He lost his job as secretary to Tsedenbal and was sent abroad, to work as a diplomat in the Mongolian embassy in the Bulgarian capital, Sofia, and then was further demoted to being a journalist. In Bulgaria, it was alleged, his philandering had been a severe embarrassment. When he was recalled to Ulaan Baatar his wife, a musician, stayed behind in Sofia. It was obvious to me that as secretary to the Mongolian National Committee to the UNESCO Silk Roads Project, Ariunbold had been in an ideal position to intercept any state patronage for the venture and make sure that he was selected to lead the preliminary sector within Mongolia. Reluctantly I also had to admit the possibility that he regarded the expedition as a chance to reverse the downward spiral of his career. In an unguarded moment he let slip that he intended to use it to his personal advantage as a way of gaining publicity in Mongolia and then to enter politics.

His approach to organizing the new phase of the expedition was dismaying. He disappeared from Ulaan Baatar for weeks at a time and made no contact with either Gerel or Bayar, who did not know where to find him. He also failed to make sure that the new equipment required for the ride was ready. It was obvious that a new tent was needed to replace the tattered wreck that had been used in the Hentei. Ariunbold boasted that he had obtained some special lightweight cloth from a Japanese television company and would arrange to have the new tent made by seamstresses. But then he vanished before the tent was finished, and when he returned he ordered the trio of cheerful Mongol seamstresses to devote their energies to sewing fancy costumes for the Mongol team members. Paul and I went to the apartment where they were doing the stitching. What we found was not encouraging. Ariunbold, who had not been seen for weeks, put in an appearance in order to try on his costume, and primped and preened in front of the mirror so that it was all too obvious that the glamour rather than the substance of the project was his interest. Three special saddles had also been ordered. They would be replicas of medieval Mongol saddles. But I was depressed to observe that Ariunbold selfishly made sure that his own saddle would be ready on time. He did not seem to care that the saddles for his Mongol companions were still pieces of wood and leather only a day before the expedition was due to leave Ulaan Baatar. I said nothing because I did not feel it was my place to intervene in what was still a Mongol-organized venture inside Mongolia, and the day was rapidly approaching when we should all go to the starting point of the main ride—the former imperial capital at Karakorum.

Karakorum lies at what is virtually the center of Greater Mongolia. If one were to draw a series of lines diametrically across the main area of Mongol-speaking peoples, they would converge in the hilly countryside of the upper Orhon River, not far from the site of present-day Karakorum. This pivotal position is the reason why for centuries Karakorum was the notional, if not always real, hub of the Mongol empire. Genghis Khan himself never had time to establish his capital there because his headquarters remained mobile, shifting with the seasonal migration patterns and moving from place to place in response to the foreign campaigns he was fighting. But his grand camp must have been set up regularly in the vicinity of Karakorum,

and by the time his son Ögodei became Khakhan in 1229* it had been
decided to build some permanent structures there so that the imperial
caravan would have somewhere to halt, conduct business, and—not
least—entertain the visiting ambassadors and tribal leaders who rode
in from the far-flung provinces. It was to the area of Karakorum that
Carpini's guides hastily brought their elderly, overweight and half-
martyred Franciscan charge to be at hand for the enthronement of
Ögodei's successor Güyük. And here in 1254 came the man who
next described the Mongol empire for Europeans: Carpini's fellow
Franciscan, William of Rubruck, whom we shall shortly meet. Even
when Genghis Khan's famous grandson, Kubilai Khan, became
Khakhan in 1259 and preferred to maintain his capital in China,
Karakorum remained nominally the focus of the Mongol empire and
the center of the homeland to which all Mongols were attached emo-
tionally at that time and ever since.

Three weeks before the official start of the main sector of the
expedition in July, Paul and I had gone to Karakorum to reconnoiter.
The town itself was an example of the small drab Mongolian country
town which we would see several times in the next few weeks. There
were one or two ugly concrete municipal offices set beside the central
square, an antiquated coal-fired electricity power station with its rusty
metal chimney held up by guy wires, a fuel dump on the outskirts
for passing jeeps and trucks, and several hundred *gers* laid out in town
blocks separated by potholed side-roads. Each block was surrounded
by rickety wooden palings, because a bureaucratic regulation required
that unless a *ger* was enclosed by a fence it could not have a house
number and therefore postal and other services would not be provided. Presumably this rule had been thought up by someone in
central government as yet another attempt to restrict the nomadic
inclination of the population, which sat uneasily with socialist doctrine.

Less than a mile from the edge of town stood the oldest and once
the grandest Buddhist monastery in all Mongolia, the huge lamasery
of Erdenzu. In its heydey it had housed 10,000 lamas who worshiped
at no fewer than sixty temples enclosed within the imposing outer

---

*There was a two-year interregnum between Genghis Khan's death and Ögodei's
formal enthronement as Great Khan.

wall. No other building better symbolized the former glory and recent misdirection of Mongolian life.

When the Mongolian People's Revolutionary Party took power in 1921, they inherited a country that had evolved into one of the strangest societies on earth. It was a grotesque church-state run to seed. In a land where there were only a half a dozen settled towns, there were 700 large monasteries and at least 1000 smaller ones. The king of this bizarre country was also its high priest. Further, he was a Living Buddha and was outranked only by the "Two Jewels" of the Dalai and Panchen Lamas of Tibet. That this priest-king suffered from syphilis, was going blind so that he hid his tortured eyes behind smoked glasses, and was a sexual deviant was of no particular consequence. It is estimated that four out of every ten male Mongols were lamas or serfs of the church, and the piety of the ordinary Mongols was so deep-rooted and absolute that their Lord, the eighth Jebtsundamba Khutukhtu,* or Exalted Revelation, was revered as the spiritual and effective leader of the country despite the fact that he enjoyed exchanging clothes and playing role-reversal games with one of his male servants, was paralytically drunk for weeks at a time, and had as his second consort or "the Holy Goddess" the former wife of a wrestler, who was notorious for her sexual capers with other lamas, including her hairdresser, in a so-called "oracle tent."

Unsurprisingly, the Jebtsundamba Khutukhtu's first predecessor at seven times remove had claimed to be a direct descendant of Genghis Khan. The first Exalted Revelation had filled a power vacuum left when the last emperor of the united Mongols, a much diminished version of the Great Khan, had been driven from the country by rival factions in the mid-16th century, and the Mongol homelands had degenerated for the next 100 years into little more than a cockpit for squabbling warlords. By then the huge Mongol world empire established by Genghis Khan and his immediate heirs must have seemed like a fantasy. In 1368 the Chinese had expelled the Mongol dynasty, the Yuan, which the Golden Family under Kubilai Khan had imposed on them in Peking.

Twenty years ago Chinese armies had marched into the Mongol

---

*His full title was Venerable Incarnation of Jebtsundamba, Sainted and Brightest Emperor, to which he added the reign title "Exalted by All."

homeland, burned Karakorum, and crushed the Mongol tribes. In his flight the last Mongolian emperor tried to make off with the relics from the Genghis Khan shrine in the Ordos, hoping that their possession would guarantee his return. He died in mysterious circumstances and the relics were replaced, but the Chinese made it a matter of policy that never again would Mongolia be able to threaten them with a resurrection of the Oceanic Ruler. They successfully reduced the chiefs of Mongolia to the role of Chinese vassals, obliging them to pay annual tribute, to accept Chinese governors and high officials, and to journey periodically to China to pledge allegiance. One Mongolian prince took with him to Peking six camel loads of ice, presumably to cool his food and drink. Such ostentation must have delighted his Chinese hosts as it further impoverished the ordinary Mongols who had to pay for this degree of extravagance. Mongolia was treated as China's empty backyard, a vast zone deliberately neglected on the principle that the least development was in the best Chinese interests.

According to one theory, the Chinese introduced Tibetan lamaism to Mongolia in order to sap the fighting spirit of the Mongols. But in fact lamaism dates a long way back in Mongolian history, and Carpini's successor, William of Rubruck, found a lamasery already established at Karakorum. Brother William went to Mongolia at the instigation of King Louis IX of France, who wanted him to serve as his unofficial messenger. Personally Rubruck was rather more interested in finding a group of Germans who had been taken prisoner by the Mongols and he hoped to administer to their spiritual needs. He traveled with a fellow Franciscan, Bartholomew of Cremona, about whom we hear little except that at times he complained he was so hungry that he felt he had never eaten in his life. When the time finally came to go home, Bartholomew could not face the rigors of the return journey to Europe and preferred to stay on in Karakorum and end his days there rather than suffer the transcontinental ride a second time.

In Karakorum Rubruck spent a good deal of his time poking around the lama temples and the tents of the shamans and asking questions about their religious beliefs. He was very irritated that the lamas frequently observed a rule of silence and refused to respond to his badgering, but nevertheless he supplied Europe with its first meaningful description of Buddhism. "All their priests," he wrote in the report of the trip which he prepared for King Louis:

shave their heads all over and their beards, and they wear saffron garments and observe chastity from the time they shave their heads. They live together, one or two hundred in one community. When they go into their temple, they bring two benches, and they sit on the floor facing each other, choir to choir, holding their books in their hands and these from time to time they put down on the benches. . . . They have also in their hands wherever they go, a string of one or two hundred beads just as we carry our rosaries, and they always say these words 'On man baccam', that is 'Oh God, Thou knowest.'*†

Lamaism blended easily with the Mongols' earlier notions of the spirit world, and the first Jebtsundamba Khutukhtu was seen to be very like a master witch-doctor or shaman. He was to be followed by six Great Incarnations, and during their rule the power and wealth of the church increased dramatically. Generation after generation of devout Mongols gave land and flocks and tithes to the lamaseries. Hundreds of thousands of Mongols joined the church as lamas or pledged themselves to it as serfs, either from piety or to avoid the grinding taxes imposed by the Mongol barons, who were in turn obliged to pay dues to the Chinese governors or were heavily in debt to Chinese merchants. With its ever-expanding wealth and population the church built more lamaseries in the countryside, and these in turn soaked up more pastureland and more recruits. In a land of nomads, the lamaseries were the only permanent structures, and they became the nucleus of any town, however meager. Thus Ulaan Baatar's pre-revolutionary name of Urga meant simply "the temple."

In their fiefs the head lamas wielded more power than any comparable medieval abbot in Europe. They were largely exempt from civil law and exercised power of life and death over their districts. Their lamaseries offered virtually the only education, craftsmanship, and literacy in the entire vast country, but their government was not all sweetness and light. Life in the monasteries was often appallingly brutal. Offenders against the rules were sometimes beaten to death or, to avoid the stigma of killing, were left tied up, naked, in the open air on a winter's night, which meant they were stiffened corpses by morning. Children could be taught by sadistic lamas who scratched

*Rubruck's rendering of *Om mani padme hum*—Hail to the jewel in the lotus.
†*The Mission of Friar William of Rubruck*, translated by Peter Jackson, Hakluyt Society, 1990.

the letters of the Tibetan alphabet into their scalps with sharp bamboo pens. Homosexuality was condoned, senior monks keeping catamites euphemistically described as "disciples." Some lamas operated as moneylenders who made loans to their flock at an interest of as much as 200 percent a year, and when the eighth and last Exalted Revelation was also created king, the highest ranks of lamas—an amazing total of forty-seven Incarnations were living in Urga at the time—greedily snapped up new civil as well as church titles and privileges. By way of comparison, the entire apparatus of civil government at that stage numbered just 300 people, including door guards, messengers, and storekeepers.

At the opposite end of the scale large numbers of ordinary lamas were neither devout nor scrupulous. They wandered about the countryside as beggars or made a living from the credulous herdsmen by selling them indulgences and telling fortunes. Nor were these petty lamas any more celibate than their seniors. They were held responsible for the extraordinarily high level of venereal disease, which was the major medical affliction of the country at the beginning of this century.

Erdenzu was a natural choice for the site of the first lamasery to be built in Mongolia. It was constructed close to the spot where Ögodei, Güyük, and Möngke, the second, third, and fourth Khakhans of Genghis Khan's dynasty, had held their great *quriltais*. By the time of Rubruck's visit a small town had grown up there to house the hundreds of traders and diplomats who arrived from China, Central Asia, the Near East, and even from Korea to attend the Mongol court. In the 1940s a Russian archaeological expedition found that stones from the ancient imperial buildings and the medieval town had been re-used to construct the present lamasery. The religious enclave that the monks built for themselves with this recycled material was immense. Each side of the outer wall had space for 108 stupas, paid for by subscription from devotees. Inside Erdenzu's temples the sacred effigies were said to have been fashioned by the first Khutukhtu himself. He was a renowned sculptor who, incidentally, was a married man. Folklore relates that when critics complained about his having a wife, he called to her to come out from his tent. She appeared holding a lump of molten bronze in her bare hands, and as the critics watched she shaped the soft metal into a statue of the Buddha. This silenced the complaints.

Today the outer wall of Erdenzu tries to reclaim something like its former glory and is whitewashed not from piety but because the modern government badly needs foreign currency and realized that the site would be a unique tourist attraction. Inside the perimeter wall, however, the compound is mostly a grassy void. In the distance, opposite the main gate under its tower, stand a few blue-roofed temples and a stupa or two, dwarfed by the immensity of the intervening open space. Once the compound must have been full of buildings—temples, dormitories, refectories, storehouses—and it has been calculated that to have achieved the present obliteration most of the original buildings of the lamasery complex must have been dynamited to smithereens. But there is not a single document to tell the tale. The destruction of the church-state of Mongolia, which reached a crescendo in the late 1930s, remains among the best-kept secrets of modern vandalism.

The communists waited until the last Khutukhtu-king was dead in 1924, at the age of 54. Then, with increasing severity and confusing changes of emphasis, they attacked the church like sharks tearing chunks out of a helpless whale. First the lamaseries were stripped of their lands and privileges. Then the monks were assessed for huge taxes. One cynical device was to make lamas of military age pay a special fine for not doing army service. Lamasery after lamasery was ruined financially. Others were forcibly relocated away from their parishioners and therefore withered from lack of local support. Many lamaseries were shut down by deputations of fanatical Party cadres whose orders were enforced by armed posses. From one monastery alone 400 lamas were expelled in a single day, and many of the cruelest evictions were done in the depths of winter, leaving the refugees to perish from cold. Several monasteries were bulldozed so that the lamas could not creep back. In 1937 about 97,000 monks were "reclassified." Most were resettled in towns or allocated to work brigades; some were taken away to labor camps and never seen again. A few were liquidated. The lamas' books, which included irreplaceable manuscripts brought from Tibet, were thrown on bonfires. *Obos* were flattened, and even the sacred relics plastered into the stupas were gouged out and smashed to powder. As a sop to outside criticism, a showpiece of religion was kept on. A part of the magnificent Gandan monastery in Ulaan Baatar was preserved under a complacent abbot and a handful of monks as a so-called "religious school," and the lesser Oracle Palace was fossilized as a dusty state museum. It seemed that religion in Mongolia had been destroyed root and branch.

Then, two years ago, the effects of perestroika and glasnost initiated in the Soviet Union spread to Mongolia and began to reshape the attitude of the central government toward religion. Although no one was quite sure what the official policy was toward lamaism, there were hints that religious worship would be permitted again. For a start, the great monastery at Erdenzu was to be reactivated as a functioning religious center, not just a tourist attraction, if lamas could be found. To the astonishment of no one but the most obtuse Party officials, the lamas reappeared. Not all the monks had been done away with or had fled the country during the great purges. Some of them had slipped away quietly to find refuge among the country people. For half a century they had been living unostentatiously among the herders. They wore ordinary civilian dress but kept their lama robes, and most had been secretly practicing their religion. These survivors, like exotic flowers growing up through the cracks in the state monolith, emerged to don their brilliant red gowns and yellow hats. They brought out the long thin wooden cases like long pencil boxes which contained their sacred texts written on parchment. They refurbished the drums and bells and incense-burners and brought them back to Erdenzu, though they were to find most of the shrines destroyed and the images in bits.

Twenty or thirty lamas took up residence once again. They cleaned and repaired a small building on the very far side of the square where they hung up again the holy banners. They refurbished the scaffold platform from which they sounded the conch shell announcing the call to prayer and began their chants for the well-being of the people. They were an extraordinary sight, wizened and ancient. Not one of them looked less than 70 years old, and their faces could have come from the Hobbit world of Tolkien.

Their Chief Lama was glad to help us. Either Gerel or Ariunbold must have been in touch with the local commune bureaucracy in Karakorum town to arrange our official departure ceremony, and through them had contacted the lamasery, because the Chief Lama sent word that he and his monks would bless our expedition. Also, they approved the horoscope which decided that the Hour of the Silver Horse, on the Day of the Black Horse, in the month of the Horse was the best time for their rites.

Ariunbold's mystifying failure to keep track of practical details nearly wrecked our lucky calendar. Not only did he omit to get the expedition's new equipment ready ahead of time, but he did not trouble himself to arrange transport to ferry the members of the team to Karakorum where we were expecting to find our gift horses, which had been sent ahead. It had been clearly understood by all the team members—Gerel, Bayar, Doc, who had volunteered to continue as interpreter, Paul, and myself—that as Gerel had organized the trial ride in the Hentei, now it was Ariunbold's turn to supervise the horseback journey that would take us westward from Karakorum toward the Soviet frontier. The idea was that we should follow the medieval Mongol courier road as far as the *aymag* of Bayan Olgei in the Altai Mountains, some 600 miles distant. There the horses would be left for the winter, and—if the Mongolian national committee for the UNESCO Silk Roads Project continued to give its support—a team whose membership was yet to be decided would continue on the ride toward France. But as the official date for our departure from Karakorum drew closer, we waited impatiently in Ulaan Baatar trying vainly to locate Ariunbold.

At the last minute, when Ariunbold still had not shown up, there was much scurrying to and fro to borrow vehicles to take us the eight-hour cross-country drive to Erdenzu. Eventually the Mongolian TV Film Studio offered to send Paul and Bayar ahead in a decrepit jeep. Loaded with a dozen saddles and assorted paraphernalia, it set off with Paul and Bayar, a driver, and two unidentified Mongols. Their job was to locate the gift horses which had been pastured near Kara-korum and bring them to the monastery in time for the departure ceremony. I watched as, clutching his cameras, Paul squeezed himself into the front seat next to Bayar, who was nursing a half-finished bottle of vodka. Our happy-go-lucky Mongolian film cameraman was blissfully and totally drunk and was wearing what apparently would be the expedition working rig of denim jacket and jeans, sewn with leather patches. It made him look like a tipsy Chinese laborer.

Ariunbold surfaced later the same day—still without explaining his absence—and by then Doc had taken matters into his own hands and contacted the Foreign Ministry, which agreed to the temporary loan of another cross-country vehicle. The three of us set out for Kara-korum with a fourth passenger, a handsome woman who was, rather obviously, Ariunbold's current mistress. She had the good grace to look very embarrassed for most of the drive and tactfully made herself scarce whenever we stopped, because accompanying us in a second vehicle was the Deputy Foreign Minister of Mongolia, who would officiate at our departure. He was a clever, sophisticated man and had been extremely helpful in his role as chairman of the Mongolian National Committee for the Silk Roads Project. He visibly stiffened with shock when he saw Ariunbold's companion and frostily stared right through her. To make the situation worse, the Minister was traveling with his wife and her elderly parents, who had never visited the monastery of Erdenzu before and who wanted to see the lamas for themselves. It occurred to me that when a Mongolian minister of cabinet rank was prepared to attend a public religious service at the lamasery of Erdenzu, the wheel of Mongolian politics had turned full circle.

The summer rains had begun. This was the season when Mongolia receives nearly all its annual rainfall, and much of it arrives in sudden torrential downpours. The entire countryside was waterlogged, and the rivers had flooded. There was not a single bridge on the route to Karakorum, and most of the fords were impassable. We splashed and slithered our way through the night, finally arriving at our destination in the small hours of the morning of 16 July, and were put up at the official guesthouse in town. The Minister and his family went to an upper room, and Ariunbold tactfully disappeared with his lady friend to search for our missing camp of gift horses. Doc and I were assigned to a lower dormitory. We were warmly greeted by the only other occupant, a most friendly and talkative Mongol. I offered him a tot of whisky and realized too late it was a waste. He was already totally inebriated and soon fell across his cot, where he snored and belched loudly for the rest of the night.

Paul appeared next morning, not knowing whether to laugh or groan. He had spent the night some six miles away where a herder family had been looking after our gift horses. The camp food had given him severe stomach cramps, but he was doubled up as much with mirth as indigestion. It seemed that the previous evening he had been shown the famous new tent of which Ariunbold had boasted. Nothing had been previously tried out or tested, and inevitably it was found that none of the poles fitted and that the whole design was a catastrophe. The tent sagged and drooped and looked like a collapsed balloon.

It was cold and windy and lashing with rain as we made our way to the monastery that same afternoon for the official send-off and entered through the huge wooden gates. The weather was so foul that only a small crowd had assembled. They huddled under umbrellas and plastic raincoats as the Deputy Minister made his speech in front of a small temple covered with green-blue tiles that was popularly known as "Ögodei's Temple." The speech had a suitably rural feeling. There was no public-address system and no crowd control, so everyone pressed in closer and closer to hear what was being said, until we were all in a central, soaking wet huddle. Then we squelched off to the lamas' chapel and, thankful to be out of the rain, attended their special service of blessing.

It was an exotic send-off in the semi-gloom of the chapel, a scene that Brother Rubruck would have recognized. Two rows of high, broad benches faced one another to make a central aisle. On each bench sat a line of aged lamas, cross-legged in their bright red robes. Laid out in front of them were their books of mantras and little brass prayer bells. They kept up a steady mutter of blessing, each phrase repeated again and again, rising steadily in pitch until finally there was a tremendous climax. At that moment the elderly but very sprightly lama at the end of the row seized his curved drumsticks and briskly hammered at the drum hanging by his left shoulder, while the others blew conch shells and rang their brass bells. It made a tremendous banging, sounding, clashing din to drive away the evil spirits from our venture. Then the sound died away, and the muttering chant picked up once more, gently now and from the bottom of the scale, to begin all over again.

The riding team were given seats on a second row of benches, behind the monks, and lay servants dressed in brown robes passed us large plates heaped with layers of holy bread—sweet bread made of white flour and then kneaded so there was a little hollow in the top which was filled with lumps of sugar and dark yellow cubes of dried butter. For drink they poured us salt tea from a great brass kettle. To our left the candles flickered on the small altar, and incense smoked from a metal trough. Everywhere was red. Red cloaks on the monks, pillars and ceiling painted red, red banners hanging from the ceiling, red tassels, red light reflecting from the wizened faces and the gleaming scalps of the lamas.

The abbot handed us good-luck charms, the same cheap brass frames with pictures of Indian gods that are sold in bazaar stalls, and I hung mine inside my shirt. Then we were ushered out of the chapel door and through the crush of onlookers who had been peering in. The rain had eased now, and though it was still drizzling a fair-sized crowd had assembled around our horses, which had been brought up by a group of herdsmen. The animals stood in a line, shifting nervously, while a Mongol woman dressed in national costume offered each rider in turn a dipper of mare's milk scooped from a wooden pail. She knelt on the wet grass as she offered up the milk, then rose after we had taken a sip, and tipped a dribble of the milk on the horse's head, then into its stirrup, and then on its wet rump. We mounted, the milk still trickling from our unhappy horses, and led by a young novitiate monk bearing a bright red banner on a staff we rode off in a ragged column across the grassy compound toward the great double gates under the gate tower. Someone tugged open the gates, which gave out a suitably dramatic creaking groan, and we rode out down the ramp through yet another crowd of onlookers. As we turned to our right, the lucky direction, another lama dressed in red was dipping his ladle into a bucket of mare's milk and flicking it to the skies to propitiate the spirits. The droplets of milk mingled with specks of rain and spattered over us.

Ten minutes later the heavens reopened in a massive downpour that made it difficult to see the way forward. Wet and chilled, we abandoned our horses, handing them over to the guides, and got a lift in a leaky jeep belonging to the local commune which took us back to camp. One look at the new official expedition tent, drooping and slack, persuaded Paul and me that we should again set up our little mountain tent on a properly drained spot of level ground. There we sheltered until we were summoned to the herdsman's *ger* for the feasting. Ariunbold had asked me to bring four dozen bottles of local vodka as a contribution to the expedition stores. "It will be useful as presents for our herder-guides," he had told me when I pointed out that four cases of vodka made a heavy and very fragile load for pack-ponies. I need not have worried. That evening half the entire vodka stock, intended to last the entire trip, was consumed. Next morning a sorry-looking gang of Mongols rose late and stumbled peevishly about the camp. Only Paul and I, who had retired early, were in comparatively good humor. The others were suffering from hang-overs and were sodden.

Under the night's rain Ariunbold's famous new tent had sagged still further, and water had leaked through every pore. It seemed that before stitching the tent together, no one had even bothered to check whether the material was waterproof, which it was not. So for the rest of the following day the camp was decorated with all the expedition's finery that had taken up the little time Ariunbold had devoted to the preparations—fancy tunics, *dels*, and denim jackets were hung out to dry, with the dye leaking from them.

The only Mongol team member whose medieval costume was dry was Bayar. No one had bothered to give him a trial fitting back in Ulaan Baatar, and his size had been misjudged grossly. When he got dressed up for the departure ceremony, his *del* sleeves hung a foot beyond his fingers and the skirts of his *del* almost swept the ground. He looked exactly like the circus clown dressed in outsize clothes, and when he tried to hitch up his *del* with a leather bandolier containing the battery pouches for his film camera, he became a parody of "Mongolia meets the Wild West." With a grimace and a wink in the direction of Paul and me he abandoned his fancy garb and never wore it again.

It was a sorry and bedraggled start to Ariunbold's sector of the project, and I found myself wondering whether matters would improve as they had done on the trial ride in the Hentei. Ariunbold was boasting that it would take the vaunted Mongol horses no more than four weeks to reach Bayan Olgei. But I was doubtful. By my estimate it would require at least two months, allowing for rest days. Unless Ariunbold's amateurish performance changed for the better, it risked being a futile waste of the precious chance to explore more of traditional Mongolia.

8

A Hundred Remounts

We returned to the lamasery in the afternoon to collect our supply of remounts. We found that the three local *arats* who would be our guides had driven a mob of more than 100 horses into the vast compound of the lamasery. They were exuberantly chasing the horses up and down inside the walls, wielding their *uurgas* or lasso poles—a device like a long fishing rod with a leather loop at the end—to capture the animals they required for saddling. This meant pursuing their victims to the distant temples and back again at a spectacular gallop. It was an unconventional setting for an exhilarating and impromptu rodeo, but no one seemed to mind the commotion, least of all the lamas. The half-wild horses were stampeding in every direction and often refused to be subdued even when a lasso had them caught by the throat. The mounted herder would then have to twist his lasso pole, deliberately tightening the loop until the unfortunate animal half-choked, its breath wheezing out in painful gasps, and a herdsman on foot could sneak up, grab an ear so the horse could not escape, and slip on the bridle.

Through the Mongolian National Silk Roads Committee, Ariunbold had obtained official permission—and a small amount of funding—to try to re-create a genuine wonder of the Mongol empire: the *orto* system, which had provided the fastest and most efficient communication across Asia until the building of the railways. Genghis Khan and his heirs did not invent the principle of the *orto* system, having inherited it from earlier cultures like the Khitan,* but they developed it into an undertaking which almost beggars the imagination. The Mongols set out to create a chain of horse relay stations from the Yellow to the Black seas, an overland distance of 5000 miles. At each relay station there were local horses on standby, ready for use by travelers carrying the imperial *paiza*. Many relay stations would also offer guides and lodging, and some supplied carts and draft animals for hire. The resources required for the operation were stupendous, even for a people accustomed to owning large numbers of horses. In Mongolia alone it has been calculated that the *orto* system would have needed a reserve of 3 million animals. In addition, each relay station would have had a manager, grooms, shelter, watering facilities, commissariat, and a substantial acreage of pasture on which to keep the remounts.

The supreme effort of the *orto* system—and the source of its greatest pride—was the facility it offered to the high-speed dispatch riders. These men carried urgent imperial messages over distances that no regular system of post-riders has ever achieved, before or since. Unlike the riders of the American Pony Express who handed over their satchels of mail, one sector to the next, the crack Mongol couriers were expected to ride the full distance themselves, carrying the letter on their persons for total security. Consequently they forced their bodies to the absolute physical limits of endurance, riding day and night, rarely stopping for food or rest, their bodies strapped up tightly with leather belts to keep them upright in the saddle. A comparison between the *orto* system and the much better-known Pony Express puts this difference in perspective. The Pony Express riders could cover 2000 miles in ten days using relay stations about every 10 or 15 miles. But it was a very short-lived temporary measure, lasting just eighteen months, during which time 616 runs were made. The *orto* riders normally did 50 to 70 miles a day, or 120 miles on demand. In emergencies they galloped 250 miles a day, and their service lasted—at least in Mongolia—for seven centuries.

It was Marco Polo in his *Description of the World* who provided

---

*It was then known as the *yam* (Turkish) or *dzam* (Mongol) system.

the West with details of this astonishing communications network. He himself never visited Mongolia proper, but eighteen years after Rubruck's visit to Karakorum he traveled by a more southerly route through the western desert of China to reach the court of Kubilai Khan at Khan balik, the "Khan's City" at Peking. There he found a Mongol dynasty imposed on a Chinese culture—Kubilai Khan did not even use Chinese, but spoke Mongol—and heard about Mongolia from the Mongols at court, and saw for himself the *orto* in action as its riders kept Kubilai Khan in touch with his far-flung empire:

> When one of the Great Khan's messengers sets out along any of these roads he has to go only twenty-five miles and there he finds a posting station. . . . Here the messengers find no less than 400 horses stationed by the Great Khan's orders and always kept in readiness for his messengers when they are sent on any mission. . . . And this holds good throughout all the provinces and kingdoms of the Great Khan's empire. When the need arises for the Great Khan to receive immediate tidings by mounted messenger, the messengers ride 200 miles in a day, sometimes even 250. . . . They tighten their belts and swathe their heads and off they go with all the speed they can muster till they reach the next post-house twenty-five miles away. As they draw near they sound a horn which is audible at a great distance so that horses may be got ready for them. On arrival they find two fresh horses, ready harnessed, fully rested, and in good running form. They mount there and then, without breathing space, and no sooner are they mounted than off they go again. . . .*

The *orto* system was at the very heart of the success of the Mongol empire. Genghis Khan and his heirs had grasped the fact that fast, efficient communications gave them a clear advantage over their enemies, and that without such communications the enormous empire would be ungovernable. Indeed the *orto* system was so useful in the vast undeveloped spaces of Central Asia that it continued to be used in Mongolia long after it had died out in the rest of the world, and state relay stations with their herds of horses were maintained as late as 1949.

Retired ambassador Tsevegmid, a dignified old gentleman now in

The Travels of Marco Polo, translated by R. E. Latham, Penguin Classics, 1958.

his 80s and Mongolia's former envoy to China, whom I met in Ulaan Baatar before going to Karakorum, had told me how as a young man he had been given permission to use govenment *orto* facilities as he traveled across Mongolia to his first job. He had been one of the first formally trained teachers in the country and had been sent to report to his new school some 470 miles away. He still kept his official pass, written in red ink in Mongol script, which instructed each staging post to provide him with food and shelter, a guide, and horses free of charge. "The system worked well," he told me. "The rich families in each area took it in turns to provide the horses at the staging posts. It was a matter of pride for them. In those days we still had the *bukhia*, the specialist post-riders. They were the strongest riders of all, hand-picked, always young men, very fit and strong. Usually they came from rather poor families as the work was very, very hard. With important government messages they would gallop from station to station, not taking any rest breaks and not even touching the ground at the changeover, but jumping from one horse to the next. Because of the physical strain of their work, they wore the bandages that Marco Polo wrote about, wrapping leather or cloth belts around their bodies so tightly that they could stay upright in the saddle for day after day."

Our expedition did not intend to gallop across Mongolia at such a breakneck pace, but we did plan to change our horses relay by relay in the manner of medieval travelers carrying the imperial *paiza*. Our staging posts would be the smaller administrative centers, the so-called *somon* centers, westward from Karakorum along the old imperial routeway. Ariunbold was supposed to have visited each *somon* center and made the right arrangements so that in theory they were ready to provide us with two guides and a change of horses as we traveled across country.

Emerging from the monastery with our remounts, we must have looked more like a small contingent of Genghis Khan's army than relay riders, because our guides insisted on bringing along the entire herd of at least 100 spare horses, including several mares with foals. Once again we turned right for luck and this time, after making half the circuit of the outer wall, headed for a landmark that I had specially requested that we should visit—the largest and most impressive relic of the days when Karakorum had been the center of the Mongol world empire. This was the statue of a massive stone tortoise carved

of granite and set in open land about half a mile to the northwest.
Into a slot in the tortoise's back had once fitted a stone tablet, its text
proclaiming the Great Khan's edicts or, according to another theory,
a charm against flooding. Now the stele is gone, and the back and
head of the stone tortoise are heaped up with small pebbles balanced
there by Mongols as an offering to the spirits of the place. According
to the conclusions of Russian archaeologists published in 1965, the
tortoise had been one of a pair standing on each side of the main
gateway into the town of Karakorum when Rubruck arrived.

Rubruck found Karakorum town disappointingly small for what
was effectively the capital of the world. It was no bigger than the
suburb of Saint-Denis in Paris, he wrote, yet there were so many
courtiers that 105 cartloads of drink had to be hauled in to supply the
Khakhan's guests at a single banquet. Abutting the town and the sole
reason for its existence was the royal enclave, protected by its own
triple wall. Here Rubruck did find something to gape at. Dominating
the imperial grounds was a magnificent pavilion standing on a raised
mound of beaten earth. The interior, he reported, was like a huge
church with a middle nave between rows of pillars. Visitors entered
through one of three doors on the southern side and found themselves
looking down the length of the great hall to the imperial dais at the
far end. There sat the Great Khan in magnificent state on a spotted
panther skin. To his right his son and brothers occupied pews lifted
up to form a sort of balcony, and opposite them, on the Khan's left,
were similar elevated seats for his wives and the palace women. Access
to the Khan's throne platform was by two stairways, up which
climbed the imperial butler carrying the imperial drinking goblets,
because the entire pavilion was really no more than a huge banqueting
hall. The Great Khan, who remained a nomad, used it only twice a
year as he passed by Karakorum on his annual migration between the
seasonal grazing lands. The Russian excavations revealed that the
pavilion was very grand, measuring 165 by 135 feet, its floor covered
with light-green glazed tiles, and the colonnades resting on painted
and lacquered granite bases.

The main item of furniture was so curious and splendid that its
fame had spread as far as Persia. It was an ornate contrivance devised
by a French jeweler named William who had been captured in Hun-
gary and now lived in Karakorum, and it was placed near the main
entrance. In the shape of a tree, everything was made of solid silver—

leaves, branches, fruit, trunk. It was a human-powered drinks dispenser. At its base were four silver lions which gushed out white mare's milk, while above them four branches decorated with hollow curling serpents of silver were ready to spew forth wine, distilled mare's milk, mead, or Chinese rice wine. When these drinks were needed, the chief steward signaled to a man crouching inside the gadget, who puffed into a tube that led to a mechanical angel at the top of the tree. The angel raised a trumpet and sounded a note. This was the signal for the palace staff, who were standing ready outside the hall, to pour the different drinks into their respective conduits so that the pipes of the tree could deliver the drinks into silver basins.

William was by no means the only Westerner living in Karakorum at the time. Attached to the imperial court was all the human flotsam swept up in Mongol military campaigns across half the world—prisoners of war, slaves, mercenaries, interpreters. From Europe Rubruck met Russians, Hungarians, Georgians, and Armenians, and what with Chinese merchants, Tibetan priests, Arab and Persian traders, and Central Asian envoys, Karakorum was an international rendezvous where Rubruck was just one of many foreign visitors. He excited attention only when, as a friar, he insisted on walking about barefoot. In the cruel Mongolian climate, this caused some surprised comment. But as Rubruck himself confessed, the weather eventually got so bitterly cold that he feared he would damage his feet irreparably and so took to wearing warm footwear like everyone else.

With our 100 horses we circled the enigmatically smiling stone tortoise for more good fortune: Paul and myself, Ariunbold, Gerel, who because of pressure of work was able to ride with us only for the first day, and the three sturdy herdsmen-guides. Bayar and Doc had gone on ahead with the entourage of friends and well-wishers to our first staging post. The other permanent member of our team was Delger Saihan, a young man who had been looking after the gift horses near Karakorum. Paul and I immediately recognized him from our earlier ride to Burkhan Khaldun, where Delger had been one of the youngest and most active herdsman volunteers, full of the energy of youth and a tireless worker. His name meant "Broad Good" and he was only 17 years old,* though he looked barely 15. His father

---

*By Mongol count, 18, for the Mongols consider an extra year in the womb as part of a human life.

now lived in Ulaan Baatar, but Delger had been brought up in the
countryside by his grandmother. Gerel and Ariunbold had hired him
to care for the expedition's small squad of gift horses, though the
animals we would borrow at the relay stations were to be the responsibility of the herder-guides. With his rumpled *del*, runny nose, grubby
face and smelling of horse, Delger could have been a feckless and
cheery stable lad anywhere in the world.

What with arriving late at Karakorum for the departure ceremony,
collecting our remounts, recovering from hangovers, and drying out
the drenched equipment, it was not until the following morning, 18
July, that we moved onward, heading west toward the first *somon*
center where we would change our relay horses. Once again we were
behind schedule, and so once again we rode off at a tearaway pace.

But this time, instead of traveling through the frozen brown scenery
of the Hentei in late May, we were entering the Hangay mountain
massif of Central Mongolia at the beginning of the summer, and the
contrast could not have been greater. Now the weather was like an
English spring day, and the countryside was a vivid green and carpeted
with millions upon millions of wild flowers. It seemed that nature
was thrusting with maximum effort to grow, flourish, and mature in
the brief space of the Mongolian growing season. The explosion of
blossom was so overwhelming that the flowers would have seemed
vulgar and overdone but for the fact that they had seeded themselves
naturally and were in proportion to the sheer scale of the landscape.
They grew in colonies so that there were solid blocks of different
colors, from bright yellow to purple, with patches of pale violet and
occasional dark red. When we were not riding across this extrava-
ganza, the horses' hooves sank into the lush spring grass or kicked
up the smells of mint and thyme.

Beatrix Bulstrode had caught the glory of a similar countryside
when describing her ride into Urga: "range upon range of mountains
disclosed themselves as we ascended among a perfect wilderness of
flowers. Peonies, roses and delphiniums, Japanese anemones, blue
columbines, red and yellow lilies—a background of dark pine forest,
and away in the distance blue mountains beneath a canopy of soft
masses of rolling clouds."

We began by riding up a long and well-favored valley, where clusters of three or four *gers* were placed at intervals along the edge of
the river. Floodwater had overflowed the banks to make backwaters

and temporary ponds. Thunderclouds drifted across the sky, and whenever the shafts of sunlight broke through, the flocks of sheep glowed a bright white against the green pasture. The herds of horses beside every *ger* were sleek and glossy, and every animal had its head down and was gorging itself on the lush summer grass as if frantically compensating for the long winter famine. There were young animals everywhere—foals, calves, lambs. The wild Siberian cranes, which scurried out of our path like oversize guinea fowl, were followed by broods of chicks. When we splashed across a small stream, wild ducklings were ushered clear by their alarmed parents.

At first the ride was exciting and spectacular. There was the constant rumble of 100 sets of hooves, the shouts of the herdsmen, the mob of horses surging forward, the flow of animals shifting and changing their positions, and the sheer exhilaration of riding at a fast pace across an unspoiled countryside. As the sides of the valley closed in, steep crags of deeply fissured rock rose to our left. Large birds of prey perched on the rocks, and kites wheeled over the river, which, now that it was more constricted, was flowing in a dangerous flood. Whenever a horse tried to approach the bank, the herdsmen-guides galloped up and drove it back, for any animal that slipped into the water would have drowned.

Sure enough, after three or four hours, the well-remembered riding aches and pains set in. First the knees began to hurt, then the base of the spine, and finally the ribs. Each source of pain became more and more insistent, however much you changed position in the saddle. The hammering, jarring, flat run of the Mongol horses was as excruciating as ever, and the five-minute rest breaks offered very little respite. I understood why the Mongol dispatch riders had found it necessary to strap up their bodies in tight bandages, and I could not help noticing that our gift horses brought from the Hentei were the laggards among the herd. There were five of them and they ran together as a group, always at the back, for they were slower and clumsier than the rest. They were an ugly gang. Two had milky eyes, one was definitely elderly, and not one of them could be described as well proportioned.

We kept up this speed all morning and well into the afternoon, and the pace was faster than anything we had attempted during the trial ride in the Hentei. I began to be suspicious, and during a rest break

Ariunbold admitted that he was trying to make up time. He had learned nothing from our experience in the Hentei, when we had nearly ruined the horses by going too fast on our second day of riding. Now, because we were two days behind schedule, he intended to put in a double day's distance to catch up. There was no use pointing out that, once again, we risked damaging the horses, particularly as the animals were unfit at the start of this sector. Ariunbold was stubbornly determined to press ahead, and for the time being the herdsmen-guides followed his lead. We got back into the saddles and rode forward, but not until I had found a chance to take Ariunbold to one side and tell him privately that unless he acted more sensibly I could not see the expedition living up to the high-flown public announcements that he would ride all the way to France. For the moment, I warned him, the venture seemed very unprofessional, and it would be better to slow down and take matters more thoughtfully. His reaction was such a flat-eyed stare that it made me wonder whether he genuinely did not understand my lame Russian phrases.

We reached a place where a spur of land thrust out into the narrow valley and deflected the course of the river, making a precipice at the water's edge that forced us to turn away from the river. We chivvied the herd up a steep hill and then slithered down the far slope in a clattering avalanche of shale. Whenever we came to a patch of flat land by the river, however small the area, a *ger* had been pitched on the little meadow and we needed to deflect the thundering rush of our horse-herd to keep a safe distance so that we did not disturb the daily routine of the nomads. Nevertheless the guard dogs would rush out, barking and snarling, soon to be followed by the occupants of the *ger*, who would emerge from the door and stand there shading their eyes and watching the unusual spectacle of 100 horses streaming past.

At first I thought that in our headlong passage we would inevitably pick up stray horses, attracted from the local *gers* by the excited herd. But like shoals of fish passing and intermingling in the sea, our animals and the local horses seemed to have a sense of identity. The local animals would be swept up in our herd, run for a few hundred yards with us, and then disentangle themselves and go trotting back to their customary pasture. Only the local stallion would maintain his defiance. Racing up to defend his territory as we first arrived, he would challenge our horses and finally chase along behind us, convincing himself that he was driving off the intruders.

As we penetrated deeper into the hills of the Hangay, we came across signs that showed how this central Mongolian massif had nurtured nomad empires long before the rise of Genghis Khan. In one pass, placed so that it could be seen clearly against the skyline from a great distance, was a gray stone pillar. It was a standing stone, a weatherbeaten and indecipherable shaft which most likely dated from the era of Turkish nomads who had once wandered this land. Breeders of cattle and horses like the Mongols, Turks and Huns had raised their herds in this remote land until, for reasons not clearly understood, they had felt the urge to migrate outwards and burst violently upon the settled lands of the perimeter. The valley of the Orhon River which we were following had been a cradle for such movements, and nothing had altered the landscape in 2000 years.

It was still a nomad's Shangri-la of open land, lush pasture, and sweet water, and we rode by the monuments left by the nomadic tribes just as they had wanted them to be seen. There were the whale-backed burial mounds of Turkish tribal chiefs rising from the valley floor, and in a side valley we caught sight of a complete graveyard of some forgotten Central Asian tribe. Turning aside to investigate, we found that the grave builders had employed the natural slabs of rock which had tumbled off the nearby cliff, sledged them to the site, and then set them on edge to mark the graves. There were at least forty tombs, and grave robbers had been at work, for there were signs of digging and many tombstones had fallen to the ground or been overthrown. But the classic, 200-year-old Central Asian patterns of antlers and interlocking fronds could still be seen etched into the gritty rock.

It was half-past 3 o'clock in the afternoon, and we must have come at least 30 miles at the scrambling, ill-advised pace when we came in sight of what I supposed to be our destination. A small cluster of tents and *gers* had been erected close to the spot where the river Orhon ran down over some rapids and turned a sharp corner. On the far bank a tributary joined, and the resulting headland made a theatrical setting. The tents were very different from anything we had encountered before. There were six tents of an old-fashioned square design, rather like miniature marquees. Some were blue and white, others striped in yellow. In two lines they led up to a brand new *ger*, much larger and finer than usual, its white felt roof decorated with a bold red pattern. The eaves of all the tents were fancifully scalloped and the fringes rippled in the breeze. At each corner of this flamboyant ensemble had been planted staffs bearing crimson banners which waved jauntily. In a remote and virtually uninhabited valley, it looked as if someone had been preparing pavilions for a medieval tournament.

Thankfully we rode our horses the last few hundred yards, tied them to a low fence, and removed their saddles. Horses and riders were totally exhausted.

The exotic encampment turned out to have been organized by the local agricultural cooperative. It seemed that the region was famous for the manufacture of tents, and so a local committee had decided to set up a display. They had certainly picked a wonderful location, but the chances of attracting a potential customer were virtually nil. It was hard to imagine more than a dozen passers-by in a week. Nevertheless the local committee had appointed a local family to act as guardians, brought in a tiny selection of tourist souvenirs, and equipped the big *ger* as a hospitality center. The floor was covered with hand-embroidered rugs, the walls hung with antique saddles and harness, and a low table was set with hand-crafted bowls for drinking mare's milk. The young man who had the job of guardian got over his surprise at seeing us and invited us to come in to rest and refresh ourselves. After hastily putting on full traditional costume, he appeared with his wife and handed us bowls of sour mare's milk and sweets. Then all of the expedition riders stretched out flat on the rugs and fell asleep from sheer exhaustion in these strangely opulent surroundings. Only our three herdsmen-guides, as matter of fact as ever, kept apart watching over the horse-herd.

We were awakened after about two hours by the arrival of two jeeps bringing Bayar, Doc, Gerel's family, Ariunbold's mistress, and various hangers-on. There followed some rather incoherent discussions, and then the jeeps disappeared. Doc explained to me that Ariunbold had failed to arrange for any food supplies, so the jeeps had gone to the nearest settlement to see what could be obtained. They returned after another hour to announce that there was no food to be had, but Gerel's sister-in-law, who lived in the next settlement about 10 miles away, was waiting for us. Thereupon Ariunbold announced that we should saddle our horses again and ride on.

I could scarcely believe what I was hearing. Only a fool would

have ignored the fact that horses and riders were worn out. On the
first day of riding we had already come much too far. To continue
any further was doubly stupid. Any horses that had sore backs would
be ruined; weak horses would need extra time to recover. I suggested
to Ariunbold that it would be better to send the jeeps to bring back
a supply of food from Gerel's sister-in-law. Then the team could rest
at the hospitality *ger* and ride on in the morning. Ariunbold was
stubborn. We were to ride on. Those who did not want to or felt
unable to do so could go forward in the jeep. Neither Paul nor I were
prepared to give Ariunbold the satisfaction of saying that we had held
back. Gerel, however, had had enough. He scowled with irritation
and then strode off, looking disgusted. He left with the others in the
jeeps.

Ariunbold then summoned the herdsmen, who had been noticeably
absent from the discussion, and ordered them to ride forward. They
looked angry and began to mutter amongst themselves. Ariunbold
mounted his horse and rode out. Paul and I grimly followed, leaving
a decent interval between ourselves and our fatuous leader. Ariunbold
kept glancing over his shoulder, and then stopped. We rode past him
and turned to see him galloping back toward the herders, gesturing
frantically that they were to mount up and follow him. They did
nothing of the sort and turned their backs. It was quite evident that
they had mutinied. They were setting up their own camp and turning
out their horses to pasture for the night. As far as they were concerned, they had gone far enough. In the context of the Mongolian
arat's easygoing nature and his usual willingness to fall in with whatever plan is put to him, this was dissatisfaction of a very high order.
It was quite apparent that they had no further time for Ariunbold,
and though he shouted and waved at them to come forward, they
studiously ignored him.

Paul, Ariunbold, and I rode on. Our horses were so tired that it
was another two hours' slow ride to the *somon* center, and Paul was
seething with anger. I was merely intent on finishing the extra distance
without too much pain. Halfway to the *somon* center, we came to
another small tributary of the main river. It was in flood, and Ariunbold, who was still riding in the lead, urged his horse into the stream.
It was largely a matter of guesswork, because the dirty brown water
concealed any deep holes, and first Ariunbold's horse and then mine

Praying to the image of Genghis Khan at the stone pillar erected to commemorate *The Secret History of the Mongols.*

Novitiate lama prays to the image of Buddha carved on the rock face at Mandal.

Aged lamas, survivors of the great religious purges of the 1930s, bless the departure of the expedition from their great lamasery at Erdenzu, the oldest in Mongolia.

Lamas blow conch shells to call to prayer at Erdenzu.

Traditional costume for a young participant in "The Great Birthday Party" celebrating Genghis Khan's birth, ending fifty years of the communist government's policy of denying Genghis Khan as Mongolia's founder-hero.

Loading a reluctant pack-horse at Mandal.

Riders at the Naadam races, which are run over distances of between eight and sixteen kilometers.

Pouring mare's milk on the head of an expedition horse to bring good luck to the journey.

A traditional Mongol saddle.

Riding across the Hentei wilderness in May on the way to Burkhan Khaldun, the Mountain of the Shaman Spirit, where Genghis Khan hid as an outlaw.

Horses at evening camp, Hentei. The horse in the foreground is hobbled in the traditional Mongol manner, three legs roped together.

Dampildorj scraping a charred sheep's head for breakfast.

Nomad woman ladles water to cool the distillation of *arkhi*, the homemade alcohol made from mare's milk.

Tents of a work brigade of Kazakh nomads in the Altai Mountains, close to the border with China.

Inside a Kazakh tent with
Hojanias, our musician guide.

The valley at Dzag, horse-
herders' paradise.

floundered across safely. By now Paul's mount was so worn out and moving so slowly that he was riding some distance behind. When he reached the riverbank, Paul decided to turn upstream to try to find a more shallow crossing. He went up the bank to where the water looked less dangerous and rode in. The current caught the exhausted horse and began to carry it diagonally downstream. The animal was too tired to resist and swam feebly. By the time it reached the far bank, the horse had been carried past the low section of bank on the opposite side and no longer had the strength to climb out unaided on the steeper shore. It began to flail weakly at the bank with its front legs. Paul slid out of the saddle and literally threw himself on the grass on the far side, keeping hold of the reins. Then, walking downstream with the exhausted animal, he managed to find a spot where he could coax it out of the water. The wretched horse stood there, head hanging, soaking wet, a picture of misery.

At that point Ariunbold rode back to inquire what was the matter and to tell Paul that we had five or six miles to ride. Paul lost his temper and yelled abuse. Couldn't Ariunbold see that the horses were half-dead on their feet? That he had pushed the animals until they were suffering? It was impossible to imagine a worse-organized first day. Ariunbold flinched and then pretended to have difficulty understanding. Slowly Paul simmered down, but he bellowed at Ariunbold to clear off and said that he preferred to walk the rest of the way, leading his horse. Ariunbold rode off looking sheepish.

Ariunbold had managed to achieve the almost impossible. With record speed and during his first day as team leader, he had lost the respect of the herdsmen, who would travel no further with him; he had forfeited the enthusiasm of his Mongol companions, who had gone on ahead; and he had reduced his traveling party to two foreigners, one of whom was in a towering rage. In short, he had lost all credibility. I wondered if all graduates of the Higher Party School, selected for their family connections, were quite as worthless and ineffectual. But I knew we were stuck with him. It was Ariunbold who had allegedly organized the chain of relay stations with the remounts ahead of us, and it was Ariunbold who had been assigned by the Mongolian Silk Roads Committee to conduct this sector of the ride. If the expedition was to continue westward, all that could be done was to keep calm, go along with the unhappy team, and hope that matters improved. This was still a Mongol project on Mongolian territory, and Paul and I were observers who would have to make the best of it.

But one did not need to be a foreigner to have misgivings. Next morning Gerel, too, expressed his opinion of Ariunbold's managerial skills. Standing in front of his sister-in-law's *ger* he gave vent to a very public display of anger. He abused his co-leader roundly, telling him that he was lazy, selfish, and incompetent. To no one's surprise it had turned out that the supply of fresh horses Ariunbold was supposed to have arranged in advance with the local authorities had not been organized properly, and we would have to wait. Gerel turned on his heel and stalked off, fuming.

9

Crossing
the Hangay Massif

This awkward situation was relieved, temporarily at least, by Ariunbold's personal political ambition and his sense of self-importance. When two new herdsmen arrived shortly before noon with a change of horses, he was nowhere to be seen. He had gone off, Doc told us, to follow up a rumor that a roving correspondent from the Russian news agency Tass was in the vicinity. Ariunbold wanted to locate the journalist and provide him with an interview about the expedition. "It will give him a chance to promote himself," sniffed Doc, whose hay fever had been aroused by the huge amounts of pollen from the wild flowers, "and I suggest that we get on without him." In his competent fashion Gerel, who seemed equally glad to be rid of Ariunbold for the time being, helped to sort out the saddles and equipment. Gerel was obliged to leave us that day and return to his studio in Ulaan Baatar, where he had to complete a major state commission on the much-photographed equestrian statue of Mongolia's revolutionary hero, Sukhebaatar the herdsman-soldier. His statue on its prancing horse was the centerpiece of Ulaan Baatar's main square, but it had been hastily made in such shoddy material that it was crumbling to pieces. Gerel and a team of sculptors were replacing it with a more durable copy in stone.

I was sorry to see Gerel leave, because he had shown his worth in the Hentei ride and he might have had enough official authority, if matters under Ariunbold got any worse, to replace or restrain him. Bayar was not in a position to exert much influence, because he was on assignment from his bosses at Mongolian Film Studio and had to get on with the job at hand. Nor was he by nature someone who would wish to intercede. He was an extremely competent and hard-working field man, always cheerful, but he did not see himself in any way as a leader.

Doc, for his part, was powerless, as he had no formal standing in the group and was coming along merely to help Paul and me as interpreter. Indeed I rather feared that Doc would be the one who would suffer the most strain if Ariunbold proved totally inadequate. Doc's role as interpreter put him in a particularly stressful position, because Ariunbold had the habit of avoiding unpalatable advice by pretending not to understand what either Paul or I was trying to say. Then Doc had to re-translate slowly and carefully, only to be ignored once again by Ariunbold. Doc himself, who was highly intelligent, could see precisely where and when things were going wrong and was suffering from the inevitable frustration. There was no question of Doc's overall ability as an interpreter. He was much more than a mere translator of words. In our conversations with herdsmen he could give a simultaneous running commentary, interspersing the direct translation with extra information drawn from his wealth of knowledge about his own country, and he was a man of both sophistication and enthusiasm.

I found myself hoping that when our little group had got properly under way in the open countryside, without distractions like the journalist from Tass, then perhaps everything would settle down, Ariunbold would grow into his job as leader of the Mongol team, and our circumstances would improve.

Before Gerel left, he introduced us to our two new guides: the Drunk and the Quiet Man.

The Quiet Man rarely said a word, but he watched everything with sharp eyes that constantly flicked from one person to the next, and he never missed anything. He had a friendly, rather pointed face like an engaging fox, very dark brown and deeply lined, and he was totally self-effacing. He kept shyly in the background and dressed inconspicuously in an old khaki *del*, with a khaki beret worn flat across the top of his head. He was to reveal that he was by trade a master maker of *gers* who normally led a work team of four men who shaped the lattice sides, door, roof poles, and all the wooden fittings, painted and ready to order, along with the felt covering. The management committee of the local *somon* center had asked him to provide sufficient horses and to guide us over the next sector of the Hangay route.

His companion, the Drunk, was the exact opposite in character. He was noisy, cheerful, rough, and extrovert, and the local committee sent a veiled warning that we would be wise to see that he kept away from the bottle. He arrived in high good humor, grinning cheerfully and equipped with a large radio-cassette player stuffed into the front of his *del*. We set out with the Quiet Man trotting along discreetly in the rear and with the Drunk in the lead, ambling along with the distorted music blaring out from his chest as he swayed slightly in the saddle. The music stopped, but only briefly, when all the batteries were jolted free and cascaded to the ground. They were recovered and held firmly back in place with yellow camera tape provided by Paul. Then the genial Drunk managed to snap his riding crop, which, too, needed a yellow tape splint. Finally he requested an extra strap to tie on his raincape and borrowed a length of brightly striped colored webbing, also from Paul. Thus, highlighted in multicolors, he jogged on, tunelessly howling Mongol songs.

Theoretically it was all wrong for a serious cross-country expedition, but the pace was wonderful after the previous day's excess—a gentle amble that spared the horses and covered the ground perfectly adequately. The sun shone, the Hangay scenery was lovely, and of Ariunbold there was no sign. It was the happiest, most carefree sector so far.

We camped that evening at the Falls of the Orhon, where the river plunges over a 60-foot cliff and drops into a rock gorge with much noise and white foam and the changing colors of a little rainbow shimmering in the spray. It was one of Mongolia's most famous beauty spots, a natural phenomenon that could not help evoke the deep-rooted Mongolian shamanistic reverence for the spirits of water, rocks, and sky. A rickety post-and-rope had been stretched round the lip of the chasm to prevent visitors from falling into the abyss, but right at the best vantage point to view the Falls there was a large, flat-topped boulder, and in a hollow on top of it lay a scattering of offerings left for the deities of the place. It was exactly the same sort of altar we had seen in front of the wigwam *obo* at the foot of Burkhan Khaldun. On the opposite rim of the chasm, seen through the mist of the Falls, was the characteristic cone of another *obo* rock cairn, and when I had clambered down to view the Falls from below I found a third *obo*, a large tree branch that had been propped against the cliff at the foot of the cascade. From every bleached branch hung the same array of strips and rags of cloth offerings we had seen at the wigwam *obo*, and as I looked back upward to the lip of the gorge I saw a solitary Mongol standing on the rim facing the Falls. He was a stranger, probably a tourist. As I watched, he put his hands together and bowed his head in reverence.

The next day's riding took us through countryside more spectacular than anything we had seen before. The views were positively Alpine, but so unspoiled as to appear as the Swiss or Austrian highlands must have looked 1000 years ago. Once again the hillsides were smothered with wild flowers from one slope to the next, so that in the space of a mile we would pass from an area that was purple, to a slope that might be yellow, and then to a third hillside white with so many edelweiss that from a distance it seemed that it had snowed in the afternoon. The flowers came in every shape, from tall spiked columns to tiny blossoms as small as forget-me-nots. For six hours we rode on a flowery tapestry except where our horses had to thread their way around the debris of an ancient lava flow that had oozed down the valley and congealed, leaving a jumbled moonscape of dark brown rocks.

A small lake had formed behind the lava flow and here we stopped for our noonday break. A group of four *gers* had been placed close to the water's edge, and the Drunk led us eagerly toward them, knowing the hospitality we could expect. The welcome would be the same at nearly every *ger* throughout our summer ride: we would enter, nibble a little food, and drink vast quantities of mare's milk and alcohol. Gone were the hungry days of boiled mutton and cold thin tea, for now we were in the brief season of high summer when the flocks and herds were giving ample milk, and the Mongol diet was virtually pure milk. To turn away a stranger at such a time of richness was unthinkable. Hospitality was given, and taken, for granted. My own inclination was to hover outside and wait to be invited into a *ger*, but our Mongol companions did not even pause for an instant. They would ride straight to the tether line between its two poles, tie up their horses, stroll over to the largest and most important *ger*, push open the door, and walk in as if it were their own home.

The scene inside was always the same. A metal stove, about half the height and the same shape as an oil barrel, stood directly in front of the door with its metal chimney rising up through the smoke hole in the apex of the felt tent. Three or more iron bedsteads were arranged in a semicircle around the back and sides of the *ger*, and the spaces between them were filled with chests of drawers usually painted orange and decorated with flowery bands. The host's seat was at the farthest point away from the door, and the most senior guest would be placed on his right while the other guests either sat on the beds or made themselves comfortable on the ground within reach of a low table set before the host. On the table there was always a dish ready and waiting, piled with sugar lumps, hard biscuits, and sun-dried lumps of curd. The latter were a tooth-cracking ordeal to chew as they were, in Rubruck's words, "as hard as iron slag."

Usually as we arrived the wife would already be stoking the fire to boil up milk and water for salt tea. But *ayrag*, mare's milk, was what our companions wanted, gallons of it. "Mares's milk is all they care about," Rubruck had written tersely,* and it became clear how the Mongols had earned themselves the nickname "the drinkers of mare's milk." The quantities of *ayrag* our companions consumed were almost beyond belief. It was not unusual to see them drink 17 to 20 pints in a day, and, as social etiquette expected every visitor to drink three bowls of milk before leaving the *ger*, neither Paul nor I escaped the orgy of milk consumption. The *ayrag* was kept ready either in a barrel or usually in a leather sack hanging on a frame just inside the door. It was not drunk fresh but half-fermented, so that it had a sour and sometimes slightly fizzy taste. At intervals the woman of the house would take the wooden paddle whose handle stuck out from the milk bag and beat air into the brew with a hollow squelching sound to aid the souring process.

*He called it "Cosmos" from the Turkish name for mare's milk, "*qumiz*."

Nothing had changed since Rubruck's day. Mare's milk, he noted, "is made in the following way":

> They stretch above the ground a long rope attached to two stakes stuck in the soil, and about the third hour [nine o'clock] tether to the rope the foals of the mares they intend to milk. Then the mares stand beside their foals and let themselves be milked peacefully. In the event of any of them proving intractable, one man takes the foal and puts it underneath her to let it suck a little, and then withdraws it while the milker takes its place.
>
> So having collected a great quantity of milk, which when it is fresh is as sweet as cow's milk, they pour it into a large skin or bag, and set about churning it with a club which is made for this purpose, as thick at the lower end as a man's head and hollowed out. As they stir it rapidly, it begins to bubble like new wine and turn sour or ferment, and they keep churning it until they extract the butter.
>
> Next they taste it, and when it is moderately pungent they drink it. While one is drinking it, it stings the tongue like wine from unripe grapes, but after one has finished drinking it leaves on the tongue a taste of milk of almonds. It produces a very agreeable sensation inside and even intoxicates those with no strong head; it also markedly brings on urination.

Rubruck's two theories, that drinking *ayrag* "markedly brings on urination" and also makes you drunk, are still heard from both Mongols and foreigners. But both ideas, from my own observation, are only partly true. The main reason for the large output of urine must simply be the stupendous quantity of mare's milk that is consumed. It was hardly surprising that as our little group rode from *ger* to *ger*, stopping at each felt tent for every man to drink another three or four bowls of liquid, 5 or 6 pints at a session, the herdsmen were obliged frequently to empty their bladders as they rode on to the next *ger*. The *ayrag* may have been diuretic, but it was the sheer volume that mattered.

Nor, as far as I could tell, was *ayrag* noticeably intoxicating. Sour mare's milk may perhaps be mildly alcoholic, but it would take so long to drink the necessary amount that any intoxication would be slow and feeble. We were consuming gallons of milk day after day on our ride and did not feel inebriated. Just an hour's riding in the fresh air would soon sober up any drinker, though perhaps to drink a similar quantity and not take any exercise might produce a state of inertia and drowsiness.

Yet the Mongols do have a ferocious reputation as habitual drunkards, whether they were humble herdsmen or Great Khans, and this notoriety has a very long history. The tales range from sad descriptions of alcohol-sodden beggars crawling through the streets of 19th-century Urga, to the last Khutukhtu, Jebtsundamba, who was drunk for a week at a time, to the Khakhan Ögodei, who, so the story runs, became so addicted to alcohol that his brother Chaghatai warned him that unless he cut down his daily intake he would kill himself. Chastened, the Khan swore that he would halve the number of goblets of strong drink he drank, and even agreed to have a servant keep a check on the number of drinks he took every day. But he promptly doubled the size of the royal goblet. Knowing the childlike deviousness of country Mongols, the story has a certain ring of truth. Despite his good intentions, Ögodei died of alcoholism, as did his successor as Khakhan, Güyük.

Oddly, few commentators seem to have taken much note that the Mongols do have ready access to a source of alcohol, easily derived from milk, which they consume with gusto. This alcohol is far more likely to have been the reason for their reputation as dipsomaniacs. Rubruck reported that a clear and "really potent" drink he called "black cosmos" was reserved for the wealthy Mongols. He believed it was made by churning mare's milk until it was free of all solids, but it was almost certainly the tipple that modern Mongols call *shimiin arkhi*—"essence or steam *arkhi*"—to distinguish it from commercially made vodka, which is also called *arkhi*. In the countryside we found nearly every family making it by simple distillation of milk boiled in an open bowl on the iron stove. A large tube, often no more than a plastic drum with the ends cut off, is placed upright in the bubbling milk, and the top end is closed with a bowl of water kept cool by constant ladling. The vapor rising from the steaming milk condenses against the bottom of the water bowl, dribbles back, and drips into a small jug suspended in the center of the tube.

Any type of milk can be used in this simple pot-still—variously we drank *shimiin arkhi* made from milk of camel, yak-cow, goat, and mare—and the liquor may be distilled a second time to increase its strength. Each type of *shimiin arkhi* has its own reputation: the best is said to be from cow's milk, the strongest from mare's milk. Camel and goat's milk *arkhi* were described to me as "sweet and sliding down easily." Colorless and refreshing, *shimiin arkhi* seemed to be about as strong as sherry or another fortified wine. Two or three small bowls should be enough to mellow a normal drinker, and any more soon produces real intoxication. For country Mongols the drink is cheap, enticing, and available in virtually unlimited amounts. Seventeen pints of milk will produce almost a tumblerful of *arkhi*. And when a guest has drunk his obligatory three bowls of sour mare's milk, it is considered polite to top it off with a draft or two of *shimiin arkhi*. Of course, our singing companion the Drunk would happily quaff a pint at a session.

His drunkenness drew no disapproval. The *arats* were very tolerant of such behavior. They saw nothing wrong in intoxication, and during that particular midday halt our visit was interrupted by a very obvious drunkard who threw open the door of the *ger*, tripped over the threshold, and lurched into our circle. He was too inebriated to stand and sat down clumsily on the ground, sweating heavily, peering at the newcomers, and breaking directly into the conversation. Everyone listened to him patiently and answered his questions, even when he repeated them three or four times. No one tried to silence him or to bundle him out. "He's still drunk from the night before," Doc told me quietly. "It seems that he and his friends have regular drinking sessions and spend most of their time intoxicated." Our own Drunk had found a kindred soul. When we left the *ger* and continued on our way, he was missing. He had been lured to another *ger* to join a second bout of *arkhi* drinking, and it was another half-hour before he came galloping up in our tracks, visibly the worse for wear. "He's got no need to worry," said Doc, "a Mongol herdsman stays in the saddle drunk or sober, and his horse will not care. It's quite normal for two Mongols to ride back ten miles to their own *ger* after an evening drinking session with their neighbors, clinging to one another for support and singing loudly while their horses trot along side by side, through the darkness, quite unconcerned."

Poor Doc was having a wretched time. He was determined to travel with us as our interpreter, and he was by far the best-qualified man for the job. But he was a city dweller by habit and preference, and an ungainly rider. So he was suffering more than anyone else from saddle sores, weariness, and all the aches and discomforts of cross-country travel and camping rough. Worst of all, his chronic hay fever was getting really acute, a terrible affliction in such a pollen-rich landscape. All day long his eyes streamed tears. He blew mournfully on a succession of huge handkerchiefs, and his nose had swollen until it was a bulbous raw blob. It was impossible not to pity and admire him at the same time. His enthusiasm never diminished and he was generous with his ample knowledge of Mongol lore. To try to protect his tortured nose he wore a white hospital face-mask as he rode, and this, together with his grey felt stetson hat, made him look like some unsuccessful outlaw from the Old West.

By now our numbers had stabilized to the official traveling team—Gerel we would not see again until we returned to Ulaan Baatar. That left Ariunbold, who had reappeared, presumably after giving an interview to the journalist from Tass, Bayar, Delger, Doc, Paul, myself, and the two guides for that sector—the Drunk and the Quiet Man. Once again, Ariunbold seemed unable to mix in with the rest of the team and kept off to one side. This, if anything, was a relief, as the rest of us got on with the humdrum tasks of saddling horses, making camp, cooking food, and so forth. Our five gift horses were looking very lackluster. We seldom rode them or even used them as pack-animals in case we overtaxed them. "Make sure that we always ride the herdsmen's horses," Ariunbold ordered cynically. "If their horses get sick, that is not our problem." So Delger drove our sorry little gang of gift horses along in a sluggish group, shouting and whistling and prodding them with a long slender goad he had cut from a forest branch. I was beginning to doubt whether, even unridden, the animals would last the distance. They were aged and sickly, and the worst of them were really so awful that it was difficult to believe that they would stand the pace.

The land was steadily rising as we penetrated deeper into the Hangay massif, the peaks around us reaching as high as 9000 feet. We spent the night beside another lake, this time camped on the broad sweep of a magnificent grassy slope that looked southward over the water where flocks of wild ducks were feeding. They belonged to the large rust-brown and white species the Mongols call "lama ducks" from their color. The Mongols refuse to hunt them, saying it would bring bad luck to kill them. At the previous *somon* center we had been given another sacrificial sheep and still had half the carcass with us, dripping blood from its gunny sack on the pack-pony. Now we cooked it in the usual boiling pot. We had no firewood for the portable stove, so the Drunk leaped into the saddle and galloped off to a distant *ger*, returning with a sack of firewood across his saddle-bow. He had found new friends, and soon afterward disappeared to them for yet another *arkhi* session. Bayar, whose cheerfulness and fieldcraft were proving more and more an asset, had taken over the role of cook. Ariunbold had gone to lie down in the tent, leaving the rest of us to summon him when the meal was ready.

Paul and I were nursing hopes of a new and succulent dish. With Doc we had been amusing ourselves by gathering the wild mushrooms we had seen during the afternoon's ride. It was typical of Mongolia's burst of summer fertility that the crop of mushrooms was more bountiful than any I had seen in another country. Ordinary field mushrooms sprouted by the hundreds in untouched rings, and the individual specimens could be enormous, sometimes 15 inches in diameter. The puffball mushrooms were solid meaty globes, and there was a variety of small bright-red mushroom that looked as if it lacked only a garden gnome. Our Mongol colleagues ignored all of them and were positively shocked when I plucked and nibbled one raw. But Doc pointed out which varieties were edible, and we had collected 11 or 12 pounds of prime mushrooms and waited for Bayar to do them justice. We should have known better. When the water was boiling, he just tossed them in to stew. Our Mongol guides even went so far as to avoid eating them, fishing them out of the bowl with expressions of distaste. I was reminded of Prjevalski's remark that when his Mongol guides saw him eating roast duck, they were very nearly sick.

Sitting quietly in the battered tent after supper that evening, I wondered at how little Rubruck or Carpini would have found that was different from their day. Bayar was in one corner, noisily demol-ishing the fat tail of the sheep. He would thrust a large portion of the tail into his mouth and carve off a gobbet with his knife, narrowly avoiding nicking his snub nose. Then he would chew away with gusto, glancing over at us with twinkling eyes, the fat sliding down his chin and the sounds of small bones crunching between his strong teeth. Doc lay in a semi-coma, having swallowed so many antihista-mine tablets that he was sound asleep and could not be roused. Ariun-bold was polishing his personal silver bowl; Delger was mending harness; the Quiet Man was just sitting quietly watching. As the moon rose in a cloudless sky, there were so many holes in the thread-bare canvas of the old tent—the fancy blue Japanese version had long ago been abandoned—that it seemed there were twice as many stars in the sky as usual.

The wild Hangay scenery hid an occasional surprise. Next morning I deliberately lagged behind to do some filming with the lightweight camera I carried in my saddlebag and let the main group ride ahead around the soggy margin of the lake. Spurring to catch up, I rode my horse in their wake through a shallow. But the bog was not as substan-tial as I or the horse thought, and without a guide to warn me I galloped straight into a giant mud hole. The horse stepped as if on air, flailed with its legs a half-second, then tilted forward, and the next moment was submerged at a 45-degree angle, its head buried past its ears in gluey mud. I tugged the poor creature out before it suffocated and rode on with a high-water mark of slime until I could clean up the unlucky animal in a stream. I did not need to hurry. My colleagues had already found another little group of gers and were having a late breakfast. Here, at last, Mongol cuisine had a happy surprise. In addition to the usual three bowls of sour *ayrag*, the deadly *shimiin arkhi*, and bone-hard lumps of dried curd, we were offered plates heaped with clotted cream. Paul and I fell upon the treat in ecstasy, using our fingers to scoop up great dripping lumps. Bayar probably thought we were as uncouth as he had appeared to us eating his sheeptail fat.

The surge of nature's fruitfulness during the brief Mongolian sum-mer had given me a fresh way of looking at why the Mongols had failed to sustain the heartland of the empire that Genghis Khan founded. Scholars have long held that the collapse of the great empires which the Central Asian nomads imposed on the settled lands of their perimeter was caused in part by the weakening of their warrior spirit. It was said that when the nomads lost touch with their harsh home base in the steppes, they became softened by the easier life in the settled lands and soon were ripe to be overthrown and ejected. By extension, it has also been mooted that if the Mongols or any other nomad society had maintained their rigorous way of life, they would have survived in power far longer.

But now, seeing the vital importance of the brief summer to nomad life in the steppe, it became obvious that the Mongols had no choice. If the Mongols, or any other nomad people, mustered and sent out an army beyond its territory in summer—the normal time for campaigning—they would strip their homeland of the essential workforce at the most vital season of the year. The steppe nomads needed to use the brief summer to raise the young foals and calves, gather the milk products, store food, and prepare for the long winter months. If the menfolk were away fighting a war at this time, the work would not be done adequately, and the nomads would find it difficult to return to their homeland and survive the winter. In short, the Mongol campaign of expansion under Genghis Khan was a one-way commitment. By the time they had conquered the surrounding territories, it was very difficult for them to return home because their nomad economy had been interrupted. Sustaining life in the harsh midcontinent did not, in effect, allow time for making war.

It was now six days since we had ridden out of the great gate of Erdenzu's lamasery, and we were crossing the most favored part of Mongolia. Nowhere else is better suited for horse-raising than the lush valleys of the Hangay in high summer. The pasture is rich, the forests provide timber, and the rivers and streams offer abundant water. We found that every valley had its scattering of *gers* tucked away in some favored south-facing glen, with a herd of mares and foals grazing contentedly nearby. The herders regarded this interval of ease in their hard lives as a god-given privilege. Sometimes we eavesdropped on a herdsman clear across the valley, singing and hallooing at the top of his voice from sheer joy as he rode flat out over the summer pasture. He might have been going somewhere with a purpose, but just as often, when he came in sight, he was simply tearing across the superb countryside for the sheer pleasure of being alive in such wonderful surroundings and feeling his horse galloping away beneath him. Such moments explained why, despite its grim climate and utter isolation, the Mongolian herdsmen are so intensely proud of their land. It was inconceivable to them that anywhere else could be as beautiful or as bountiful as the mountain pastures in high summer.

The renaissance of Genghis Khan was here, even among these remote herding people. I was surprised to see that there were *arats* in the heart of the Hangay who wore cap buttons and badges bearing the image of Genghis Khan. They had moved with their families and flocks and herds into regions where they probably would not see a permanent dwelling for three or four months. Yet they were sporting the image of Genghis Khan. Where they had obtained their Genghis Khan buttons was impossible to learn. When asked, they just said that they had seen someone wearing the badge and managed to get one for themselves. After half a century of official obscurity not only had Genghis Khan become a symbol of national identity but deep in the countryside his image had taken on the quality of a good-luck charm. When they heard that our little team was riding through their isolated valleys to celebrate the old way of Mongol life, they looked thoroughly approving and wished us every success and a safe and lucky journey.

The lives of the herder families could be read in their collections of faded black-and-white photographs. Every *ger* had them, framed and displayed over the chests of drawers at the back of the *ger*. Here were the obligatory portraits of the father and mother, the picture of the school class in the *somon* center, perhaps a snapshot taken of one of the children dressed up as a jockey in the Naadam races, and maybe a picture from a well-remembered visit to Ulaan Baatar. The latter would usually have been taken in the great central square, with the Sukhebaatar statue in the background, by the portrait photographers who lined up with their old-fashioned wooden tripods and ancient cameras waiting for the country visitors. But the most frequent photograph of all was the picture taken during army service. Sometimes it was a self-conscious studio portrait of the young man dressed in his private's uniform, but just as often it was the picture taken on the day he came home on his first leave. Still dressed in his uniform, he would be mounted proudly on one of the family horses.

The only other decoration inside the *gers*, apart from the painted colors of the chests and the scroll patterns on the slim pillars holding up the roof wheel, were hanging embroideries suspended over the beds and around the walls. Simple outlines of naïve art, they showed animals and human figures, flowers and uncomplicated patterns, stitched in bright colors on plain white backgrounds. The most frequent subject was horses—horses running, horses tethered, foals prancing. Even the Mongol women who chose the designs and stitched the pictures gave pride of place to horses.

All the next day we climbed, first along the narrow gorge called the Valley of the White Stallion, and when that route petered out against a steep hillside, we turned aside and scrambled up a mountain path until we were above the tree line. Because the paths were narrow, we usually rode in a long, strung-out line, bunching together only on the valley floors. Mostly we rode in silence, occupied with our own thoughts, and aware that every evening there would be ample time to discuss the day's events. Occasionally Paul darted ahead, looking for a vantage point for his photography. Delger was always hurtling back and forth, roaring and whistling at his gang of gift horses to make them move along and stay on track. Ariunbold had faded into the background and made little impression, while Bayar kept going with his usual high spirits, clowning and giving impersonations of drunken *arats* swaying in the saddle. Our two herder-guides insisted that we stop regularly to rest the horses, and at least twice a day they changed the pack-animals, loading the baggage onto fresh mounts. Our march had finally settled down into some sort of routine, broken only when a new pack-horse bolted. By bad luck the animal was carrying on top of its load the metal chimney pipes for our stove, and they tumbled to the ground with loud clangs that frightened all the other pack-ponies. They disappeared at a panicked gallop into the trees, pursued by Delger waving his goad like Don Quixote's lance and cursing vehemently, but obviously glad of a little excitement.

We had crossed the watershed by late afternoon and began descending the far mountainside cautiously. It was so steep and treacherous that when a clumsy gift horse lost its footing it rolled down the slope for 10 yards before scrambling back to its feet. At the base of the hill we came across a single *ger*, set at what was clearly the upper limit of summer pasture. It was occupied by a young couple so poor that all they owned was the smallest size of *ger*, its canvas cover ripped and faded, a dented stove, a bed, and two wooden cases. They possessed no other furniture, no mirror, no wall hangings, and the earth floor was bare. Yet they already had three children under the age of 3, and the site was so high that the local stream was still banked with hard blue ice in late July. It brought home the harsh fact that Doc had earlier pointed out: beneath the splendid Hangay with its magnificent forests and summer meadows, the bedrock lay permanently frozen because the altitude of the massif made it one of the world's most southerly regions of permafrost.

Even here we were expected to spend a few polite moments and accept three bowls of *ayrag*. Then we descended the valley for another twenty minutes and found a much more prosperous family where the wife, a huge, bustling, laughing woman who clearly dominated her family, directed us to a small *ger* which turned out to be used only for cooking and storage of food. There she lit the stove and cooked us a series of buttery chapattis, spread with clotted cream, and again it seemed to Paul and me that Mongol cooking did have its compensations. Her husband volunteered to come with us for the next few miles, saying that the rivers were badly flooded and the fords were dangerous. When Bayar mentioned that we would be camping out that evening and had very little food, the wife sent us on our way with a small metal churn of liquid cream which the herdsmen lashed on top of the packs. Unfortunately the canteen lacked a top, and although the herdsmen tried to seal it with a strip of cloth, the jiggling motion of the pack-pony's trot meant that an occasional spray of cream flipped out and spattered anyone close by. It was a measure of the jerky motion of a Mongol pony's gait that when we set up camp two hours later we discovered that the trotting motion had turned the cream to solid butter.

The Drunk also managed to locate a small plastic container and get it filled with a gallon of *shimiin arkhi*. He clasped it to his bosom as he rode and kept beckoning us to share his good fortune by taking swigs until finally the Quiet Man succumbed to the temptation. Once we had waded the hazardous fords and were back on a level valley floor, he and our local guide rode in line abreast with Delger and the Drunk, passing the container up and down the line and chatting amiably until the Drunk, who was already half-pickled, was totally inebriated. Our local guide pointed out the next high pass we should cross and turned back for home, but we had left our attempt too late. Halfway up the mountain it became evident that the horses were too tired to make the long climb and we would find ourselves in the wilderness after dark. So we turned round, descended down the mountain, and found ourselves a rather indifferent campsite on a squelching slope where two small streams emerged from the rocks.

Looking back down the valley we had traveled, we had a view that extended uninterrupted for at least 15 miles. Yet there was no sign of human life, not a single *ger* or domesticated animal. We were in one among scores of valleys in the Hangay, and the sense of isolation and emptiness was overwhelming. Overhead a griffon vulture hung motionless in the sky as it scanned the ground for carrion. Earlier we had ridden past a flock of these scavengers ripping the bloody remains of a dead calf. Each bird stood as tall as a man's chest and had a 12-foot wingspan. Yet in that vast landscape even these huge creatures seemed insignificant.

That evening Paul and I tried to intercept Bayar's cooking. Doc had discovered wild onions earlier in the afternoon, identifying them by their bright purple blossoms, and we had dug up at least two dozen bulbs, as well as gathering another couple of pounds of small round mushrooms. Paul and I borrowed the pot and some newly churned butter and fried onions and mushrooms for Bayar's usual mutton stew. It was another disappointment. The onions were stringy and tasteless, and the mushrooms disappeared altogether once they had been added to the mutton stew. Hopefully spooning out what I took to be a solitary and succulent mushroom bobbing to the surface, I found myself eating, once again, a blob of soft fat from the tail of the inevitable sheep. But by then I found myself quite fond of the taste and texture.

10

Cattle-herders

On the brow of the pass, which we reached at 11 o'clock next morning, stood the biggest *obo* we had yet seen. There must have been about 40 tons of small rocks and stones heaped up in a great pile by passers-by thankful to have toiled up to the end of their climb. Adding a stone to an *obo* or walking in a circle respectfully around it assisted the remission of sins and led toward a better reincarnation, according to Buddhist belief. Years of human effort and piety were represented in that untidy mass of rock, which continued to accumulate, and its sheer size and permanence made a mockery of the scheme once fostered by Party activists that all *obos* in Mongolia should be dismantled and leveled as they were objects of empty superstition.

Also you could see why the place was so significant to travelers that they had wished to raise a monument there. We had come to a natural dividing line in the land. After we had ridden our horses in a clockwise circle around the cairn, we paused to rest the animals and, looking back, saw that we had crossed a country of deep narrow valleys and forested mountains. Ahead there were no more trees. From where we stood the land descended in a series of gradual folds with the higher slopes covered only with rough grazing or bare screes of broken shale. Here and there layers of harder rock thrust out as jagged ledges or made coxcombs on the skyline. Below us the pasture on the valley floors was much paler than before, insipid and dotted with round boulders. This was a landscape harsher and more barren than the better-favored central Hangay, and in the farthest distance where the hills ended lay the beginning of the Great Mongolian Desert. Somewhere beyond that again, another 500 miles of riding, lay the province of Bayan Olgei where Ariunbold and Gerel had originally planned to leave the horses for the winter.

As if to emphasize the more austere character of the countryside, the first *ger* we reached after we had ridden downslope for three or four miles was a truly melancholy place. A man and his four small children were living in very reduced circumstances. There was no color in the *ger*, no decoration, only a functional collection of pots and pans, a stove, and a few blankets on the bedsteads. The children were quiet and spiritless. They stood staring at us as though in mild shock, showing little animation. "Their mother died recently," Doc explained in a low voice. "The family unit is still together, but they are living through very difficult times. Unless the father finds another woman quickly, he will not be able to continue this way of life. He will have to leave the children with their grandparents and go to the city to get work, or maybe stay in the local *somon* center as a laborer. A herdsman must have a wife to share the daily tasks. Without a woman to help, he cannot make his living."

It was a bleak statement of the knife-edge existence of the poorer *arat* who lived in a society where the resources were so meager and the environment so unforgiving. The price of being employed, fed, and provided with basic shelter by his commune was that a humble *arat* had to be an economically viable unit in return, and there were plenty of other married men in the commune who would take on the cattle-herding job. An *arat* received only tiny amounts of cash, never enough to build up savings and provide a degree of personal security or independence. But there was very little for him to purchase in the *somon* center where he probably spent most of the winter in a *ger* or visited occasionally during the summer pasture season. As for a trip to the city, that was even more rare, organized by the commune or perhaps when he could get a lift on a supply truck. Sadly, the other reason to go to the city would be to move there permanently, seeking work in what was already an over-supplied labor market.

We found that we were passing from the land of the horse-herders to the land of the cattle-herders. The valley of the Wild Yellow River which we were now following opened into wide skimpy grassland.

Here, instead of one or two *gers* tucked away in secluded glens with their horse-herds, we came across ten or twelve *gers* at a time, set up beside the track. Grazing beside these hamlets were yaks and hainags, black-and-white crossbreeds between yak and Central Asian oxen, which kept the former's flyswat tail and long hairy fringe on the belly but added the latter's extra size and better milk yield. The hainag bulls with their shaggy heads, hump shoulders, wide horns, and stupid glare looked very like three-quarter-sized bison living on the prairie, and were very skittish for such ungainly animals. At the last moment, as we rode up to them, they would react in fright as if they had been absentmindedly thinking of something else and had only just noticed our presence. They would suddenly leap into motion, looking utterly ridiculous, huge lumps of beef cavorting away in a see-saw gallop, their tails stuck out horizontally, snorting noisily as their fur fringes swayed from side to side.

The *gers* of the cattle-breeders were bigger and more solidly furnished than the felt tents of the horse-herders, and it was clear that the cattlemen did not shift them so readily. Outside their *gers* stood motorbikes, as well as the favorite pony hobbled and waiting to be ridden. I eyed the ponies enviously, for they were the pick of the local horseflesh, neater and more alert than our collection of part-worn nags. Indeed one of our gift horses was now limping steadily. We had been obliged to use it as a pack-pony and, coming down the *obo* hill, the animal must have strained a shoulder muscle. We changed the packs to a remount, but I began to wonder how much longer we could continue without a proper stopover to rest and recuperate our feeble animals.

I also realized that we had seen the best of the Hangay, Mongolia's most beautiful scenery by reputation, and feared that our daily forward slog was becoming repetitive without being particularly instructive. Each day was much like the last. We had established a steady routine. After breakfast, we took down the tent, loaded the packhorses, saddled up, and rode, rode, and rode, with stopovers at hospitable *gers*, until we were ready to set up camp again eight or ten hours later.

While it was important to Ariunbold that he traverse the entire country, I knew that there was so much more to see and research in Mongolia that Paul and I might be using our time more wisely. Behind this sense of growing frustration was the knowledge that Ariunbold had no real idea how long it would take us to reach the far west of Mongolia. He was still convinced that we would be near the Soviet border in another three weeks, but he was not allowing for rest days for the horses or delays due to bad weather or mishaps. It was more realistic to suppose that he would reach his winter quarters some time in early September, and by then the snow would impede the travel and research that I hoped to do among the tribal peoples of the higher ranges of Altai, some of whom had not been visited by a Westerner in their entire lives.

For our afternoon meal we were invited into the largest and most prosperous-looking *ger* of the cattle-herders. The owner, more enterprising than most of his colleagues, had harvested some of the bountiful crop of wild mushrooms and left them to dry on the roof, the only time we ever saw such an initiative. Courteously he offered us a smoke from his long-stemmed pipe. It was two feet long and the tiny bowl could not have held more than half a cigarette's worth of tobacco. By now we had learned to anticipate the correct formalities. I accepted the proffered pipe with right hand outstretched, admired the workmanship, took a symbolic puff, and then passed it back while holding my right elbow in my left hand. Our host then smoked contentedly while we waited for the meal to be prepared. Apparently we would have dried rather than fresh mutton, but the taste proved to be much the same as always. Only the lumps of dried fat were different. They had a pleasantly smoky flavor if you could ignore the unfortunate fact that they bobbed and twirled on top of the boiling broth like eyeballs.

Ariunbold was becoming a bore and an embarrassment. He had now taken to posturing in front of the herdsmen. As a rule when we arrived at a hamlet, he would stride self-importantly into the main *ger*, settle himself in the place of leading guest, and look around in lordly fashion waiting to be served. Then, as soon as the herdsmen had arrived to meet the strangers, he would launch into a speech about the grandiose purpose of his mission, and produce his knick-knacks, the medals and *paizas*, and hand them round to be admired. I was reminded of a medieval pardoner selling false indulgences and fake religious mementos to gullible peasants. The herdsmen were, by and large, unsophisticated and credulous, and they were usually impressed.

The more Ariunbold behaved like this, the more uncomfortable I became, although I could not explain why. I knew that there was something wrong and suspected that Ariunbold was somehow duping the herdsmen. Doc confirmed my fears. Apparently Ariunbold was telling his listeners that he was already on his way by horse to Europe and would soon be famous. He was also on the scrounge, always angling for free supplies and never offering to pay for anything. Doc found this constant cadging as distasteful and demeaning as I did, and he too remarked how Ariunbold seemed to be living in a puffed-up delusion of a dream world. In the evening when we halted to make camp, Ariunbold would do no work but stand around idly and wait for everyone else to erect the tent. Then, once the tent was up, he would order Delger, whom he began to treat like a servant, to carry in his saddlebags, spread out his sleeping bag, and lie or sit waiting for the meal to be prepared. He never cooked and very rarely cleaned up or offered to help.

His laziness in practical daily chores would have mattered less if he had been making any contribution by way of leadership or initiative. But here he was a bungler. He had a detailed Soviet army map of the region, and from time to time would spread it out and pore over it portentously. These map-reading sessions seemed oddly inconclusive, and after a few days I realized that Ariunbold—a product of that élite Higher Party School—did not know how to read a map properly and was largely play-acting. That afternoon I happened to suggest to him that if our two guides wanted to go home early to their families, we could manage to find our way to the next *somon* center by ourselves. We could, I told Ariunbold, go across country simply by following the map. Ariunbold shot me a look of pure venom. "Only a Westerner would say that," he said. "In Mongolia it is impossible to find your way without a guide. Mongolia is different." I was sure that he genuinely believed it. He was one of those unhappy people who have been promoted to a precarious position beyond the scope of their intelligence or their training. He feared being made a fool of and resented his own limitations. The result was that he became sullen, withdrawn, and stubborn and did not seek help which would have been given him. Each day he would go off by himself and try to mark in the day's progress on the map in pencil. Always he drew the line wrongly. It was either in the wrong place, too short, or too long, and he was so churlish about accepting any correction that eventually it was easier to ignore him and his map altogether. Paul was growing more and more exasperated with him, but I still felt strongly that we should respect our position as observers and not interfere. And this fitted in with the attitude of the other Mongols—as usual they were phlegmatic and patient and simply got on with their daily chores.

On the afternoon we spent with the cattle-herders Ariunbold must have felt that he had finally mastered the techniques of map-reading. He announced that we had another 38 miles to ride before we reached the next *somon* center. Paul and I glanced at each other in disbelief. Thirty-eight miles seemed much too far. Ariunbold spread out the map and pointed out the distance. "Thirty-eight miles," he announced firmly, measuring across the grid lines. My heart sank. Ariunbold was wrong twice over. He could easily have worked out our progress by ordinary common sense, but after all our efforts in the Hentei and after riding across the Hangay it appeared that he still did not know how many miles we were riding on average each day. Just as bad, he did not understand the scale of the map, though he had been using it for a week. It took careful explanation, using bits of string and matchsticks as measuring devices, to show him that what he thought was 38 miles on the map was in fact 19 miles.

The map showed that we should ride down the left bank of the Wild Yellow River, keeping to the main valley, to get to the next *somon* center. So when we left the cattle-breeders' hamlet Paul, Doc, Delger, and I rode our horses across a shallow ford and headed down the valley. When we looked back for the others, we were puzzled to see that Ariunbold had not followed us. Instead he was leading Bayar and the two herdsmen-guides along the opposite bank at a fast trot, apparently abandoning our little group. By then we had such a low opinion of his geographical sense that we let him go his own way. As the valley grew wider, the little band of riders on the far bank dwindled in the distance and, sure enough, we watched as one after another the two herder-guides and then Bayar realized that Ariunbold was leading them astray, turned their horses aside, and rode back across the valley to join us. Ariunbold was left to his own devices. To our astonishment we saw him continuing on his own way in solitary state. Then, instead of following the main valley, he abruptly turned to the right and disappeared up a side valley.

It was baffling. We thought that he must have some special reason for such an odd detour—perhaps he had seen some *gers* he wanted to visit. But no, Ariunbold not only lacked an idea of scale and could not read a map; he had no sense of direction either. He thought he would find the *somon* center up the side valley, and he was selfishly prepared to leave everyone else to look after themselves. After another hour we saw him riding back, obviously knowing that he had made a clown of himself. By then it was too late. As with the original set of herder-guides who had refused to take their horse-herd any further at the end of our overambitious first day's ride from Erdenzu, the Drunk and the Quiet Man had now lost all confidence in Ariunbold. They looked the other way when he announced that we could expect to reach the *somon* center the following day. Half a mile further on, we topped a rise and the small town was there below us, a five-minute ride away.

Unlikely though it may have seemed in the middle of Mongolia, the place was a health spa. The river flowed past a steep hill and on the right bank there were hot mineral springs oozing plumes of steam. Facing them across the river stood a hideous sanatorium which resembled a bedraggled factory block that had been constructed to the standard rectangular design of cheap Soviet architecture and had then been allowed to fall into neglect. Further along the hillside, to complete the rape of the scenery, were thirty or forty ugly little wooden cabins painted in various colors which had once been sickly and were now merely drab and faded. We had finished a long day's ride and were looking forward to setting up camp and resting ourselves and the horses. But Ariunbold insisted on making us wait for an hour and a half while he disappeared into the sanatorium. A bureaucrat to the core, he wished to announce his presence to the officials of the administration and consult with them. Maybe, he said to Paul and me as he left, he would be able to arrange for us to meet some of the invalids. Behind his mask, Doc groaned with despair.

In fact the sanatorium officials either had nothing to offer or did not even want to see Ariunbold, because he came back only with the grand announcement that he had arranged permission for us to make camp on the far bank. As the far bank was the usual empty Mongolian countryside which stretched unused for several hundred miles, it seemed a rather hollow concession.

We set up camp and helped Doc catch grasshoppers for fishing bait. All day the grasshoppers, brought out by the warm sunshine, had been swarming in their millions on the pastureland. There had been so many of them that they jumped up in thick clusters around every hoof-fall. The effect was as if the horses were trotting through shallow water and kicking up grasshoppers instead of spray. Another species of insect, similar in size to a small cricket and usually living singly, had the startling habit of leaping up suddenly out of the grass and hanging in the air, whirring its wings frantically and giving off a series of loud ticking sounds, exactly like countdown clicks from an anarchist's round black bomb in a cartoon so that you expected a loud explosion at any moment.

Disappointingly, Doc had no luck with rod and line. It seemed that the hot springs drained into the river and the effluent killed the fish. So Bayar cooked us a scratch meal, and we were promised a resupply of food when we got to the next relay point. Ariunbold it seemed had not troubled to think about bringing reserve stores with us but was depending entirely on scrounging free meals from the herders.

Equally irritating, he had failed to bring along a small kerosene stove that I had noticed in our camp at Karakorum on the first day. At the time I had suggested that the little stove should be taken as a reserve cooker, but he had refused, saying that we would always cook on the collapsible stove using firewood. Now, of course, we had passed out of the forested zone and firewood was extremely difficult to collect. We were reduced to begging firewood from the local people or doing as they did and burning cattle dung. Unfortunately it was the rainy season and to burn properly the dung, which lay scattered about the prairie, had to be completely dry. So once again we were reduced to dependence on the local people and asking for help, this time for gifts of dry cow-dung patties from the reserve supply they kept in little canvas-covered stacks beside their *gers*.

When I asked Ariunbold if perhaps we could obtain a kerosene stove locally, he informed me sullenly that there was no point because Mongol horses would never carry paraffin as they objected to the smell and would be frightened by the sound of liquid sloshing around in bottles in the packs. I pointed out that the paraffin could be carried in properly sealed bottles which did not leak or give off a smell, and

there was no difference between the sounds made by a bottle of
kerosene and a bottle of *arkhi*, sixteen of which still remained. Mulish
as ever, Ariunbold simply repeated that Mongol ponies would never
carry paraffin.

The next morning began with the discovery that a second gift horse
was limping. This time the trouble was an infected foot. The guides'
remedy was to tip out the stove on the ground and make the horse
stand with its sore hoof in the hot ashes. This rough-and-ready blistering had no noticeable effect. Then it was found that the horse I
had been riding had a cut leg. A remount was selected, but when I
approached the half-wild horse with my saddle, it took fright, reared
up, and lashed out with its front hooves. Oddly enough, I never saw
a Mongol pony try to kick a human with its hind legs. Bayar then
tried to tame the horse and failed. So too did the Quiet Man. It was
left to the very hung-over Drunk to take my saddle from me, walk
unsteadily over to the horse, and, with one quick motion, throw the
saddle on the animal's back. I was disappointed: I had begun to flatter
myself that after nearly 200 miles I had begun to radiate the same
aura as a Mongol herdsman, but now I knew that I still had a fair
way yet to go.

On what proved to be our last full day with the Drunk and the
Quiet Man we finally hit our stride by ignoring Ariunbold, who rode
in the rear by himself. Despite the lame ponies we made 30 miles,
riding much faster now that the terrain was not so hilly. We pushed
along briskly, with the Mongols encouraging their animals with occasional shoo! shoo! noises which made it seem as if we were all suffering
from head colds. As we progressed, the change from the green grassland of mountains to the more arid downlands became even more
noticeable. It was now 23 July and already the short Mongolian
summer was beginning to ebb away. The vegetation was languishing.
The wild flowers had begun to wither and droop, and the wild grass
was dying back. Now the green whorls and loops of mushroom spore
systems stood out vividly against the dry grass on the hillsides as if a
wandering giant had been scribbling cryptic messages in some unknown hieroglyphs.

We reached the *somon* center of Erdenzot late in the day, and the
guides advised us to set up camp on the river flats some distance away
from the town. In this way, they said, we would avoid being pestered

by curious visitors and also, if Bayar was to be believed, thieves. Bayar
and Ariunbold then rode off into town to find the local committee
and ask about the next relay of horses and if there was any food.
Surreptitiously I gave Bayar some money and suggested that he buy
us emergency stores. He managed to purchase a small quantity of
sugar, two jars of Russian jam, and a loaf of stale bread, as well as
the real treasure—seven pounds of corn flour. It meant that at last
we had some proper traveling rations. We turned the corn flour into
tsampa, mixing it into an uncooked paste with tea and butter and
sugar and either eating it at breakfast, after which we hardly felt
hungry again for the rest of the day, or rolling it up into small balls
as a snack to be carried in our pockets as we rode.

In the meantime the Drunk and the Quiet Man had ridden up the
valley to scavenge. They came back with a broken plank for firewood
because all the *argol*, the cattle dung dotted around the floodplain,
was wet from the heavy rain that had begun to fall. It was still raining
next morning when a small truck drove up to our bedraggled little
camp. Riding in the back of the truck were a sheep and a wizened
old woman. The driver brought a message from the *somon* committee
to say that it would take them a little time to get together our new
horses but the sheep was a gift so we would not go hungry. The wet
animal was manhandled out of the truck and dragged into the tent.
There the Quiet Man toppled it to the ground and dispatched it,
rather more messily than usual, on a dirty piece of tarpaulin. The
old crone's special function, it turned out, was to squeeze out the
undigested food from the guts before filling them with blood and
placing the offal into the inevitable cauldron of boiling water. The
scene was timeless. There were nine people crammed together,
crouching inside the rickety, threadbare tent, with the rain drumming
on the stained canvas or spitting and dripping in through all the holes
and rips, and the fire smoke blowing back into our eyes. We were all
damp and smelly and had specks of horse dung stuck to our clothing.
Naturally we ate the intestines of the sheep first of all, each man using
a knife and his soot-blackened greasy fingers to saw and wrench away
tubes of intestines from the steaming mass scooped out of the cauldron
and thrown on the soggy ground. The rest of the sheep—fleece, head,
and disjointed sections of carcass—lay in a bloody heap behind one's
elbow. If you were thirsty, you could wash down the tripes with

entrail soup made by the old crone. Again, our situation would have been familiar to Rubruck or Carpini or, indeed, to Beatrix Bulstrode.

The Drunk and the Quiet Man set off for home that evening, taking their horses with them, and we settled down to wait for their two replacement guides. This pair quickly earned themselves the nicknames of the Whistler and the Shy One when they showed up early next morning with the best group of horses we had seen so far—a dozen ponies which were very robust, even though a purist would have complained that they were rather short in the leg, to the point that the animal with the longest back and the shortest legs was a sort of equine dachshund. All of these new animals were a uniform dark chestnut in color, and I could only suppose that each *somon* region tended to breed its distinct type and color of horse.

The calm and competent way in which the two new guides loaded up the pack-animals was very encouraging, and within an hour we were ready to set out for our next relay point at the *somon* center of Galuut, the Mongol word for Goose, named for a nearby lake known for its wild geese. The guides pressed us to get started as soon as possible, because they were worried by the recent heavy rain. Any more rain in the next few days, they said, would cause the rivers to flood until they were impassable. So we set out by 9 a.m., and as if to make the point our most elderly gift horse, a mealy-mouthed skewbald with a milk eye, a maverick disposition, and as ill-favored as Don Quixote's Rocinante, nearly drowned in the first hundred yards.

We had to cross the river on whose bank we had camped, and Doc searched up and down for a few minutes to find a suitably shallow spot, using his experience as a fisherman. All the horses followed him across safely except Rocinante, who had been straggling along behind the little herd of remounts. The skewbald took its own independent line and strayed into deep water. In an instant the current had plucked the animal off its feet and carried it off into a channel where the floodwater was at full strength. For a while it did seem that Rocinante would not be able to get back on shore. Swimming feebly, the horse was carried farther and farther downstream until a lucky current swung it into a backwater where the poor beast at last had a chance to heave itself out very slowly and stiffly onto the shingle before rejoining us, looking even more abject than before.

On previous occasions when we changed to a new relay of horses, Ariunbold had made sure that the guides saddled for him the best animal in the herd. He clearly felt it was his due. But this time he had slipped up. He found himself aboard a real plodder, a leaden-footed animal with an iron mouth and a stubborn temperament which refused to be hurried. So Ariunbold trailed along some distance behind us, growing more and more angry, sweaty and frustrated as he whipped and kicked his horse ineffectually. It did not seem significant at the time, but it was to lead to a near-crisis later. For the moment, all of us were relieved to be spared Ariunbold's presence, though we were sorry for his wretched mount.

Up to this point in our ride it had been noticeable that the *gers* we visited were as well kept and clean as circumstances would allow. It was very difficult to look after a dwelling where everyone came in and out wearing boots that had tramped through the horse dung of the tethering places just outside. Yet on the whole the *gers* were no more messy than the kitchen of a working farmhouse. So it was an unpleasant shock when our next halt was at a *ger* so squalid that it would have turned even the most hardened stomach. When we rode up, the owner was seated beside his half-dozen children as they sat in the open air, chopping scrap wood into kindling. The children were unkempt and dressed in filthy clothing, and a spattering of human excrement revealed that no one bothered to go more than a few yards from the *ger* to relieve themselves. The owner was already tipsy and his wife, who appeared soon afterward, was an alcoholic slattern in a foul temper. When the owner was helped to his feet we realized that he had lost a leg, and he hopped ahead of us insisting we enter his *ger*.

Inside the *ger* the scene was more depressing. A drunken and straggle-haired sister-in-law propped herself on one elbow and watched us blearily from one of the cots, trying to focus, while the slattern wife grudgingly offered us bread and rancid clotted cream from filthy plates. The inevitable *arkhi* was proffered in a grimy glass that stank. To cap it all, one of the unwashed small children was tied to a cot post with a leash like a dog and, fortunately bare-bottomed, proceeded to squat and defecate copiously on the floor, an act that was totally ignored by the drunken parents.

It was a nightmare of exactly the sort which, even by medieval

standards, Rubruck had found gross. On hot days he and his companion Bartholomew of Cremona would seek shelter from the sun by
sitting under the wagons, and the Mongols, curious to see strangers,
"would crowd in on us so persistently that they trampled on us in
their desire to see all our effects. If they were seized by an urge to
void their bowels, they moved away from us no further than one
could toss a bean—in fact they would do their filthiness next to us
while talking to one another. And they did a great deal more that was
excessively tiresome." Rubruck also complained that the Mongols
"never wash their clothes, for they claim that this makes God angry
and that if they were hung out to dry, it would thunder. In fact they
thrash anyone doing laundry and confiscate it. They are extraordinarily afraid of thunder. In that event they turn out of their dwellings
all strangers and wrap themselves in black felt, in which they hide
until it has passed."

Glad to be breathing fresh air again, we left the repulsive place and
rode farther up the valley until it ended abruptly in a great slope of
dark-purple rock. The extraordinary color of the rock was matched
in the underbellies of the thunderclouds which now rolled across the
sky and seemed to close down like a lid, shutting us into the end of
the valley. The two guides warned us that we would be faced with a
difficult climb, for they had brought us by an unusual route in order
to try to avoid the worst of the flooded rivers. The mountain pass
would be taxing for the horses, but we would save at least five hours'
riding if we went over the mountain. The storm struck as we were
halfway up, toiling along the zigzag path and leading the horses. The
wind battered at our faces and brought an angry slanting rain that
chilled us in a few moments. Paul and I had brought ex-army ponchos, but they proved to be worse than useless. They failed to stop
the rain from soaking through to our clothes, and they were almost
impossible to put on. The half-wild Mongol ponies were terrified by
the flapping of the ponchos and the strange smell of the rubberized
material, and reared and plunged until they were unmanageable. We
had no choice but to dismount and wait until they had calmed down,
and then we plodded up the mountain leading them by their reins.

Fortunately it was the only stiff climb of the day, and beyond the
ridge the land again sloped down to the west, allowing us to ride with
gathering momentum, faster and faster, toward the camping place the

guides had recommended. They intended for us to stay at another location known for its mineral springs, but instead of the previous ugly sanatorium building we found an attractive open valley where a random scattering of *gers* had been erected near the watercourse by families and herdsmen who were treating the region as an agreeable summer grazing ground. Led by the Whistler, Paul and I rode down to a suitable spot where we could make camp. There we hobbled our horses and waited for Ariunbold to catch up. We were joined by Delger and Doc, and we could see Ariunbold a mile behind, as usual bringing up the rear. To our surprise he once again rode straight past, no more than a hundred yards away and ignoring us altogether. The Whistler, who had already unsaddled his horse, did not conceal his indignation at these bad manners. He refastened the girths, leaped in the saddle, and rode furiously after Ariunbold. More accustomed to Ariunbold's uncouth ways, Paul and I and the others remounted more slowly and followed. We were not surprised when we found Ariunbold sitting on a convenient rock half a mile farther on. He had picked a much less suitable camping spot on rough ground and was waiting for Delger and Bayar to put up the tent for him while he went down to the river to wash. The Whistler was boiling with anger and I realized that it had taken Ariunbold less than a day to antagonize one of the two new guides. I anticipated glumly that before the two guides had finished the usual three- or four-day stint with us, both would be as disheartened as their predecessors.

The rain had stopped and we were quietly sitting in the camp in the gathering darkness when a pair of strange horses appeared from nowhere and stampeded past the tents at full gallop. They were followed a moment later by two unknown Mongol riders who charged through the camp, hallooing wildly and weaving from side to side. As it was virtually dark, this was a thrilling display of horsemanship, as the two strangers hurdled ditches and dangerous rocks with insane bravado. It took a moment to realize that the two whooping riders were two-thirds drunk and worked up to a great pitch of excitement.

They had scarcely vanished into the gloom when we again heard the drumming of hooves, and the runaway horses, who must have circled around, flashed through the camp once more. This time one of the chasers pulled up and shouted to Delger, who leaped to his feet, ran across to his lasso pole, picked it up, and handed it to the rider, who snatched it from his grasp and went careering off once again. For another moment or two the pursuit continued crazily around our camp, and then the runaway horses ran off into the darkness still followed by their drunken herders at a gallop. Delger yelled something which must have been a request for the return of his lasso pole, only to be answered with a shout that was clearly an insult as the drunken stranger made off with the pole as a prize. The theft obviously transgressed some basic rule of behavior among herdsmen, because Delger responded as if he had been slapped across the face. Red with anger, he ran to the nearest of our horses, flung a saddle on its back, and in a moment was riding in pursuit of the thief. The Whistler also saddled a horse and galloped off behind him in support. What had been a quiet evening in camp had erupted into activity and now subsided back again into quiet as we waited for the riders to return.

After two hours our two colleagues came back, carrying the lasso pole but still very miffed. There was a great deal of muttering and grumbling, but Paul and I considered the matter to have been resolved and had gone to sleep when, once again, there was a tremendous commotion. This time there were many voices, all quarreling and spitting with anger. The arguments swung back and forth. Some of the voices were incoherent with rage. Then came the sound of deliberate blows. Someone was being given a heavy beating, and we could hear the thump of blows, followed by high-pitched wails of pain. The beating continued steadily for a while, and when it stopped the whimpering faded away as the sobbing victim left camp. Then there was silence.

In the morning Doc tried to explain what had happened, though the story was still confused. Apparently Delger and the Whistler had found the missing lasso pole at a nearby group of *gers* but were told that the thief came from a different camp. There was already bad blood between the two camps, and allegations of slander and rumor-mongering were flung. Both groups then met at our camp to settle their differences. One group accused the other of being horse thieves who were intending to steal our horses and to lay the blame on the other camp. Tempers had run high, and two of the younger Mongols had been set upon and beaten up.

It was one of the very few occasions when Doc's interpretation and explanation fell short, and I was left puzzling over exactly what was going on. From time to time during the trip Delger and Bayar had made references to the dangers of thieves and horse rustlers, but I had found it difficult to take their warnings very seriously. The difficulty of making off with stolen horses in such open countryside, or of being able to account for them to the commune authorities when a headcount was made at the end of the grazing season, would seem to make horse-stealing rather impractical. And, in my unstated opinion, our gift horses were such a ragbag lot that no one would want to steal them anyhow. Perhaps there was still some cachet to be gained from being able to steal someone else's horses, or perhaps there was a parochial disdain for strangers from another *somon*. But I had not detected any regional rivalry, and the whole affair of the nighttime chase, the arguments, and the ensuing beating seemed haphazard, impenetrable, and unnecessarily brutal.

11

The Lamas
of Mandal

A thread of pitilessness runs throughout Mongol history. When Beatrix Bulstrode visited Urga's prison, she was shaken to discover that many of the prisoners in the dungeon were padlocked inside heavy wooden chests like ironbound coffins, 4½ feet long and 2½ feet deep. A small hole in the side of the chest was the only means of ventilation. The hole was big enough for the prisoner to put out his manacled hands for food and, if his skull was narrow enough, to thrust out his head and look around. Descending into the gloom where these humans were kept in their boxes, she observed that:

> one's eyes growing accustomed to the darkness—the only light that penetrates it is from the doors when they are opened—one became gradually aware of wild shaggy heads poking through the round holes in the coffins' sides. I was standing, quite unconsciously, close to a coffin when, glancing down, I saw a terrible face, nothing more, almost touching the skirt of my riding coat. Beside one coffin was a pool of blood which told its own tale. Within it there was a poor devil coughing his lungs up.

The majority of the prisoners, she was told by the warders, had never been brought to trial but were incarcerated for life on suspicion of being pro-Chinese.

Under Genghis Khan's direction this pitilessness had been an instrument of state policy, and he employed it with a ruthlessness that appalled even the most hardened contemporary observers. His Mongol troops were neither sadistic nor depraved, and there is no evidence that they enjoyed killing. But they were butchers, and they were prepared to put people to death on a massive scale and without remorse. It was an established custom that before Genghis Khan's generals attacked a city, they offered to spare the lives of the inhabitants provided they surrendered without a fight. If, however, they resisted, they could expect no quarter. The Mongols kept their word. If the city agreed to these terms, it was thoroughly pillaged but the population was spared. If it put up a defense, the citizens were put to the sword *en masse*. The killing was comprehensive and businesslike, and not done in blood lust or rage. The civilians were marshaled in batches for execution, as in a well-organized abattoir for humans.

The annals of the countries attacked in this callously efficient way by Genghis Khan's armies are full of horror stories of the Mongol invasions—whole areas depopulated, cities overthrown, sacred shrines defiled, precious works of art smashed. But the authors of these reports give no hint that the terrible Mongol conquerors relished the destruction for its own sake; they seem to take it for granted that the Mongols were insensible to the terrible tragedies they were causing. For its part the Mongols' own saga, *The Secret History of the Mongols*, makes it clear that the purpose of victory was to despoil the enemy and bring home in triumph his desirable women, horses, cattle, and movable valuables, to enslave the able-bodied, and to hunt down and kill the chief of the rival clan. Usually there was no lasting vendetta. Children of the rival clan might be adopted into the families of the victors, and it was quite normal to recruit the defeated clan as junior partners for the next raid farther afield. Genghis Khan applied these same principles on a continental scale. When his army took the ancient and holy city of Bukhara, the Mongols looted its wealth as if it were a neighboring nomad camp. They rode their horses into the courtyard of the great mosque, and drunken troopers dumped rare copies of the Koran on the ground so that they could use the wooden Koran cases as mangers for their horses, and obliged the terrified Muslim scholars to hold the animals while they fed. Within weeks they were recruiting more Muslim allies to continue their campaign of destruction.

One of the stranger twists to the Mongol story is that the damage to Islam fueled a rumor that Genghis Khan was a long-awaited champion of Christendom. Rubruck and Carpini traveled to Mongolia half-hoping that they might find Prester John there, the paladin of Christianity. Prester John was a fantasy figure of the medieval imagination who had surfaced in the middle of the 12th century. He was said to be a descendant of the Magi, a pure and invincible priest-king who ruled over a distant Christian nation somewhere in the East and was capable of putting into the field a matchless host of warriors. The rumor was probably based on confused reports of a major battle fought in Central Asia near Samarkand between the Seljuk Turks and the army of the Kara khitai, a people who lived alongside the Mongols before the time of Genghis Khan. The Seljuk Turks, who were Muslim, lost the fight, and it was presumed in the West that the victors must therefore be Christians, though the Kara khitai were more likely to have been either heathen or Buddhist.

In any event the Pope wrote a letter to the victorious "Prester John" hoping to establish contact and asking for details of his version of Christianity. For the next hundred years the rumor of this distant Christian monarch persisted and became particularly popular among the hard-pressed Crusaders in the Holy Land fighting off the counter-attacks of the Muslims. Somewhere beyond the hostile ring of their Islamic foes, it was said, was this potential Christian ally (Prester John, of course, was ageless). If only a messenger could get through to him, a great combined operation could be organized against the Muslims. With the rise of Genghis Khan and the resounding success of his army, reports of a new Central Asiatic superpower hostile to Islam began to filter through to the West, and the notion arose that this could only be the long-awaited Prester John, or possibly his grandson, King David.

Carpini quickly realized that there had to be some mistake. The savage Mongols he met could not possibly be the followers of the saintly priest-king. The people he encountered worshiped human effigies made of felt which they put up on each side of their tents. Underneath they hung a model of an udder. These, they said, were the guardians of the herds and ensured that there would be plenty of foals and milk. They also venerated the sun and moon, fire, water, and earth, and had a very special reverence for an image they had dedicated to Genghis Khan. When a visiting Russian prince, a Christian, refused to bow down to this image, the Mongols kicked him in the stomach until he was half-dead and then decapitated him. These ungodly people, Carpini surmised, must have chased the real Prester John out of Central Asia and into India, where he should now be looked for. Rubruck, though he was skeptical, never entirely gave up hope. When he failed to find Prester John ruling in Karakorum, he set about trying to verify the rumor that the Great Khan had been baptized and was a secret Christian. So he went about Karakorum on the lookout for signs of Christians—a cross over a *ger*, the sound of church bells, a gesture of respect from a Mongol toward a Christian symbol.

Rubruck was not entirely wide of the mark. As it happened, two of the Mongol tribes, the Keraits and the Naimans, had been deeply influenced by Nestorianism, a form of Christianity dating back to the 5th century which had been spread into Central Asia by missionaries based in Persia. Many leading Kerait families had been baptized, and one of the Great Khan's chief wives was interested enough to attend Nestorian services held in a portable chapel. Probably under her influence, the Khakhan Möngke, third in succession to Genghis Khan and ruler of Karakorum when Rubruck was there, sent word one day that Rubruck should be brought before him and demonstrate his Christian rituals. Rubruck took along an illustrated copy of the Bible and a breviary and recited a psalm and intoned a chant. Then he showed Möngke, whom he called Mangu, the pictures in the holy books. The Great Khan was interested in the pictures but no more, and his consort spoiled the solemnity of the occasion by drinking too much. She finished up befuddled and "climbed into her cart, to the chanting and wailing of the priests, and went on her way." Rubruck did not hear from her again on the subject of royal Christianity.

If Rubruck had been less starry-eyed, he would have noticed that the Khakhan was a true Mongol pragmatist. Fundamentally Möngke believed in the power of the great ancestor Genghis Khan and the spirit world of the shamans. But that did not exclude the possibility that there might be some merit in other religions. So Möngke allowed Christians,* Buddhists, and Muslims to practice and preach their

---

*There were some very odd religious hangers-on at court, including a fake Armenian priest called Sergius who claimed he had come from Jerusalem at God's command to convert the Mongols. Sergius was "swarthy and lank," wore a haircloth tunic over an iron girdle, and, making claims to medical skill, doctored with a rhubarb stew the French goldsmith who made the drinks dispenser. The victim barely survived.

faith openly at his court. Rubruck was very disappointed that the representatives of Christianity were so poorly prepared. The Nestorian priests, he complained, did not understand their own texts, which were written in the Syriac language. Furthermore they were usurers, polygamists, and simoniacs who demanded money for religious services, and they took to the bottle. Because their bishop arrived in such a remote location only about every fifty years, Rubruck claimed the bishop had the presumptuous custom of going round and anointing all the children, even down to the smallest baby, thereby guaranteeing a future supply of priests.

Rubruck need not have been so reproving. The Nestorians understood that the Mongols were unlikely to be converted by moral example or illuminating sermons. The Mongols preferred to stay with their time-honored customs. They consulted their shamans, whom Rubruck called "soothsayers," on all immediate matters, such as the best spot to set up camp or when to go to war; they laid offerings in front of the images of their ancestors; and they practiced the art of divination with the shoulder bones of sheep. These were scraped clean and placed in a fire, and a qualified shaman then read the future by interpreting the lines and cracks which appeared in the bone as a palmist reads the lines on a hand.

I was unexpectedly reminded of Rubruck's vain quest for Christianity in Mongolia as we approached Galuut. That day, 27 July, Doc informed us that we had entered the former territory of the Naiman Khans, the same people who had taken to Nestorianism. Several times in the afternoon we passed broad circles marked out in the grass with small rocks. They were the remnants of the royal pavilions that had once stood looking across the prairie of the western Hangay. And at the end of the day we rode past a large tomb of what must have been an important Naiman chief.

Galuut itself beckoned us from a distance. Almost any permanent structure would have seemed enticing when there had been no building for more than 60 miles. But on closer inspection Galuut proved to be just another undistinguished *somon* center, and as the Whistler and the Shy One were both eager to get home we did not bother to enter the settlement but halted about a mile short of the town so they could turn back with their horses. We had just waved goodbye to the two guides when a deputation came out of the town to tell us that our remounts were to be collected, not at Galuut, but 10 miles farther

on at the old monastic settlement of Mandal. So Paul, Doc, and I
hitched a ride in a municipal truck while Bayar, Ariunbold, and
Delger brought on the gift horses.

Mandal gave us a bonus. We had spent the night at a disused camp
of shepherds and were waiting for our remounts to show up when a
young man rode into camp and shyly asked if we would like to see
the holy sculptures. He turned out to be 16 years old and had decided
to become a lama, now that the central government was allowing the
church to practice openly. Already he had started his preliminary
religious instruction, and in the autumn he would shave his head, put
on his robe, and enroll as a novitiate. We asked what his parents
thought of the idea that he was entering the church, and he replied
without hesitation—"It makes them happy."

Our camp had been placed in the lee of a low cliff, and the young
man and his younger brother now led Doc, Paul, and me along the
base of the cliff. After about half a mile we came upon lines of Tibetan
script carved into the contours of the living rock close to ground
level. Our young guide told us they were religious texts sculpted by
the former monks of Mandal, which had once boasted one of the
finest lamaseries in Mongolia. The lines of writing continued sporadically until we reached the first of the sacred figures. It was a picture
of the Buddha seated on a lotus, chiseled into the rock-face. There
were traces of the original paint which had picked out the details in
red, blue, and brown. Farther on a small stream ran along the foot
of the cliff, and here were more pictures of the Buddha, and then a
drawing of a Demon Defender riding a dragon lion, and finally the
portrait of an Ayush Baksh, or Woman Saint. We counted nine such
rock-carvings, but the lad told us there were a total of nineteen
distributed along the rock-face. The carvings did not look any older
than 19th-century, but they made up a fine devotional gallery where
the vanished monks of Mandal had turned the vertical wall of rock
into a lasting monument of their faith. Just before we turned to retrace
our path, the young man pointed upward. Fifty feet up, a string of
small white objects was draped around a rock that projected from the
cliff wall. They were human bones, he said, the pieces of a lama's
skeleton that had been strung on a rope and hung like a necklace
against the rock.

By the time we got back to camp, the new relay of horses had

arrived. They had been brought in by a large and openly curious band
of local *arats*, and there was the usual bustle and chaos of making
pack-ponies out of the half-wild animals. I was glad to see that, once
again, the two men who would be our guides were very methodical
and sensible about the loading, and I waited until they had assigned
me a horse to ride. The owner of the animal they finally selected
looked very worried. He thought his horse was too skittish and, like
all Mongol herdsmen, he was convinced that all foreigners had never
ridden before. I tried to reassure him that I ought to be able to manage
his horse, but he hovered around looking very nervous. When I
produced my saddle, he insisted that he should fit it. As usual, the
foreign saddle attracted great interest, and all the *arats* clustered
around and were looking on with great fascination when I produced
the crupper strap and explained to the owner of the horse how the
strap should be attached from the back of the saddle and around the
root of the horse's tail. The Mongol looked horrified. He had never
seen a crupper strap in his life. I got Doc to explain that the strap was
necessary to prevent the saddle shifting forward. Doc translated, then
laughed. "He says that the strap is some sort of perversion, or it will
damage his horse. He does not believe the horse will ever permit such
a thing."

"Tell him that I insist, and that crupper straps are used on horses
all over the world, in many countries. Without it the saddle will slip
when going up and down hills."

I could see the herdsman was unconvinced. But I was adamant that
the strap had to be fitted, and reluctantly he agreed. However, he
wanted to fit the strap himself. I showed him how the loop at the end
of the strap should slide over the stump of the horse's tail. Gingerly
he picked up the tail to slip the tail loop in place, but he was so
nervous that he failed entirely. The horse sensed his hesitation and
scuttled out of reach. The herdsman tried again to fit the strap around
the tail and again fumbled the job. It was absurd that a man who had
worked with horses all his life, and had probably picked up that
particular horse in his arms time and again when it was a foal and
taken it to its mother, could not now lift up its tail and fit the crupper
strap because the task was utterly unfamiliar to him. As politely as
possible, I took the crupper strap from him, lifted the tail, and slid
it in place. The horse did not even stir. The owner of the horse looked

astonished, and his circle of colleagues guffawed with delight. I suggested that he might like to try riding in the saddle, and he mounted and rode around. He still could not believe that the horse did not object to the crupper strap, so he reached back and tugged on it several times. The horse paid no attention, and finally the herdsman gave a grin of pleasure and a nod of approval.

With no more than a couple of dozen small *gers* behind their wooden palisades, the reason for Mandal's existence was still its lamasery, just as it had been in the days before the wholesale destruction of the Mongolian church. Three pagoda-like buildings with upswept roofs of green tiles formed the monastery complex. Presumably they had once been chapel, dormitory, offices, and stores, but now the structures were dilapidated and empty, so it was impossible to identify their original function. There was grass growing on the roofs, beams had come away from their joints and fallen askew, sections of tile had slid to the ground and lay broken in heaps, and there were gaping holes in the mud walls through which cattle wandered to use the interior of the main temple and the adjoining residences as byres. But the lamasery could be restored without too much difficulty. It had not been bulldozed or vandalized, and the buildings were basically intact.

What was important was that a tiny monastic community was again in active occupation. There were just six lamas at Mandal, plus their Head Lama, and because the main buildings were uninhabitable they were conducting their services in a new, immaculate white *ger* planted in the very center of the old monastery complex. A notice above the painted wooden door to the *ger* announced that it was the temporary Mandal monastery.

I enjoyed the irony of this little *ger*-lamasery. Forty years earlier a feature of the great anti-church campaign organized by the communists had been their "Red *Gers*." These were indoctrination centers set up in the villages by Party cadres. In the Red *Gers* they had preached the Party line, enrolled herdsmen, and consolidated their control over the region. Now, from what might be called a White *Ger*, the counter-reformation was taking place. As we sat inside the *ger*-lamasery and talked about its future, the elderly Head Lama, who must surely have been in his 80s, wanted me to make no mistake and understand that it was only a temporary arrangement. He and his monks had been promised government funds to restore the original lamasery buildings and work would begin the next year. I asked where they had made their homes during this past half-century.

"We were living quietly among the local people," he replied gently, "and praying for the restoration of our faith."

As our riding team prepared to move on, he and his elderly colleagues hobbled out of the *ger*-lamasery and assembled in a group to say a formal farewell. Some of the lamas were so bent and elderly that they needed staffs to support them as they lined up. As they stood there in the sunshine, wearing their brilliant robes, I was irresistibly reminded of Beatrix Bulstrode's observation that the "deep red, mid orange and pale cinnamon colours" of a lama congregation "suggested great borders of parrot tulips."

The track out of Mandal led past the monastery's twin "guardians," a seated Buddha and a ferocious green-painted monster sculpted into the flat sides of large boulders which flanked the trail. An hour's ride further on, a camp of cattle-herders gave us a belated lunch of clotted cream and bread, and their leader presented us with another gift horse. Paul, who had to ride it the next day, claimed that it was a nasty tearaway beast which swerved erratically and dangerously, but at least it was fit and eager and that made a change from our previous lackluster mounts.

After that we saw no more herdsmen all day, for we entered on a great expanse of rolling downland where there was no surface water. Everything was on an overwhelming scale. The occasional boulder stood as high as horse and rider, and lordly falcons well over two feet tall sat on the ground and glared at us as we passed, not bothering to flap away even if we rode by 20 yards from them. The soil was increasingly sandy, and the drought had turned the wispy grass to a pale sage-green except in the patches where the ground squirrels made their burrows. Perhaps the ground squirrels disturbed the soil so that it held rainwater better, or maybe they picked the moister patches of land for their homes, but you could identify their colonies from the telltale patches of brighter-green grass. We tried to avoid these spots, for they were honeycombed with the small burrows and treacherous. When a running pony put his foot into a hole, horse and rider went sprawling.

Our guides were real drivers, and as the evening drew in we did not halt, but went faster and faster, ending with a mad flailing gallop into an approaching thunderstorm, with the horses pounding upwind into the gale, the breath whistling through their nostrils. It was an exhilarating end to the day and we hurried to erect the flapping, slatting tents before we were drenched by the rain. A hundred yards away a team of shepherds, the only humans we had seen in 20 miles, were looking after a pump well from which they gave us water for the horses.

We kept to ourselves that evening, eating in the shelter of the tents without going near the shepherds. It seemed strange to be standoffish in that featureless land, surrounded by mile after mile of open, meager grazing, with absolutely nothing in sight except the rolling contours of the uninhabited downs. But I supposed that our guides did not want to impose on the hospitality of the shepherds or risk upsetting their horses by coming too close with our half-wild animals. In any event, we were getting on with the job of saddling up our horses next morning, which had dawned sunny and clear, when there was an incident which finally destroyed what little hope there was of continuing in Ariunbold's company.

The relay horses that Ariunbold had been riding for the past week had all been laggards. This was pure bad luck, since normally he made sure that the guides gave him the best horse among the remounts. But for the last few days matters had been very different. He had been riding a series of glue-footed mounts and had been left trailing along in the wake of the main party that he was supposed to lead. He had flailed away with his whip trying to get his mount to go faster, but with little success. No one had paid him much attention, and most of us were rather glad that he was safely in the background while we got on with covering the daily riding distance. Ariunbold had become increasingly irritable, and his temper was fraying to the point that he seemed to have spent most of the previous day beating his horse with a dull and mindless monotony. A couple of times on the previous day he had managed to ride past us at a slow gallop, his face set grimly, and steadily thrashing his sluggish horse.

When Ariunbold approached this same horse that morning to put on its saddle, the animal balked. It reared up and tried to escape, obviously detesting the man who had ridden it so callously all the previous day. Ariunbold, who was holding the halter, was suddenly jerked off his feet and ignominiously dragged for a few yards. Delger

gave a shout and ran to the rescue. He calmed the rebellious animal
and handed it back to Ariunbold, who had dusted himself off and
once again tried to put on the saddle. Again the horse flung back,
trying to escape its tormentor. Delger was obliged to restrain the
animal with a hobble while Ariunbold put on the saddle. By now the
rest of us were ready to ride out and were watching Ariunbold. He
put the saddle in place, removed the hobble, and, when the horse
again tried to run away, successfully restrained the animal with the
lead rope. He was just about to mount when the horse, realizing that
it could not break free, showed its objection by lying down. It was
an act of pure stubborn rebellion, and a mark of the animal's intelligence. It simply folded up its forelegs, dropped to its knees, rolled
on one side, and lay there flat on the ground, not moving.

Ariunbold stood there, looking uncertain what to do. Delger called
out something. He was probably telling Ariunbold to give the horse
a stroke of the whip to show who was master and to get it back to
its feet. Ariunbold still had the free end of the rawhide lead rope in
his hand. Now he walked to the head of the prone horse and, with
all the strength he could muster, he leaned across and slashed the free
end of the rope spitefully three times across the animal's face. It was
the first time I had ever seen a Mongol hit a horse in the face, and I
could sense shock waves of disapproval coming from the herdsmen
beside me. But more was to come. The horse flinched at the blows,
lifted its head briefly, but then lay back, still refusing to get on its
feet. When the horse's head touched back on the ground, Ariunbold
seemed to forget himself. He went into a black rage. Standing over
the horse, he began to beat the horse steadily and viciously with
blow after blow across the face. It was an act of wanton malice and
committed with deliberate cruelty. The horse now could not have got
back on its feet even if it had wanted to, and Ariunbold must have
known it as he stood there aiming lash after lash deliberately at its
head as it lay on the ground.

There was a shocked silence from all the rest of us as we watched
in disbelief, thinking that each blow would be the last. No one moved
a muscle, we were so taken aback. But Ariunbold kept going, hitting
his victim, oblivious of the appalled audience. He stopped only after
twenty or so systematic blows and then stood back to allow the horse
to get up.

Beside me, Paul was livid with rage, and I thought for a moment that he was about to run over and assault Ariunbold. I hissed at him to hold still. From the way everyone else avoided looking at Ariunbold as he climbed into the saddle, I could tell that we were not alone in thinking that he had behaved atrociously. Clearly, what he had done was not the Mongol way of chastizing a horse, and our companions were very embarrassed. It was characteristic that our herdsmen-guides had not intervened to stop him. That was not the Mongol way either. But no one would see Ariunbold in quite the same light again. For my own part, I decided I would prefer to continue my Mongolian journey in less distasteful company. There was too much that was worthwhile to do and see in Mongolia without wasting time having to put up with such a traveling companion. Also I now knew that if the Mongols wanted a civilized and presentable leader for their team, they would have to look elsewhere than Ariunbold. It was a pity, because there was great potential to the notion of a transcontinental ride to France, but in its present structure the Mongol expedition was sure to leave a bad taste if it should ever venture out beyond their borders. My responsibility was to advise the Mongolian National Committee for the UNESCO Silk Roads Project to think again about whom they should select as leader. Meanwhile, I wanted to get on with the far more interesting task of investigating the survival of Mongolia's traditional culture. To do that, Doc, Paul, and I should leave as soon as it was convenient.

We rode for most of that morning in an uncomfortable silence. When I caught his eye, Bayar shook his head disapprovingly. His usual frivolity was gone. Paul was muttering under his breath that he would like to flog Ariunbold with the same halter he had used on his horse, and Doc, who, despite being a poor rider, was very adept at gentling and calming horses, clearly considered that Ariunbold had shown himself to be barbaric. Even Genghis Khan would have disapproved. Never, he had ordained, was a Mongol to strike a horse on the head.

Doc himself was worn out. He had still not adapted to the rigors of cross-country riding and from time to time was obliged to get down and limp beside his horse to exercise a very painful knee joint. Our two guides, Good Happiness and Bold, kept up an exacting pace. I suspected that they too had had enough of Ariunbold and wanted to finish their stage of the journey as quickly as possible and be rid of him. So it was not yet 4 o'clock when we emerged from the dry downland and saw we had reached the rim of a wide shallow valley. Approaching us at a fast trot across the floor of the valley were about twenty mounted men. They were members of the local work brigade of the little town of Dzag and had been sent by the *somon* committee to escort us across the river, which was flooded and hazardous.

On the far bank a reception had been organized in the felt tent of the champion *arat* of the region. The committee of his commune considered him to be such a successful herdsman that they had allocated him a herd of 400 horses which he and his family were to look after on behalf of the commune. In return for managing the herd, he could expect to receive preferential treatment in the allocation of resources such as fuel, materials, and foodstuffs brought into the *somon*, and he would be allowed to keep a small private herd of his own horses whose milk he could use directly or sell to the commune. We were taken inside his *ger* and given the standard reception of dried curd, rancid butter morsels, and sugar lumps, together with the usual huge quantities of mare's milk and *shimiin arkhi* chasers. We ate glumly and in silence, still depressed by the events of the morning, and when the chairman of the *somon* committee asked us for our plans it was Bayar who made Ariunbold take into account that four of our gift horses were now sick or lame, and we would have to halt and rest them.

I watched as the Mongols clustered around the lamest of the gift horses. It was one of the sherry-colored animals with the black eel-stripe down its spine and the faint zebra bars on its legs which Mongols say are telltale signs that the animal is descended from the Wild Horse. They pressed and tapped the shoulder, and squeezed and felt the injured leg, but again, in typical Mongol fashion, no one would venture a firm diagnosis of the injury for fear of being considered self-opinionated or, later, shown to be wrong. It was not until next day when all the onlookers and hangers-on had departed that the champion herdsman did show up quietly at our little camp on the hillside above his *ger*. The injured horse was led off to one side, and he nicked one of the major veins in the chest so that a steady jet of blood spurted out for about half a minute. The horse stood there motionless, except for occasionally lifting the injured leg, almost as if pressing the vein closed. Then the bleeding stopped of its own accord, and the veterinary treatment was considered done.

Doc found a way for me, Paul, and himself to extricate ourselves from the unhappy situation. Next day was to be polling day in the first free elections to be held in Mongolia since the communists took power. A *ger* at the base of the hill was one of the rural polling stations, and a jeep would be coming to collect the ballot box. Doc arranged for us to hitch a ride back with the jeep to the *somon* center. There the polling results would be collected next dawn by a "Bee," one of Air Mongolia's fleet of venerable yellow-painted Antonov 2 biplanes, and taken to the provincial capital. If the local *somon* secretary agreed, we could hitch a ride on the plane and get back to Ulaan Baatar with minimum delay and then find a way of traveling forward to continue our researches in the far west of the country, in the Altai. Doc was eager to get going, and our departure would not hinder the riders. Rather the reverse, for if three of us left, Delger would have our extra horses, which would reduce the dependence on remounts, and our happy-go-lucky groom could take Ariunbold forward. Bayar was the person I felt sorry for. In theory he too had the option to leave, but there was little to attract him back to Ulaan Baatar and he would need the permission of his bosses at the Mongolian TV Film Studio. When Doc explained the situation to him, Bayar, after much heart-searching, decided that he would have to stay with Ariunbold until he reached the next provincial capital and could telephone his office. As matters turned out, he was told to continue. Paul and I liked Bayar very much, and to our regret we were not to see him again.

We spent our final field day preparing ourselves mentally to eat a marmot. As usual it was Bayar who knew how to cook the creature properly. Two hunters had brought in a pair of marmots, neatly shot through the head, and Bayar and Delger skinned their carcasses down by the river. Bayar then heated up some stones in the fire and placed the hot stones together with chunks of marmot in the pot. That was all. There was no cooking, no boiling, no spices, and Bayar had promised us a feast. Paul and I waited dubiously. We were not entirely convinced that we could bring ourselves to swallow bits of the chubby and engaging marmots, which before they were flayed had the faces of rather confused and costive aldermen. But we could not resist the chance of trying to vary our monotonous diet of sheep meat. Bayar lifted the pot lid and hooked out two blackened lumps of marmot. They looked exactly like oversize portions of rabbit. Paul and I gingerly took our rations in our fingers and bit into the flesh. The marmot meat was unexpectedly tough and stringy, but that was not the real disappointment. Pot-roast marmot was very bland. Indeed it had barely any dectectable flavor whatsoever, but if it tasted of anything at all—it tasted like mutton.

Later I commented on this disappointment to the local government official who came to pick up the ballot box next evening. We were driving to the *somon* center in his jeep and he chuckled. "You shouldn't tell me that you were eating marmot. I ought to arrest you! The hunting season for marmots does not open for a couple of weeks. But of course it's difficult to keep any sort of control on the *arats*." He was a man in his early 40s, energetic and businesslike, one of the new-style officials in regional government who were much less doctrinaire than the Party faithfuls who had formerly run the *somon* centers with a dead hand. Of course there was still a Communist Party machine in place, with a local Party chairman in each *somon*, but the central government was now sending professional managers to run the local administration and often they were men of high caliber. Our companion, Chief Councillor Gombo, had grown up in the *somon* and was glad to be back there after a career in Ulaan Baatar. He was not unduly concerned about the results of the election. The country people, he explained, were very conservative. While there was much talk in the capital about the formation of new political parties and a democratic movement in Mongolia, the *arats* had barely been affected. The fledgling opposition parties had made little contact with the remote *somons*, and he expected that the two candidates put up by the local Communist Party would win by a comfortable majority. "Who are the candidates?" I asked. "One of them is me," he answered with a smile, and then began talking about his hopes and plans for the development of the region.

His strategy was down-to-earth. Here was no empty Party theorist. His *somon*, he explained, could never be anything but an agricultural zone. It spanned all four types of Mongolian terrain—Gobi, valley, steppe, and mountain—but it had no mineral wealth, and the climate placed a strict limit on the numbers of cattle it could sustain. In winter the temperature fell to minus 40 degrees, but luckily the snow was seldom more than 16 inches thick. If it was deeper, then the cattle could not reach the pasture underneath and there were severe cattle losses. The most the *arats* could hope for would be a few small factories to process their own foodstuffs, but our friend did not want to see them give up their herding and move away to Ulaan Baatar. Their lives, he felt, were much richer and freer in the countryside. The single greatest improvement he would wish them was somehow to bring electricity to the ordinary herdsmen so they could watch television and begin to understand the outside world. Already a few of the wealthier *arats* had bought Japanese portable generators, and in the south of the *somon*, in the Gobi region, there were pioneer experiments with small windmill generators for individual *gers*. It seemed a modest enough ambition.

The Chief Councillor made us welcome that evening in the official guesthouse, a government *ger* pitched in the center of the little town. There we had the luxury of beds, clean towels, and a table. Before toasting the future of Mongolia in *arkhi*, he dipped the tip of the third finger of his right hand into the drink three times. Once he flicked a small drop of the alcohol away in the air, once toward the hearth, and once to the ground. It was a ritual gesture we had seen many times, the customary offering to the spirits of sky, fire, and earth. But he explained two extra details: the third finger was employed because it was the cleanest and least-used finger on the hand; and folklore said it was a test for poison in the cup. The poison would burn the fingertip.

The take-off of the "Bee" was delayed next morning while we waited for a motorcycle dispatch rider to bring the late results from the outlying polling stations. "How did you get on in the election?" I asked our host as he waited with us in the shadow of the venerable biplane. Above our heads the Mongol pilot was casually leaning out of the cockpit window, looking like a prosperous market gardener in his greenhouse. "I was elected," he replied. "In this *somon* the Party received eighty-five percent of the vote."

12

The Sage

Before Carpini and Rubruck ever set foot in Central Asia, another priest had already made the long and uncomfortable journey across Mongolia. But he came from the opposite direction—from the east.

Ch'ang Ch'un, Taoist Master of the "Golden Lotus" school, was the living embodiment of that famous stereotype: the venerable oriental sage. His wisdom was so renowned that in 1219 he received an invitation from Genghis Khan requesting that he come to Mongolia. Genghis Khan wrote to say that he had heard of Ch'ang Ch'un's sanctity and erudition and wished to consult the learned master on some unspecified but very important subject. To escort the Taoist scholar across the Gobi Desert he had dispatched an adjutant and a special guard of twenty men and had issued a gold *paiza* so that all men would treat the Taoist Master as if he were the emperor himself. Ch'ang Ch'un was then 71 years old and had retired to a life of quiet contemplation at a retreat in the mountains of Shantung province. Indeed he had been considered a sage for so long that Sun Hsi, the Taoist monk who published Ch'ang Ch'un's story, was astonished to learn that the old man was still alive. As Sun Hsi put it in his introduction, he had thought that Ch'ang Ch'un must have "long ago soared up to heaven, and after his transformation lived in the company of the clouds in the high spheres of the universe." When the admirer actually met the Master, he was even more effusive. When Ch'ang Ch'un sat, he said, "his position was immovable, like a dead body.

When he stood upright he resembled a tree. His movements were like the thunder, and he walked like the wind. . . . There was no book he had not read."*

Ch'ang Ch'un hesitated. He had already turned down similar invitations to visit the court of the Sung, the native Chinese dynasty still ruling south China from Hangchow. With good reason he feared that the 700-mile journey to Mongolia would be too much of an ordeal, and then there was the awkward matter of Genghis Khan's young women. The same caravan that he was to join was bringing back several young Chinese women destined for Genghis Khan's royal harem, and Ch'ang Ch'un felt it was not fitting that he should travel in the company of these girls. He sent back a prevaricating reply. But Genghis Khan was not a man to be put off. His secretariat firmly repeated the summons, and presumably the girls went by another caravan, because in February 1221 Ch'ang Ch'un set out on the "Journey of Ten Thousand Li" as his amanuensis and disciple Li Chih-ch'ang called it, and thereby provided us with a unique eyewitness account of what Central Asia was like immediately following the most traumatic phase of the Mongol conquests—the complete overthrow and subjection of the empire of Khwarazm, the most splendid Islamic power in Central Asia, whose lands included all the great oasis cities of Transoxiana as well as what would now be Turkmenistan, Kirghizia, and Uzbekistan in the Soviet Union, and part of northern Afghanistan, Iran, and Pakistan.

Traveling sometimes by cart, sometimes on horseback, the little group of Chinese—Ch'ang Ch'un, his nineteen disciples, and their Mongol escort—plodded off first across the Inner Gobi, where they passed across a great battlefield strewn with human bones. It was the spot where Genghis Khan had annihilated the hapless Chinese army sent to block his first thrust into China in 1211. Ice was still covering the lakes when they reached the clustered black carts and white tents of the camp of Temuge-otchigin, Genghis Khan's youngest brother. There on the great grassland they witnessed a Mongol wedding where the noblemen rode in with their gifts of mare's milk, and their ladies wore pointed headdresses so tall that they had to walk backwards, stooping, as they entered the doors of their felt tents. There, too,

* *Medieval Researches from Eastern Asiatic Sources*, E. Bretschneider, London 1988.

they heard the unwelcome news that Genghis Khan was far in the west campaigning against the Khwarazm Shah Muhammad II. It meant that they would have to travel on for perhaps another 3000 miles to reach the "Universal Ruler."

Leaving Temuge-otchigin's camp, the Mongol guides took their charges along virtually the same route that Paul and I were to travel seven centuries later, following the courses of the Kerulen and the upper Orhon rivers and wending their way through the Hangay mountains. They traveled at the same time of year and their reactions were much the same. They found the weather bitterly cold and commented on the wild onions, the grave mounds, and the traces of sacrifices to the spirits, presumably *obos*, which they came across in the high passes. The grandeur of the Hangay mountains made a powerful impression on them:

> In the valleys splendid pine trees were growing, more than a hundred feet in height. The mountains stretched to the west in a continuous chain, all covered with tall pine trees. We were five or six days travelling in these mountains, the road winding round the peaks. It was magnificent scenery, the slopes of the rocks covered with noble forests, with the river gliding through the depths below. On level places pines and birches were growing together. Then we ascended a high mountain which resembled a large rainbow, overlooking an abyss of several thousand feet deep. It was dreadful to look down to the lake in the depth.

Their path now veered south to cross the Altai mountains, where they saw evidence of an army's passing: an astonishing supply road cut through these desolate mountains by Genghis Khan's engineers. The army had gone through two years previously, accompanied by 10,000 Chinese artificers and engineers equipped with all their machines of siege warfare. The excruciating labor needed to haul all their equipment through the mountains can be imagined from the fact that the hundred Mongol riders escorting Ch'ang Ch'un and his disciples had to heave their carts up the stony paths using ropes attached to their horses, and then fasten drags on the wheel to prevent them running away downhill. Worse was to come: the little caravan crossed a vast stony plain littered with black rocks which brought them to the edge of the Great Sandy Desert. There, said Li Chih-ch'ang, neither man nor beast could travel in the heat of the day, for the sun killed all living creatures. So they began the march in the evening, after their Mongol guides had rubbed blood on the horses' heads to keep away the desert goblins which they believed would seize them in the dark, and traveled all through the night in order to reach the first oasis town by noon. The largest sand dunes "seemed to swim like big ships in the midst of waves," and the exhausted bullocks could go no further. They were abandoned by the roadside, and henceforth horses, six at a time, pulled each cart.

On the frontier of what had once been the kingdom of the Khwarazm Shah they again saw evidence of Mongol military efficiency. Coming to the Sairam Lake they found forty-eight bridges that had been constructed to carry the siege train through a land of snow-peaked mountains and deep ravines. Each bridge was wide enough so that two carts could pass side by side loaded with the machines for hurling rocks and giant arrows, flame-throwers, and cannon designed to fire stone cannonballs which Genghis Khan unleashed on the subjects of the Shah.

The cities of Transoxiana had never expected to face anything like this onslaught of advanced oriental war technology. Worse, their overlord made the fatal mistake of trusting to their fortifications. The vainglorious Sultan Muhammad II, Shah of Khwarazm, liked to compare himself to Alexander the Great, even adding the name "Iskander" to his coinage, and he commanded an army three times the size of the Mongol invasion force. But he took no counteroffensive action and scattered his forces disastrously. His 300,000 troops, mostly mercenaries from Turkish-speaking tribes, had been distributed among the great cities—Urgendj, Merv, Bukhara, Samarkand, Balkh—and they closed the gates and waited for the Mongols to beat in vain against their fortifications. Almost contemptuously, Genghis Khan split his army into four sections and selected a target for each. The first objective was the frontier city of Otrar, which he selected for particular vengeance. In 1218 the governor of Otrar, a man called Inalchuq, had arrested a caravan of 450 men and 500 camels arriving out of Mongolia. Inalchuq may have been no more than an official brigand or else, as he later claimed to his overlord Muhammad II, he genuinely suspected that the caravan included Mongol spies on reconnaissance for Genghis Khan. In any event he decided that all the men in the caravan should be killed, including one who was an official Mongol ambassador, and then the caravan's valuables were sold on the open market. Muhammad Shah did not stop him.

If this was not enough to bring down Genghis Khan's wrath, Muhammad Shah then flouted the diplomatic status of the three-man delegation which Genghis Khan promptly sent from Mongolia to protest about the Otrar outrage. One delegate was beheaded, and the other two were sent back to Mongolia with their beards shaved off, an open insult.

After such provocation, the citizens of Otrar knew they could expect little mercy from the Mongols and put up a despairing resistance. The Mongols, initially commanded by two of Genghis's sons, Chaghatai and Ögodei, made no effort to disabuse them of their eventual fate. When part of the garrison left the city to plead for clemency, the Mongols lined them up and executed them on the spot. Otrar was to hold out for five months, and the citadel under the personal command of the doomed governor managed to resist for a full month after the main town had gone down. But in the end Inalchuq was taken alive as Genghis Khan had ordered and, according to the Muslim historian Nasawi, the avaricious ex-governor was put to death by molten silver poured into his eyes and ears.

Genghis Khan, meanwhile, had switched his lethal attention to the far bigger and richer target of Samarkand. It was the largest and most splendid city of the entire region, and its population must have been close to half a million. Muhammad II had recently made it his capital and had ordered that a new wall should be built to protect its lush oasis. To complete such a grandiose scheme, the wall would have needed to be 50 miles long. But although the taxes were raised to pay for it, nothing had been done by the time the Mongol army arrived, and the invaders quickly showed that they had fine-tuned the techniques of siege warfare.

For a start, the citizens of Samarkand were duped into thinking that the city had been surrounded by enormous numbers of the enemy. Genghis Khan had brought along all his prisoners to increase the apparent size of his forces and had made them set up camp in military formations as if they were part of the main army. He also called in his reserves, placed a blocking force to fend off any rescue attempts sent by Muhammad Shah, who had cravenly abandoned his capital, and made a personal reconnaissance of the defenses. The wretched prisoners were then used as human shields in a direct assault, pushed ahead of the Mongols to soak up arrow fire and projectiles hurled from the walls. The Chinese-directed cannon bombardment must have sapped the faith of the defense in their city walls, because on the third day of the siege the greater part of Samarkand's garrison troops launched a mass sortie. Genghis Khan promptly employed the classic Mongol technique of withdraw-and-ambush. The Mongol cavalry fell back, luring on the Turkish garrison troops until they were clear of the city walls and had entered the hollow square of the Mongol killing formation. Then the Mongol cavalry wheeled their horses and began the slaughter. Half the garrison, about 50,000 men, lost their lives. Forty-eight hours later the city surrendered, leaving only a couple of thousand diehards to shut themselves in the citadel and continue their defiance. Genghis Khan's officers barely paused to accept the surrender of the main garrison. They closed on the citadel and quickly overran it. A thousand defenders broke through the Mongol noose and escaped, but the rest were dead. From start to finish the siege of Samarkand had taken Genghis Khan's war machine just five days.

It took longer to organize the pillage. Genghis Khan loathed turncoats, so the 30,000 or so Turkish mercenary troops who had volunteered to desert the Shah were lined up and killed in batches. Then the entire civilian population of Samarkand was moved outside the city walls so that the city could be looted more efficiently. The population was graded like cattle at market. Craftsmen, artisans, and those with technical skills were deported to Mongolia to work there. Men of military age were assigned to the "human shield." The old and infirm were left to fend for themselves. When Ch'ang Ch'un reached Samarkand a year later, only a quarter of the population had seen fit to reoccupy their former homes; Samarkand had had its heart torn out. It would not regain its former magnificence for another 180 years until, ironically, it achieved the status of Golden Samarkand under the warlord Tamerlane, Marlowe's "Tamburlaine the Great," who consciously copied Genghis Khan and claimed a common ancestor. He even married into the "Golden Family" so he could call himself "son-in-law."

The rapid fall of Samarkand revealed to Genghis Khan just how fragile was Muhammad Shah's grip on his sprawling realm. The Mon-

gol Great Khan realized that the Khwarazm Shahdom was not just
ripe for plunder but that much of it could be incorporated into a
Mongol empire. So he sent his sons rampaging up and down the land
in command of Mongol field armies to impress the natives with the
fact that they were now subject to Genghis Khan and his family. All
cities were fair targets for pillage, but if circumstances allowed they
were to be preserved as future Mongol possessions. As the months
passed, a pattern of Mongol behavior began to emerge. The luckiest
cities and towns were those where a Mongol flying column simply
did not have time to stop for more than a day or so. If food and
supplies were produced immediately, such places got away with no
more than a quick trawl of the best booty. Less fortunate were those
places which, as the Mongols approached in less of a hurry, surrendered as soon as a Mongol envoy demanded their submission. In such
cases, as at Samarkand, the population was ordered to leave so that
the plundering could be done undisturbed. This might take a week
or more and then the people went back to their houses and continued
their lives under a Mongol-appointed governor, impoverished but
thankful to be alive. However, if a city rejected a Mongol demand
for capitulation, it was attacked without compunction. Most of the
garrison could expect to be killed, and a brutal sack followed. The
standard selection of useful prisoners was sent to Mongolia, and the
rest were enslaved or left to rebuild their lives in what was left of
their homes.

The most savage treatment of all was the result of three conditions:
no city could expect a shred of mercy if its citizens dared to kill the
Mongol envoy sent to demand its surrender, if it rebelled after initial
submission, or, worst of all, if a member of Genghis Khan's immediate family was killed during the fighting. The great Afghan city of
Herat was treated quite leniently when its governor submitted in
advance to Genghis Khan early in his campaign of 1220. Some of the
garrison had threatened to put up a fight and were executed, but
the majority of the citizenry was left undisturbed. Six months later,
however, Herat unwisely rebelled after a local Mongol force suffered
a temporary defeat. The punishment the Mongol general meted out
was calamitous. As soon as he had retaken the city, he gave instructions that every single one of its citizens should be beheaded. It took
seven days of butchery to lop off all the heads of everyone who could

be found. The Mongol army then rode off, and a miserable handful of Herat's survivors crept out of the ruins to bury their dead. They had been tricked. The Mongols sent back a punishment brigade which suddenly swooped in, herded together the survivors, and hacked off their heads as well.

Farther west, the city of Nishapur in the northeast of Iran seemed to have got off very lightly in the summer of 1220 when it promptly resupplied a Mongol flying column. Unfortunately the mood of the citizens had changed by autumn and they resisted when the Mongols reappeared. In the fighting a Mongol commander by the name of Toquchar was killed. Toquchar was a member of Genghis Khan's family, and the Mongol vengeance was terrible. When Nishapur finally surrendered, every living creature was put to death, including the cats and dogs. Toquchar's widow took part in the slaughter of the entire human population, and the severed heads were set out in neat lines by age and gender. Afterward the walls and buildings of Nishapur were pulled down, and the order was given that destruction should be so complete that the ground could be plowed where the city had previously stood.

The mass punishment exacted for harming a member of the Chingizide family was a deliberate means of spreading the extraordinary awe now surrounding the person of Genghis Khan himself. Though the Mongols could also claim that there was the mandate of Tengri the Sky God for them to subjugate the world, Genghis Khan himself had acquired his own godlike status. He was considered invincible and divine, and this adulation may have influenced his decision to summon Ch'ang Ch'un. In the autumn of 1222, when the Taoist sage finally reached Genghis Khan's camp in the mountains of northern Afghanistan, he found that Genghis Khan had brought him all that distance in order to ask one question: did Ch'ang Ch'un have a medicine that would give eternal life? With admirable honesty, Ch'ang Ch'un replied that "there are means for preserving life, but no medicine for immortality." Genghis Khan does not seem to have been unduly disappointed, and treated the old man kindly. He had a special tent erected for his accommodation so that he could stay with the camp and even listened to three tutorials given by the sage on the principles of Taoism. He also seems to have found out that Ch'ang Ch'un was a vegetarian, because he sent him fruit and vegetables for his diet before he eventually made arrangements for another Mongol escort to ride with Ch'ang Ch'un all the way back to China. It was a return journey which, according to Li Chih-ch'ang, the sage made with complete equanimity, sipping only rice water for sustenance as he crossed the Gobi of Inner Mongolia. From a position of such lofty detachment, it was not to be expected that Ch'ang Ch'un himself would comment on his meetings with the Great Mongol, but he must have made a favorable impression on Genghis Khan, because the Khakhan made an edict exempting Taoist masters from paying taxes and gave an order setting aside an area of the royal park in Peking for Ch'ang Ch'un to establish his own monastery.*

There was a very down-to-earth need for Genghis Khan to promote the prestige of the "Golden Family." The extravagant success of the Mongol invasion of the Khwarazm empire was now exceeding even his capacity for energetic government. The Mongols ruled or were about to launch military campaigns in Mongolia, north and central China, and all of Muhammad Shah's former domains. Already they dominated half of northern Asia, and there was no obvious limit to the expansion of their empire. Genghis Khan could not be everywhere to direct operations, so by distributing the mystique of his authority among his sons he could continue the phenomenal rate of expansion. He also realized that the Mongol army of some 130,000 men was far too small to control such an immense area. Cities and entire provinces were falling to them in every direction, and there were simply not enough Mongol troopers to go round. The policy of following quick victories with shocking massacres was one way of easing the problem. Opponents became paralyzed with fright at the mere thought of fighting the Mongols. Captured garrisons often outnumbered their Mongol executioners as they stood meekly with bowed heads waiting to be decapitated.

But still the Mongol war machine did not have enough manpower. At the start of the attack on the Khwarazm empire Genghis Khan had been obliged to boost his troop strength with non-Mongol allies drawn from Turkish-speaking tribes hostile to Muhammad II. Now, with the empire growing larger and larger, he permitted his sons to

---

*Ch'ang Ch'un died there in the same month of the same year as Genghis Khan, August 1227.

recruit more and more foreigners. After the initial phase when renegade Turkish troops who tried to switch sides were killed, the Mongols began to welcome Turkish confederates into the Mongol armies.
The Turks were, after all, a related people who had their origins in
the same steppe and mountain country of Mongolia. Even those who
had adopted Islam retained many of the same tribal customs. The
Mongol cavalry still comprised the loyal core of any strike force,
particularly when speed of attack was required. But with a siege train
that was already largely Chinese, and with thousands of Turkish
riders, Genghis Khan's army was becoming multinational. In fact,
without the help of the Turkish-speaking tribes who pledged allegiance to the nine yak-tail banner in increasing numbers, the Mongol
empire could not have continued its headlong expansion.

13

Eagle Hunters

Today a sizable Turkic minority still lives within Mongolia. Ninety thousand Kazakhs, a Turkish-speaking people, inhabit Mongolia's mountainous and most westerly *aymag* of Bayan Olgei. Carpini and Rubruck had described Turkic as well as more Mongol customs, and both travelers frequently used Turkish words in their writings, which they would have picked up from the Turkish-speaking peoples whom Genghis Khan had included in his empire. Given the extreme isolation of the Kazakhs of Bayan Olgei, it seemed possible that they retained some of these Central Asian traditions, so I was eager to meet them. But there was one problem: Bayan Olgei lies right against the Soviet frontier and is a sensitive area politically. The gigantic Soviet Republic of Kazakhstan is on the far side of the Altai, and its people are racially and linguistically identical to the Kazakhs in Mongolia. Both the Soviet and Mongol governments were alert to the possibility that one day the Kazakhs might demand the political union of their people. Unsupervised travel by foreigners close to the international border had been discouraged in the past. I fretted that we might be hindered from going there freely and discussed the problem with Doc as we made our way back to Ulaan Baatar. In the end we took the matter into our own hands. Up to that point everyone in authority in Ulaan Baatar had been so helpful and so enthusiastic about my plans to explore Mongolia's traditions that I felt I could presume on the continuing understanding of the authorities. So Doc simply bought us three tickets aboard the

52-seater Soviet-built turboprop aircraft which made the daily run to the regional center at Bayan Olgei, Beautiful or Rich Olgei. We had no special authorization from the authorities; we made no prior arrangements; and we had no contacts. We would trust to luck and see what happened if we arrived among the Kazakhs unheralded. And there was an advantage to arriving there without the Mongol riding team: there is mutual distrust between Kazakhs and Mongols. The latter often regard the Kazakhs as potential defectors and, besides fearing that the Kazakhs might take Bayan Olgei out of Mongolia, do not like to mix with them in the workplace. Among the Mongols the Kazakhs have a reputation for being clannish hard-workers who, if they were allowed into any job, acquired all the best posts and then filled any vacancies with fellow Kazakhs. In return, the Kazakhs resented being treated within Mongolia as a minority, largely ignored by the central government. Even such an easy-going person as Bayar pulled a disdainful face when he talked about Kazakhs, and Delger, who knew that Kazakhs ate horse flesh, believed they would devour his Mongol horses given half the chance.

On 2 August Doc, Paul, and I flew directly westward for four hours from Ulaan Baatar toward Bayan Olgei, looking down at the terrain we had covered so slowly on horseback. The flooded plains around the capital gave way to the rumpled mountain scenery of the Hangay, and then the mountains faded away imperceptibly to steppe and then Gobi. It was a drab country of low sculpted hills and dried watercourses. Very occasionally there was a lake. Seen from 20,000 feet it had exactly the same tan and yellow colors which mapmakers use to depict areas of uninhabited low semi-desert. Nor was there any visible settlement except for a solitary *ger* every 30 or 40 miles. At very rare intervals a ridge or a valley might have the slight tinge of green that indicated some sparse grazing. In such spots there was sure to be a line of *gers*, eight or nine of them arranged cheek by jowl on a nearby bluff.

The capital of Bayan Olgei was a sprawling, dusty, pebbly town of 20,000 inhabitants, little charm, and the usual functional architecture of four-story apartment buildings and government offices. Here, too, there was a suburb of felt tents behind wooden palisades. The barren foothills of the Altai pressed in on the south and east. The town's name is usually shortened to plain Olgei, and in truth there was nothing Beautiful or Fertile about it. Nor, when we arrived on a dull, overcast day, was there anyone on the streets. Ninety percent of the population had departed to spend the best of the short summer in the surrounding hills, leaving the featureless boulevards behind them. The population would return in mid-August.

The first vehicle we saw was a jeep with Soviet registration plates which must have come across the border from Gorno Altaisk District, just two hours' drive away. If the driver and his passengers had been hoping to do some foreign shopping in Bayan Olgei, they would have been disappointed. The few shops in town had virtually no stock. The first we visited had a total range of about twelve items, including cheap combs, dolls of Chinese plastic, and—for some odd reason— a line-up of a dozen old-fashioned photographic enlargers displayed in a dusty row. The grocery store next-door offered watery straw-berry jam, countless bottles of a greenish yellow soda drink, and a bin a quarter full of stale bread loaves. We were looking for supplies for ourselves as well as presents to give the Kazakhs, so we bought a magnificent embossed brick of Chinese tea, a packet of sugar lumps, and some boiled sweets. The shop had no coins in the till so our change was given in handfuls of sun-dried apples and plums from another larger wooden chest. The dried fruit had come from across the border, from Kazakhstan itself. We scorned the insipid strawberry jam, and regretted it, for when we returned three days later every jar had gone, and we were hungry.

It took three days of patient negotiation to extract the hire of a jeep from the local administration. As everywhere in Mongolia, vehicles were in desperately short supply, extremely battered, and most of them belonged to government organizations, which in Olgei were starved of equipment. The Mongol officials in Ulaan Baatar regarded the province as *ultima Thule*, the end of the line and very low on the list of priorities for investment or resupply. The happy result, we were to find, was that Ulaan Baatar did not interfere much in Bayan Olgei and let the Kazakhs run their own local affairs. In consequence the Kazakhs were very proud of their own achievements and made great efforts to keep their customs and language. There was a Kazakh-language newspaper, a Kazakh-speaking radio station, a new Kazakh theater under construction, and a small ambitious museum largely devoted to Kazakh achievements. Even the town hotel had "KOSH

KELDINIZER"—Welcome—boldly written in Kazakh Turkish in large letters over the door.

By great good luck Doc happened to meet an old friend, a Kazakh, whom he had known in Moscow when both were working in COMECON, the Eastern bloc's economic cooperation organization. In the intricate crossweave of Eastern bloc society, no one would have thought it odd that a Kazakh engineer and a Mongol cardiac specialist would have become acquainted in a Moscow office where neither of them had any enthusiasm or qualification to devise international economic programs. What mattered in the system was to make useful friendships. So now in Olgei there was a sudden flurry of introductions and recommendations, and on the fourth day we left town in a jeep that had been resurrected from the repair depot of the municipal transport pool and headed into the Altai.

If the Hentei mountains had seemed desolate in May, the lower slopes of the Altai appeared even more barren at the start of autumn. Our Kazakh driver assured us that there were no people living on the lower valley floors because they were saving the pasture for the winter feeding of their flocks. Looking around, it was difficult to see what they were preserving. There seemed to be scarcely any pasture at all, only a little scrub grass, sandy soil, mile after mile of gravel, and the occasional dried-up watercourse.

After 12 miles we stopped at a small settlement to pick up Hojanias, the brother of Doc's Kazakh friend. Hojanias was to be our contact with the Kazakh nomads. He was a big, energetic bear of a man with a strongly Turkish face. His brown eyes were much rounder than the Mongol eyes we had grown used to, his skin more fair, and he had a far broader jaw and a higher bridge to his nose which made him look completely different from the *arats* who had been our companions earlier. No one would have mistaken him for a Mongol, even if he had not been wearing a brightly embroidered Kazakh skull cap perched on the back of his shaven skull.

Hojanias immediately volunteered to take us to a Kazakh friend of his who was camped with his flocks high in the mountains, very close to the Soviet border. His friend, he promised, lived the real Kazakh way of life.

It took the rest of the day for the aged jeep to grind its way up into the mountains. We were climbing to the roof of Central Asia, a region

Passing a stone monument of the Orhon Turks, another of the nomad peoples who burst out of Central Asia and conquered the settled lands of the perimeter.

Wrestlers at Naadam, the annual national festival.

Singer in a traditional hat.

Olzvoi, deputy foreign minister of Mongolia, presents Tim Severin with a commemorative medal at the departure ceremony held at the Erdenzu monastery in front of Ögodei's Temple, said to date from the time of Genghis Khan's son and heir.

Holding up the central roof wheel while erecting a *ger*, or felt tent.

Herder family with tray of sun-dried milk curds, which the medieval traveler Rubruck complained were "as hard as iron slag."

Gerel and Ariunbold riding under the walls of Erdenzu.

Tim Severin with an *arat*, or herdsman, who served as a guide.

Tents of the Gurvan Gol expedition, whose Japanese and Mongol archaeologists are searching for the tomb of Genghis Khan.

Lunch with Mongol Kazakhs in the far west of Mongolia.

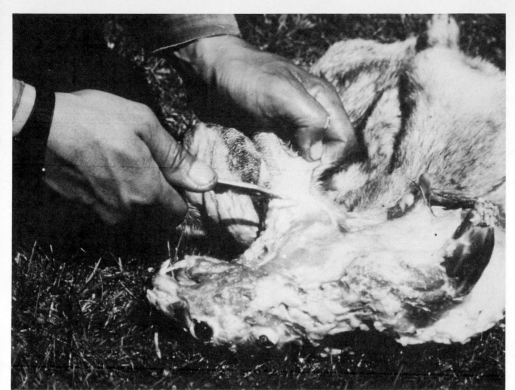

Skinning a marmot for
lunch—later it was
discovered that marmots
carry the Black Death, or
bubonic plague, which is still
widespread in Mongolia.

Samga, the shamaness or "Old
Woman," in her ceremonial dress,
praying and invoking the spirits of
wind, sky, water, and rocks.

Yaks in the snow in August.

A Kazakh eagle hunter. A fully grown eagle weighs thirteen or fourteen pounds.

so remote that it is doubtful whether any Western visitors had been in that particular locality for half a century. By late afternoon we were in sight of the tangle of mountains the local people called the Five Peaks. One of the 15,000-foot snow-capped summits marked the junction of the borders of China, Mongolia, and the Soviet Union and was part of what Soviet geographers grandly call the "World Watershed," the divide between waters which drain to the Arctic or to the enclosed drainage system of Central Asia. Our destination was another two hours' journey to the north, and by the time we came upon the first Kazakh yurts pitched in the high valleys the light was fading.

The Kazakh yurts were, to the uninitiated eye, the same felt tents the Mongols called *gers*. But even in the dusk Paul and I saw the differences immediately. The Kazakh yurts had a different profile. They were taller and lighter in construction, the roof cones were more steeply pitched, and in general they were larger than the standard Mongol *ger*. But it was when you entered a Kazakh yurt that the difference was really overwhelming. It was nearly midnight by the time we reached the home of Camran, Hojanias's friend, because he had chosen to put his yurt at the very upper end of the high valley, the last tent before the border. We needed to stop several times to ask our way, once from a Kazakh family who kept a captive wolf cub on a string. When we eventually arrived at Camran's yurt, there was a shadowy figure in the dark to greet us, and we were led inside. Camran owned a generator, and after we had sat down inside the yurt he switched it on. A single bulb hanging in the center of the yurt lit up, and the interior was suddenly a bright pavilion.

Every surface was gloriously decorated. The panels of the roof cloth were dyed red and black between the roof spokes. Long colorful ribbons of woven cloth were draped and crisscrossed behind the spokes. The floor was covered with thick carpets of white felt embroidered with bold antler patterns. The work chests were painted bright colors and inlaid with iridescent shards of metal. Every possible excuse for embroidery had been taken up. There were embroidered cushions, embroidered bedspreads, embroidered panels, embroidered wall hangings. The beds around the wall had been turned into small four-posters by the profusion of embroidered panels hung around them. And none of the embroidery was restrained. It was a tumult of hues and patterns, loops and whorls, figures of birds, flowers, and horses, abstract designs and simple repetitions. What made the exuberance and richness of the decoration all the more impressive was that Camran's wife had done every stitch herself. It was a tradition that no Kazakh wife should decorate her home with any present or purchase. When she was first married, she moved into a plain yurt, and over her lifetime she should demonstrate her skill and taste and industry by stitching all the decoration herself. By such standards Camran's wife was a paragon.

Camran himself was thrilled by the arrival of his totally unexpected visitors. We may well have been the first Westerners he had met anywhere, and I was sure that we were the first to have climbed up into the mountains to visit his summer yurt. Yet he took the arrival of foreign guests with complete poise and a real enthusiasm to make sure that we were entertained and comfortable. We noticed the contrast between the Mongols and the Kazakhs, that Camran was much more the master in his family than if he had been a Mongol herdsman. But his dignity and status did not diminish his unaffected eagerness to be a good host. He was less reserved than any Mongol *arat* as he bustled around making sure that we were at ease, asking our news, and complimenting Hojanias.

Then, while his wife prepared a meal, we all sat or sprawled on the thick off-white felt rugs with their red and purple and yellow embroidery while Hojanias sang. It turned out that our guide was a semiprofessional singer, and he produced his *dobri*, the two-string Kazakh guitar, and strummed away lustily, producing a medley of traditional Kazakh songs as well as popular tunes from Mongol and Kazakh films. Well after midnight Camran's wife served the food, and once more there was a contrast with Mongol custom. As usual, we were eating mutton, but this time the meat was tender and flavored with herbs. And the plates were carefully washed in hot water before use, something we had seldom seen in a Mongol *ger*. There was a final divergence: no offer of *shimiin*. We drank yak's milk with the meal, but the Kazakhs, though they lived in communist Mongolia and without Muslim clerics, still kept their Islamic prohibition against alcohol. They neither distilled nor drank steam *arkhi*.

At 2 o'clock in the morning we pleaded exhaustion. Camran and his wife piled up felt rugs to make a 6-inch platform. On it Hojanias,

Paul, Doc, myself, and the driver obediently lay down in a row, and our host and hostess then hauled three more layers of heavy felt rugs on top of our close-packed bodies. Around the edges, where chinks let in the icy draft, they wedged embroidered cushions to seal in the sides of the thick human sandwich. And we slept.

Four hours later I awoke and gazed up at the splendid multicolored roof of the yurt. Daylight was leaking in through cracks around the door and under the skirt of the yurt, and the light seemed unusually bright and clear. The ribs of the tall roof were more slender and longer than the roof spokes in a Mongol *ger*, and they were creaking and shifting in a strong wind like the ribs of a lightly built ship. It was bitterly cold. The elderly Kazakh jeep driver was fast asleep right against me. He was a most helpful and excellent guide, who seemed to have friends in all the Kazakh yurts, but now he was snoring loudly. Also he had bad breath. So I eased myself out of the human heap, dragged on my boots, and walked quietly to the wooden door to look out. I pushed open the door a fraction and halted.

Outside the world was dazzling white. Now I knew why the chinks of light filtering into the yurt had been so bright. An early blizzard had swept into the high Altai during the night and dropped three or four inches of snow. It said something for the efficient design of a Kazakh yurt that the weather change had gone virtually undetected as we slept. Thirty yards away a herd of yaks bunched miserably together to avoid the wind. The snow had frozen on their long coats like poorly applied icing sugar. The black pelts of the snuffling animals were in stark contrast to the brilliant white of the fresh snow. Beyond the herd the valley swept away to a clear blue sky with thin trails of high cirrus cloud. Little flurries of snow crystals skittered over the snowfield like wisps of white steam. Here we were, in the first week of August, and yet snow had already come to the high Altai. It was the first warning to the nomads that they should begin to plan their move with their flocks and herds to lower ground.

Last night it had been difficult to gauge just how high we had come in the darkness. But now, gazing across the gleaming snow, it really did feel that we were on the gable end of Central Asia. Camran's tent was so far up the valley that we were almost at the watershed. Next to us a great rock outcrop reared up like a final massive mountain pivot. Last evening Camran had pointed out two small pinpricks of light to the west. "Russians," he had said. We were, he estimated, just a couple of miles from the Soviet border. Yet no one in authority in Mongolia knew where we were, nor seemed to care. This was Kazakh land, and the Kazakh nomads came and went as they wished.

There was another yurt pitched a short distance away downslope, and a third against the side of the valley about a quarter of a mile off. During the next half-hour the Kazakh women began to emerge from them, and it was clear that an early snowfall would make no difference whatsoever to their daily chores. The women had muffled themselves in heavy felt boots and thick padded coats and wore large woollen scarves pulled tight around their heads. They pummeled and pushed the unhappy yaks to their tether lines and tied them up for milking. The wind keened past, whipping up little spirals of snow and lifting a light haze of snow crystals which streamed past the women at their work. Seated on small stools, they bowed their heads to keep the snow from their eyes, pushed their heads into the snowy flanks of the animals for shelter, and began to milk with their bare hands.

There was a sharp cold in the air, and an elderly shepherd came down from the farthest felt tent and began to trudge toward me. He was dressed in what I took to be the standard Kazakh coat, a long black corduroy overcoat with wide skirts that reached down to his heels. It was padded to keep out the wind, and on his head he wore the traditional Kazakh hat. The original bright crimson silk exterior had faded to a well-worn cherry pink. Two side flaps hung to his collar to keep his ears warm, and a long, square-cut rear flap protected his neck. The entire hat was lined with the fur from the legs of foxes, hand-stiched in bands to make a meticulous striped effect. The old shepherd was gaunt and black against the snow. His flock must have drifted away during the night blizzard, for the old man trudged off stoically across the wide snowfield to seek out his animals, his silhouette growing smaller and smaller in that huge sweep of land.

Camran pushed out of the red-painted yurt door behind me. He too was dressed in long black corduroy coat and scarlet hat, and a little spray of brown and dun feathers sprouted jauntily from the crown of his winter cap. They were owl feathers, a sign of good luck. He carried a saddle across his arm, and a bridle, and was on his way to his horse, which he had left overnight tied to a peg on a distant slope. Then he would ride across the ridge and retrieve his small horse-herd and bring them back across the mountain to be closer to the yurt. Later I saw him riding down the scree, driving about a dozen Kazakh horses before him. They were very little different from the Mongol horses, perhaps a little rangier and finer-boned.

In the early afternoon, with the snow beginning to melt, two men on horseback came riding up from the Kazakh yurts in the lower valley. They had heard about our visit to Camran and were coming to pay their respects and to gossip with Hojanias. They had also heard that I had been asking if there were any eagle hunters in the valley, and so each man made a splendid sight as he came cantering across the snow, carrying on his right arm a huge mountain eagle.

Carpini, Rubruck, Marco Polo—all the medieval travelers to the Mongol lands had noted the Mongols' passion for falconry. According to *The Secret History of the Mongols* it was how Yesugei the Brave, Genghis Khan's father, had loved to hunt in the valleys by Burkhan Khaldun, and falconry was an abiding passion of the Khakhans. The famous "pleasure dome" of Xanadu was surrounded by a nature park where Kubilai Khan, Genghis's grandson, loved to go hawking, and as Rubruck had said about his Mongol host:

> they have an abundance of gerfalcons which they uniformly carry on the right hand, and they always put a little thong around the falcon's neck which hangs down in the middle of his chest. When they cast him at the prey, they use this with the left hand to hold the falcon's head and chest at a downward angle, so that he is not hurled back by the wind or carried upwards.

During the interview with Rubruck, Khakhan Möngke had been caressing a favorite hunting bird, and when foreign ambassadors visited Karakorum they knew that the most pleasing and reliable gifts to bring were gyrfalcons for the royal mews.

Mongolia still swarms with birds of prey. Across the steppe and in the Hangay and Hentei we had seen hundreds of wild falcons and hawks thriving in the wilds. Kites swooped over our tents looking for scraps, and the mountains are the home for Mongolian mountain eagles similar to the golden eagle of the West. The semiofficial Mongolian directory even lists the peregrine falcon as a "cosmopolitan species" along with rat, mouse, sparrow, and housefly. But today the Mongols themselves have given up falconry, and it is left to the Kazakhs to carry on the tradition.

Their hunting eagles were majestic. Each bird was as big as a man's torso and weighed 13 or 14 pounds. They were so heavy that the riders used small wooden props reaching up from the saddle to support the carrying arm with its massive padded gauntlet. The hooded eagles swayed easily to the rhythm of the riders, twisting their heads to face any new sound. As the riders dismounted, the eagles shifted their stance and raised their wings to maintain their balance. Their wingspan was 5 or 6 feet, and they gave thin, high-pitched screeches. Camran now reappeared on foot. He too brought his eagle, which he had left for the night sitting on a nearby rock, and he gestured that I might like to hold it. I put on a heavy gauntlet and the superb bird was handed over. I could feel the powerful grip of the huge claws through the heavy padding of the glove, and Camran took my free left hand and brought it across so I could appreciate the massively muscled thighs of the bird. Just a foot away from my face the eagle turned its head nervously, this way and that, ducking and bobbing its head with its cruelly curved beak, a perfect stabbing and tearing weapon. The great bird was aware that he was riding on the arm of a stranger, and I was relieved that it was blind behind its hood.

The Kazakhs were immensely proud of their eagles, and although the hunting season did not start until October the birds were in peak condition. In the valley, they said, there were at least twenty men who owned hunting eagles, and more eagle hunters could be found in every other Altai group. In the autumn the Kazakhs would begin their hunting forays, riding out into the frozen land with their eagles on their arms in search of the eagle's natural prey. For the most part the eagles would be flown at fox and wolf, but the very bravest birds had been known to attack snow leopard and griffon.

Camran and the other eagle hunters were modest about their skills. It was not difficult to train an eagle, they said. The instinct of the birds was to hunt, and with patience and careful handling the mountain eagles were soon accustomed to hunt in company with humans. The owners took their birds from their nests as fledglings and then reared them by hand. As soon as they were strong enough, they were introduced to prey by being flown against rabbits. After that, they were ready. It all sounded far too easy, and I asked if there was any part of hunting with eagles that was difficult. To catch a fully grown wild eagle, Camran replied, that did take skill and cunning, but it was worth the effort. The wild eagles made better and braver hunters than birds that had been raised from fledglings, because they had learned to take their prey in the wild. I asked him how long it took to train a wild eagle to the hunt. Again Camran was quietly unassuming. About a week or ten days, he answered.

The Kazakhs loved their eagles and treated them well, and yet I could not help regretting that these magnificent birds should be restrained, even though they were well cared for and fed. Without knowing it, Camran responded to the thought. He was stroking his own eagle, preening its feathers. The eagle had its hood removed and was prancing on his arm and flapping its wings, now and again screeching its high piping call. "This eagle is three years old," Camran said. "I hope that it will hunt with me for many years, but if it gets tired I will release it early back into the mountains. When eagles grow old or if they are weary, we let them return to the mountains to live as free creatures."

Typically, Genghis Khan had perceived a practical use for Mongol hunting skills. Sweeps by teams of hunters had always given the Mongols an important supply of extra meat. On the steppe grazed deer of different species—gazelle, saiga with its strange bulbous nose, and musk deer. Also there were herds of kulan or wild asses whose flesh was edible and which were just as fleet of foot and difficult to approach. Individual hunters could stalk their prey or lie in ambush by the water holes, but the most effective method was the battue, or driven hunt. "They obtain a large proportion of their food by the chase," Rubruck noted. "When they intend to hunt wild animals, they gather in great numbers and surround the area where they know wild beasts are to be found, gradually converging until the animals are enclosed in the middle of a kind of circle; then they shoot them with their arrows."

Genghis Khan turned these small-scale battues into military training exercises on a monumental scale, in which every adult male was expected to take part as a form of war training. In advance of the operation, mounted scouts identified the size and position of the game herds, and a master huntsman selected and marked an eventual killing ground, which might be hundreds of miles away from the starting point. Then the Mongol men were sent in their military units to form a farflung cordon up to 75 miles in length, which swept across the country flushing out every living creature and driving the mass of animals before it.

Coordination and discipline had to be perfect. Foxes and even wolves were considered fair game and were caught up in the drive. The sweep might continue for weeks or even months, with sentries maintaining watch at night so that the wild animals did not slip out of the trap. A trooper who allowed even a single hare to double-back and escape through the cordon was severely punished. Signals, scouting, concealment, coordinated field maneuvers, speed of movement were all rehearsed and improved. On the battlefield the value of the Mongol soldier was much more than his endurance or personal courage. It was the extraordinary extent to which he was able to coordinate his efforts with his comrades and operate as part of an integrated team, and this ability was rehearsed again and again during the battle.

Gradually the cordon drove the animals toward the final killing ground where the Khakhan himself shot the first arrow into the mass of panic-stricken animals. This was the signal for the troopers to join in the slaughter. Echoing the Kazakh respect for their eagles' freedom, the Mongols did not kill every animal in the trap. When the Khakhan judged that enough animals had died, he gave the order for the arrow fire to stop, and the cordon opened so that the surviving game was allowed to escape back into the wild.

14

The Black Death

According to *The Secret History*, among the Mongol tribes living near Burkhan Khaldun at the time of Genghis Khan's rise to power was a people called the Orianghai. Rubruck heard about them as the people who strapped polished bones on their feet to skate or ski across the ice and snow of their remote fastness. Today the Orianghai represent only 1 percent of the population of Mongolia, and they are chiefly renowned for their skill as traditional singers and dancers. Their singing, called *hoomi* singing, is eerie. Technically classified as split-tone, it is usually performed by men, for it requires considerable muscular strength. The sounds are altered by varying the shapes of the mouth cavity, throat, chest, and abdomen to produce several voices simultaneously which are said to imitate the murmuring of streams and the sounds of wind in the mountains. Their frenzied dancing is done with a rapid shaking of the arms and shoulders. Groups of semi-nomadic Orianghai live in Bayan Olgei Province alongside the Kazakh, and in response to my request our Kazakh jeep driver promised that he would take Paul, Doc, and myself to an Orianghai camp not far from the Chinese frontier.

He drove us across some of the most unpromising terrain we had yet seen in the Altai. After leaving the Kazakh eagle hunters and dropping Hojanias back at his home, we embarked on a long, slow climb through a succession of stony valleys. The rock was a dismal slate color, and where it did not make jagged cliffs it had weathered down into sharp-edged pebbles which grated under the bald tires of the jeep. Traveling in a rickety jeep was less romantic than by horse, but it did mean that we could scour the countryside more effectively looking for the Orianghai, who proved to be elusive. At the best of times the region must have been inhospitable, but now there was no sign of life, only of death. Where our driver had expected to find Orianghai, not a single nomad was to be seen. Instead, around a rocky outcrop on the hillside, there lay the carcasses of fifteen or twenty sheep, lying in a neat swath where they had collapsed and died. They might have been killed by disease, but the total emptiness of the valley and the bare slopes told another story. Mongolia's rainfall is notoriously patchy, and whereas the Kazakhs with Camran had received a snowfall, here the valleys were in the grip of a severe drought. Our driver presumed that the Orianghai must have retreated away from their dying pastures and sought fresh grass in the highest valleys, so we bumped forward.

Eventually we climbed to a high ridge and on the far side found ourselves looking down into a broad natural bowl. The place was so bare that we might have been looking down into the crater of an extinct volcano. The dark-gray, steep sides of the bowl were devoid of vegetation. There was only scree and rock, and yet more slopes of sharp-edged pebbles. On the floor of the bowl a small, shallow lake was shriveling away into a mere skin of water. A border of cracked mud showed where the water had retreated, and that the lake was less than half its usual size. Across the far side of the valley a few patches on the hillside had a faint tinge of green. At every one of these spots were clusters of cattle and horses, bunched together unnaturally as they plucked hungrily at the few blades of grass. On the slope above the animals stood half a dozen felt tents. They were not tall enough to be Kazakh yurts, so they had to be the *gers* of Orianghai.

We drove down toward the small lake, passing two Orianghai herdsmen who were glumly driving a small herd of emaciated horses across the flat valley floor. We were 700 or 800 yards short of the lake when suddenly Doc called out to the driver to stop the jeep. He did so, and Doc told him to reverse carefully. Doc had pulled out a handkerchief and was holding it over his nose and peering anxiously over the side of the jeep. "Stop now! Stop!" he called out. "Don't go any further!" He was looking down at the ground and pointing with his free hand to what looked like a small raised mound about the size and shape of a molehill, with a hollow scooped out in the center. At first I could not see what he was so excited about, and then I noticed that there was something moving slightly in the hollow. My first reaction was that it was a dead fox, because the breeze was ruffling beautiful long, reddish-orange fur. "A marmot! It's dying," said Doc.

I could not understand why he was so worked up. There was indeed a marmot curled up in the top of the hollow, and perhaps it was dead, or on the point of death. But marmots were commonplace. We had seen hundreds upon hundreds of them everywhere in Mongolia. They were steppe rodents about the size of a small badger which sat bolt upright when they saw us riding by, whistled a warning, and then either watched us carefully until we were at a safe distance or, if they thought we were a danger, turned and darted into the security of their deep burrows. Those marmots we surprised feeding at a distance from their bolt-holes would scuttle for safety, humping across the ground rather like seals lolloping for the safety of an air hole on the pack ice. Colonel Prjevalski, who was a keen naturalist, had given a good description of how the tabargan, as the Mongols called it, spent its day:

Early in the morning as soon as the sun is up, and the air is a little warmed, it issues out of its habitation and scampers about feeding on the grass, not returning to its burrow, unless disturbed, till about ten o'clock where it remains till two or three in the afternoon, when it comes out and plays and feeds until sunset. This rule is of course not without exceptions but in rainy weather they may never stir above ground although the rain may last several days in succession. The marmot is sagacious and wary, especially when it is hunted by man. Before leaving its burrow it pokes its head out, and remains half an hour in this position to assure itself of safety. Then half its body may be seen, and again it listens and looks all round, and then only comes quite out and feeds on grass. If it notices danger, however far off, it immediately makes for its burrow, sits up on its hind legs and utters a loud, prolonged whistle. Then if the object of its fears approach nearer it conceals itself again below the ground. . . . The usual mode of killing these animals is by lying in wait for them near the burrow, hiding before they come above ground. They are remarkably tenacious of life, and will escape to their burrows even though mortally wounded, nothing but killing them outright will secure them for the hunter.

They begin to lie dormant in the second week in October, and like the European marmot a great many will congregate in one burrow.

Now, however, Doc was treating the corpse of the marmot as if it were a spitting cobra about to attack. It seemed very strange. After all, we had been eating baked marmot with Delger and Bayar only two weeks before.

"Don't get out of the jeep! Stay where you are!" warned Doc urgently, his voice muffled through the handkerchief held over his nose and mouth. "That marmot is very sick."

"What does that mean?" I asked him.

"It means that there is an outbreak of *pestes* in the valley, and we must warn the Orianghai immediately," he answered.

"*Pestes?*" Then I remembered my Latin. "Do you mean plague?" I asked.

"Yes," Doc confirmed. "Plague!"

There was no doubt that Doc was very alarmed. Paul certainly thought that he was overreacting and started to get out of the jeep to take a photograph. But Doc caught him by the arm, and it was the first time I had ever seen him really angry. "I told you. Don't go near the animal!" he ordered fiercely. "If you breathe the air near that marmot, you could die!" Paul, looking skeptical, sat back in his seat. I, too, was puzzled rather than alarmed. The marmot may indeed have been suffering from plague—which seemed extraordinary enough—but I had always thought that plague was transmitted by fleas and other parasites which transferred the sickness from rats, the carriers, to man. But this was a layman's view, and Doc seemed so intense that it was better to do as he said.

We promptly turned the jeep and drove back to the two herdsmen we had passed a few moments earlier. Doc spoke to them very seriously. Immediately they drove their horse-herd over to one side to avoid passing close to the dead marmot in its burrow. The country people, Doc told me, were so fearful of the plague that they believed you could catch the disease simply by breathing the contaminated air near a diseased marmot, and they gave all dead marmots a very wide berth. Their traditional belief is founded on the now scientifically proven fact that pneumonic plague can be transmitted aerogenically between humans by bacillus-carrying droplets expelled from the lungs.

Then we continued up to the Orianghai *gers*. The Orianghai established a small, rather scruffy camp on a bare patch of ground where the slope was not quite as steep as the rest of the valley. Physically the Orianghai looked just like other Mongols, and the camp itself had a sense of impermanence. It could not have been in position for more than two or three days, and ironically, in view of the drought, I noticed a small ditch had been freshly scooped around the nearest *ger* to divert run-off surface water. Apparently the previous evening a sudden downpour, the first for weeks, had swept through the tents causing damage and soaking all their possessions.

Nothing had been going right for the luckless Orianghai. They confirmed that there had been a severe drought for the past two months. Many of their cattle had already starved to death in the lower valley, and recently they had moved them up to the higher ground hoping to find more grass. Doc told them about the dead marmot and warned them that there was probably plague in the valley. The Orianghai looked even more despondent.

"They say it is the final blow," Doc translated. "Now they will have to abandon this valley too and try to find somewhere else for their herds. But the grazing season is almost over, and there is no pasture left. They said it is the third of their misfortunes."

"I know about drought and plague," I said, "but what is the third misfortune?"

"Look by your feet."

I looked down and saw dozens and dozens of grasshoppers crawling among the pebbles and small stones.

"Locusts. They are destroying what little grass there is left," said Doc.

It seemed as if the biblical plagues of Egypt were being visited on the hapless Orianghai, but all at one time and in one place.

There was no point in our lingering there with the Orianghai. The news of the dead marmot had cast a pall. They would move out next morning, they told us, and leave that doomed area. Doc was also eager to get out of the vicinity, and at once. He feared that as soon as the local authorities discovered there was plague in the valley, they would quarantine the area. In that case, we would be obliged to stay in the valley, forbidden to travel, for at least another month. It was better, he said, that we get ourselves farther west. The Orianghai had already seen other carcasses in the valley; small rodents as well as cattle were dying. I suspected that the cattle were dying from starvation rather than disease, but the deaths of the mice and rats could have been connected with the outbreak of plague, which, if I guessed rightly, was better known in the West as the Black Death.

As we left the valley, Doc confirmed my suspicions. He listed the classic symptoms of the illness he called *pestes*—high fever, shivering, swelling glands especially in the armpit and groin which produced an agonizing, tearing pain, giddiness so that the unfortunate victims staggered as if drunk, and delirium. Death came usually within ten days. The signs Doc enumerated were very similar to the sufferings of the plague victims described by writers in the 14th century when an estimated twenty-five million people in Europe perished from the Black Death. The standard explanation for the arrival of the Black Death in Europe was that it had been brought by diseased rats aboard ships. The first Western reports of the Black Death actually came in 1347. It broke out among the troops of the Kipchak khan, ruler of one of the fragments of the disintegrating Mongol empire. His army was besieging the Black Sea port of Kaffa when it was ravaged by the plague. In one of the first recorded instances of biological warfare, the Khan ordered his siege artillery to fling infected corpses over the city walls. The Black Death broke out in the city and was duly carried back to Europe by Genoese vessels trading in the port.

Now the shock of discovering that the Black Death still survived in the very heart of the continent, far from any seaports, made me wonder if the accusation against the carrier rats and mice was the full story of the onslaught of the dreadful disease which roared across Europe in what has been rated the worst calamity experienced by the Western world at that time. The French historian Froissart calculated that one-third of the population died. In some regions as many as three out of every four inhabitants succumbed, and Europe's population did not return to its previous levels until the early 16th century.

The illness occurred only in summer, Doc explained, usually breaking out in late July or early August and subsiding in the autumn. The *arats* called it "marmot sickness" and were well aware that the disease was somehow connected with the appearance of sick and dying marmots. The disease was so virulent that it had been known to decimate the summer communities of nomads and wipe out entire families. Apparently it could strike any area of the country, and without warning. So by tradition a precautionary formula had developed for approaching isolated *gers* during the danger season: Arriving at a strange *ger* no one should dismount from horseback but wait instead at a safe distance and call out loudly "Tie up the dog! Tie up the dog!" If someone emerged from the *ger*, then it was safe to come closer. But if nobody appeared from the door of the felt tent, then it was a warning that there could be sickness inside and perhaps the occupants lay dead. In that case the custom was to turn one's horse and ride away without staying a moment longer than necessary because the disease was so contagious. If by chance there were survivors in a *ger* where plague had struck, then it was their duty to close the ventilation flap at the top of the *ger* and leave the tail end of the rope that normally controlled the vent panel hanging across the door. This was the warning for all visitors to stay clear for fear of infection.

We spent two more days in the region, venturing to within five miles of the Chinese border. We were discreet, because officially we were in a forbidden zone, but I wanted to locate the Sixth Brigade. This was not a military formation but a *somon*'s work brigade, the field group sent out to summer pasture. The Sixth Brigade was said to be camped near the border for the summer. Doc had picked up a rumor that witch-doctor shamans were living among the herdsmen, but it was a false report; the Sixth proved to be a perfectly ordinary work brigade of Kazakhs looking after their commune's flocks and herds on the bare, windswept Altai plateau, their grazing land overlooked by small, rather grimy glaciers which clung to the crests of the dividing range between China and Mongolia.

The humble equipment around each yurt was a summary of nomad life—a makeshift wooden rack on which small blocks of curd were drying, a couple of logs to provide wood chips to start the fire in the stove, the main fuel supply of yak dung kept dry under a piece of tarpaulin, and a few sheepskins drying on a pole. Sometimes there was a hunting eagle perched on a rock. The carpet of animal droppings told you all you needed to know about their livelihood—the larger cow pats of the yaks and hainags, the medium-sized turds of sheep, and the tiny pellets of small goats. The only surprise was to note that the birdlife was dominated by seabirds. Gulls, terns, and cormorants had traveled immense distances along the river systems to finish up in the tangled knot of the Altai highlands in the very heart of the landmass.

The World Health Organization has an office in Ulaan Baatar whose responsibility is to monitor the presence of communicable and dangerous diseases. The following week, when Paul, Doc, and I had returned to Ulaan Baatar from our venture into the Altai after completing our research there, I lost no time in contacting the WHO officials for further information about the continuing existence of plague in modern Mongolia. By international agreement plague is rated as one of the most pathogenic and lethal diseases in the world, and it was the duty of the WHO office to report its presence in Mongolia. But when I telephoned to ask for information, the WHO office was evasive and refused to comment. They were not able to give any data, and told me that I should better address my questions to the Ministry of Public Health.

Once again Doc knew what to do. He knew personally the medical doctor who had recently been appointed as Minister of Health in the government reform program. We were walking toward the Ministry of Public Health building to make an appointment to see him when we met the new Minister himself, hurrying along the pavement. Yes of course, he said at once, he could spare us time to discuss the matter of plague.

Dr. Nymadawa was another of the new style of Mongolian administrators. He was well informed, decisive, and very frank. He also had a wry sense of humor. "If you had come a year ago to ask me about plague in Mongolia," he said in his excellent English, "I would have had to reply to you that it did not exist in our country. That it was impossible for such a dangerous disease to survive in a socialist society after so many decades of improving health care, and that plague had been eradicated long ago. But now, with glasnost, it is more helpful to tell the truth, because this is a subject where we need to have Western help. Yes, we do have plague in Mongolia, it is endemic, and we believe that the live vaccines which we get from the

Soviet Union are not as effective as they should be. I have read that there are dead vaccines made in the West which offer better protection. It would help if we could inoculate people living in the very high-risk areas or as soon as an outbreak was reported in any particular region, but it would still be very difficult to reach all families in time to treat them, as their camps are so widely scattered during the summer grazing season. Let me show you the extent of the problem."

An aide produced the plague file. The first document was a map that showed the areas of Mongolia where plague had been reported, either as a disease in animals or where there had been human victims of the illness. Regions where plague was endemic were colored light green; the places where there had been reported cases of human plague were shaded dark green. Starkly, the pale-green belt with its dark-green blobs extended in a broad sweep along the entire width of Mongolia. No less than 60 percent of the land surface of Mongolia, the Minister revealed, served as a natural reservoir of plague. It was, as he pointed out, a major plague zone.

The Minister was also very forthcoming with the fearful details. *Pestes* is one of the group of diseases internationally classified as Very Infectious. Because it has a very high pathogenic potential, it is also designated as Quarantinable, along with cholera and yellow fever. Because Mongolia is particularly vulnerable to outbreaks of plague, a central Institute for Contagious Diseases has been established in Ulaan Baatar which is particularly concerned with *pestes*, and the public-health office in each *aymag* maintains a section for Quarantinable Diseases. In essence, their job is to watch out for plague and report it whenever it occurs.

The problem, as the Minister pointed out, is that the disease is virtually impossible to stamp out because it is held in the almost limitless reservoir of the resident population of wild rodents. The carriers are marmots, steppe dogs, which are the equivalent of North American prairie dogs, and certain mice and rats. Even hamsters and gerbils can be infected. Nearly all these species live in burrows and hibernate, so they are impossible to root out. The disease itself can spread from burrow to burrow and, as Prjevalski had noted, the marmots live densely packed in their underground homes, further spreading the contagion. The best the Ministry of Public Health can do is to send out field teams every spring to locations where plague has previously occurred. Here they shoot or trap the carrier animals and test them for plague. If they find fresh plague signs, local warnings are issued and, in particular, hunting for marmots is banned. But of course the country is simply too vast for the whole of the reservoir area to be checked in this way, and so local plague spots may go unreported, and there are many herdsmen living in such isolation that they simply do not receive the warnings. To alert the city population to the plague danger, the government has started transmitting plague alerts on television, using simple little sequences showing a warning cross drawn over pictures of sick marmots. But the herdsmen do not possess television sets.

The Minister gave a recent and macabre example of how easily matters could go wrong. Early the previous month a boy from a herdsman's family had handled a marmot which his dog had caught alive. The lad had taken the marmot to his parents, who lived in one of an isolated group of three *gers*. They decided to keep the animal for its fur and skinned it. About a week later, several members of the family began to suffer from fever and severe headaches. But instead of reporting this sickness to the authorities, they decided to conceal the matter, because the marmot had been caught and killed outside the official marmot hunting season and they were frightened of getting into trouble. The result was that the fever spread rapidly throughout the group of three *gers*. There were often fifteen people living in the *gers*, and eleven contracted the disease. Of those eleven, five had died.

"That shows just how dangerous and how contagious the disease is," commented the Minister, "and it followed the classic pattern—a seven-day incubation period, followed by fever, and soon afterwards the deaths begin. If the disease is not treated in the first two or three days with antibiotics or sulfa drugs, then the result is almost certain death."

The worst outbreak of plague in recent times was in 1910 and 1911, when the so-called "Manchurian Plague" flared across northern China. Sixty thousand people perished, and poor communications and inadequate reporting meant that many thousands more deaths went unrecorded. The Manchurian Plague was *pestes*, or the Black Death, and contemporary research showed that it had originated in Mongolia and had been carried into North China along the caravan roads. A Russian doctor by the name of Zablotny had studied the progress and vector of the disease and had confirmed that it was resident in the population of the marmots, steppe dogs, mice, and rats, and that it was usually transmitted by the insect parasites that fed on the diseased animals and then bit and infected humans. The Manchurian Plague had spread like wildfire because it had also infected the lungs of the victims and had then been spread by air droplets. A further outbreak in 1947 had occurred in Inner Mongolia, when 30,000 people were infected, of whom 23,000 died. "You will be relieved to know that you cannot contract plague by eating marmot," Dr. Nymadawa said with a grin, "as I believe you have done . . . particularly if it is well boiled."

Some of the popular folklore about the plague was based on accurate observation. For instance, the Mongol *arats* knew long before Zablotny confirmed the fact scientifically that marmots were the main culprits. In fact the Mongol name for plague was "marmot sickness" and it had been known by this description since the time of Genghis Khan. All Mongol herdsmen knew that the presence of sick and dying marmots and the arrival of carrion birds to feed on their carcasses was a warning to stay away from the region for fear of contracting plague. Nor did any marmot hunter touch an animal that showed signs of being drowsy or was not fully alert, in case it was already in the early stages of the disease. For this reason the traditional method of marmot hunting was very special. The marmot hunters dressed in white overclothing and carried a small white flag on a short stick which they flicked back and forth as they crawled toward the marmot at the lip of its burrow. An alert and healthy marmot would immediately stand upright and watch the strange white apparition as it approached. A curious marmot would be fascinated by the flapping of the white flag, and the attraction was fatal. The hunter came within arrow range and killed his prey, knowing that he had dispatched a disease-free animal. "But now," the Minister observed a little sadly, "things have changed. There are city folk who drive out in a jeep, and simply shoot the marmot from the vehicle using a high power rifle, not knowing if it is alert or not. As for the boy whose family was infected, it is almost certain that his dog was able to catch the marmot because the animal was too diseased to run away."

The Minister then let slip an intriguing detail. His health officials regularly tested samples of the plague bacillus taken from the diseased animals. They had found that the samples they took from mice and steppe dogs were less virulent than samples taken from marmots. The plague carried by rats and mice seemed to be more akin to the milder "urban plague" reported from Southeast Asia. It was infectious and harmful but not so fatal to humans. On the other hand, the samples taken from marmots were highly pathogenic. The conclusion was that the zoobiotic reservoir of the Black Death was among the marmots, rather than among smaller rats and mice.

Two other items of scientific evidence modified the standard explanation of the spread of Black Death. In the first place it had been shown beyond all doubt that the plague bacillus was extraordinarily resilient. For example, the plague organisms were known to survive in dried human sputum for as long as three months, and under laboratory conditions they retained their characteristics in low temperatures for up to ten years. Secondly, the carriers that spread the disease could be animals, but equally they could be infected humans or the fleas themselves. A flea, for example, which sucked the blood of an infected marmot might retain the deadly bacillus in its mouth or gut for at least a month or even longer. Thus fleas infected in October could transmit the disease the following March. The disease could also be passed from human to human, either by air droplets as had happened in Manchuria, the pneumonic version of the disease, or by a parasite which fed on one diseased human victim and then carried the bacillus to the next human whose blood it sucked.

As the Minister pointed out, the Black Death or "marmot sickness" was not restricted to Mongolia but was found in a broad belt of country across the steppes of Asia wherever marmots lived. In the previous year a death by plague had been reported in Soviet Kazakhstan, 1250 miles closer to Europe, and in 1878 there had been an outbreak of plague on the lower Volga. A generation after Genghis Khan, Rubruck reported that "there are plenty of marmots there, which in those parts they call *sogur** and of which in winter twenty or thirty at a time collect in one hole and sleep for six months: of these they catch a great number." He also recorded the fact that whenever a Mongol was very sick, a warning sign was put up over his tent advising that it contained an ill person and that no one should

---

*An example of one of the Turkish, not Mongol, words Rubruck picked up.

enter. In view of my conversation with Dr. Nymadawa, Rubruck's observation now sounded to me very similar to the description of the quarantine precautions practiced by modern *arats*.

Certainly there was plague in Central Asia in the Middle Ages. Archaeologists working near Lake Issyk kul to the west of the Altai had found the graves of people who had died of an outbreak of the disease in the early 14th century. To the eastward there were outbreaks of devastating diseases in China in 1331 and again in the middle of the same century which historians had suspected could well have been bubonic plague. One scholar of diseases, W. H. McNeill,* had already speculated that there was a link between the spread of the Black Death and the expansion of the Mongol empire. Now the firsthand evidence of how the plague still managed to survive and spread in Mongolia, and how the *arats'* response was ingrained in their culture, supported a straightforward conclusion: The Black Death's murderous journey to Europe had been more by land than by sea. Infected humans and their body parasites, more than rats or mice, had carried the plague from Central Asia to Europe. The major and ineradicable reservoir of the Black Death was among the marmots of Central Asia, and it is likely that it was the Mongol armies and the merchants who traveled under Mongol protection who brought the most lethal version of the disease to the West. Thus, the legend of Genghis Khan as the warmongering destroyer of civilization is misleading. His armies may have produced havoc and destruction across two-thirds of the known world, but that was nothing compared to this ghastly legacy, a nightmare they themselves had suffered. Unwittingly the Mongols and their allies had inflicted the Black Death on Europe.

*W. H. McNeill, *Plagues and Peoples*, Oxford, 1976.

15

Shamaness

My search to find a living shaman did not end with the fruit-less visit to the Sixth Brigade near the Chinese border. Although I thought it very unlikely that genuine sha-manism—the belief in, and communication with, the spirits dwelling in earth, sky, rocks, streams, winds, and forests which had been widespread until the arrival of communism—was still practiced in Mongolia, I was prepared to track down even the most unpromising rumor. It seemed to me that if a shaman did exist, he or she must surely be the last survivor of what had been an intriguing element of the world of Genghis Khan.

Shamanism had been central to the phenomenon of Mongolia's imperial expansion. The Mongols liked to claim that it was Tengri, the shamans' Universal Sky God, who had authorized Genghis Khan to go out and conquer the world, and there is reason to believe that Genghis Khan himself had been a shaman. When he heard about the massacre of his caravan at Otrar, for example, he had withdrawn alone to a mountain for three days, a typical shaman's retreat, to commune with the gods. As churchmen, Carpini and Rubruck had both commented on the numbers of shamans—"soothsayers" as they liked to call them, though they might equally have been described as spirit lords and spell-casters—who clustered about the imperial camp and attended the royal ancestor images. Rubruck, in particular, had watched the camp shamans at work:

Soothsayers are constantly to be found outside the court of Mangu and other wealthy people (the poor do not have them)—those, that is, who are of the stock of Genghis. . . . They deliberate where the camp is to be pitched and they unload their own dwellings first of all, the rest of the camp following. On an occasion when it is a feast day or the first of the month, they produce the effigies that I have mentioned and arrange them methodically in a circle in their dwelling. Then the Mo'al [Mongols] arrive, and enter their dwelling, bowing to the effigies and worshipping them. No outsider is allowed to enter the dwelling: once I wanted to go in and was given a very sharp reprimand.

Thanks to his curiosity, Rubruck was the only Westerner to record in any detail the original shaman rites of the Mongols, and his tales amount to a mosaic of the occult and charlatanism. Apparently the chief shaman was also the court astrologer, and he predicted the times of the eclipses of the sun and moon. During the actual eclipses the entire population hid in their tents and made a tremendous din with drums and instruments, presumably to scare off the evil spirits, and once the eclipse was over they emerged and held a great feast of rejoicing. When someone died, the shamans had to conduct purification ceremonies, carrying all the dead person's effects and bedding between two fires to purge them of evil. They officiated at the major festivals, particularly the great First Mare's Milk Festival held on the ninth day of May, when the white mares from the horse-herds were gathered together to be blessed and thank offerings of the season's first *ayrag* were sprinkled in the air. Shamans, Rubruck believed, were able to influence the weather, and they were consulted as healers when someone was sick or dying. He detailed one incident which seemed pure quackery when a Mongol noblewoman fell ill with shooting pains through various parts of her body. The shamans were called in and:

sitting at a distance ordered one of her maids to put her hand over a painful spot and to remove anything she might find. So she got up and did so, and discovered in her hand a piece of felt or some other material. They thereupon told her to put it on the ground; and on being laid there it began to crawl like some live creature. Next it was put in water and turned into a kind of leech.

Rubruck feared that the shamans also had direct communication with demons, for he heard tales of how they gathered in a *ger* at night with those who wanted to consult with the devils. A dish of meat was placed in the middle of the tent, and the chief shaman "who issues the summons begins uttering his incantations and holds a tambourine which he bangs heavily on the ground. At length he falls into a frenzy and has himself tied up; and then the demon appears in the darkness and gives him the meat to eat, and he utters oracles." Rubruck himself could not witness such scenes, because if a Christian was in the audience the demon sat on the top of the dwelling and cried out that he could not enter.

Even as Doc, Paul, and I were putting a prudent distance between ourselves and the plague outbreak among the Orianghai I was still hoping that in such a remote corner of the country it might be possible that shamanism still continued. Shaman-soothsayers were still active at the court of Pi-Yin, the last Chinese emperor, at the beginning of this century, performing rituals and divination, and in Ulaan Baatar I had heard a rumor of an old woman, a shamaness, who lived some-where in the Altai in Bayan Olgei province. She had been acknowl-edged as a seer and had been visited many years ago, some said at least twenty years earlier, by a well-known Mongolian poet who had written about her mystic powers. According to her reputation she knew the ancient rituals, could predict the future, and could cure the sick. But whether she was still alive, and if so where in Bayan Olgei province she lived, no one could tell me. The only course was to keep on asking the local people.

The first clue, which had come in the town of Olgei itself, seemed to be a dead end. This was when we were told that the Sixth Brigade had shamans. But although the information was misleading, it at least took us through Tsengel, a small settlement at the foot of the mountains which had the air of a frontier town in the American West. In Tsengel it was grizzled Kazakhs in fur-lined pink satin hats and long-skirted corduroy coats rather than trappers in buckskins who stalked along the main street, leading their pack-ponies loaded with bags of flour and provisions before they headed back into the moun-tains. Here Doc again inquired about the rumored shamaness, and the initial response was discouraging. Yes, there had been a shamaness in the area, but she was very old and as far as anyone knew she had died or withdrawn into the mountains to find a lonely spot to end her days. In either case we would never find her.

One fact, however, was useful. It turned out that the shamaness was neither Kazakh nor Orianghai, but belonged to the Tuva people. Many ethnographers consider that the Orianghai and the Tuva are one and the same people under different names, but as far as the ordinary Kazakh or Mongol is concerned this is not the case. They regard the 25,000 Orianghai who live in Mongolia and use mostly Mongol words in their speech as being Mongols, while the people they call Tuva are more closely associated with their tribal cousins across the border in the Tuva Associated Socialist Republic of the USSR, who speak their own Turkic language of Tuvinian. As with the Kazakhs, I got the impression that the handful of Tuva artificially isolated within Mongolia had retained their ancient customs more faithfully than their fellow tribesmen in the Soviet Union. In the past the Tuva combined all three ways of life characteristic of Central Asia—herding sheep and cattle on the mountains, growing millet in the valleys of the upper Yenesi River, and in the north raising reindeer which they saddled and rode like horses. What was more encouraging from my point of view was that the Tuva homelands included the Siberian forests, the heartland of Asian shamanism.

The Tuva of Bayan Olgei, we were warned, were reticent with strangers and kept to themselves. There was, however, one Tuva, by the name of Magsa, who had recently retired from a career in the government service, and he might be prepared to help us with our inquiries. Fortunately the Kazakh driver of our jeep, who seemed to know everyone in the region, was acquainted with Magsa and thought that he could take Paul, Doc, and me to his camp, which he shared with a small group of fellow tribesmen in the valley they called the Valley of Mirages.

The Tuva deserved their reputation for closeness. Halfway along the valley we stopped at a Tuva felt tent to inquire where we might find Magsa, the retired civil servant. Our reception was chilly. There was no man in sight, and the Tuva woman who was outside the tent doing her wash in a tin bowl curtly waved us to enter her *ger*. For the next ten minutes she ignored us completely. She then came into the *ger* and dumped a bowl of stale bread in front of us and wordlessly handed out some rancid milk. After that she stumped out the door and continued doing her work, paying us no further attention. It was only with great tact that Doc managed to coax her into giving directions.

Magsa's *ger* was a couple of miles farther on, perched at the upper end of a steep side valley above a line of Kazakh yurts which had been set along the narrow stream bed. The interior was half-Mongol and half-Kazakh. The animal figures on the little wall hangings were Mongol in character and style, but the floor was spread with embroidered Kazakh rugs. On the low table was Kazakh bread and a Kazakh type of boiled and dried curd like lumps of yellow pumice, but also a typically Mongol mixture of sugar lumps, biscuits, and clotted cream. Magsa himself was distantly polite rather than welcoming, and his attitude was explained when he asked us rather wearily if we wanted the family to put on their national costume for photographs. It seemed that for the past year the Tuva minority in Mongolia had been attracting media attention. Japanese and Mongolian journalists and a television team had recently come to the valley to interview them and had disrupted their lives. Magsa, I suspected, felt that he and his people were being treated as curios and resented the fact.

To try to overcome this poor start I asked Doc to explain that we had come there only because we were interested in any traditions which survived from the days of Genghis Khan, and that we had been riding through the Hentei and Hangay with the herdsmen as part of our research. This seemed to impress Magsa, and he began to be more cooperative.

As he talked about the Tuva, I began to sense that Magsa's people had retained more of the medieval traditions than any other people we had met in Mongolia. For example, when Magsa was a child his Tuva family still regarded the hearth fire as sacred. The fire was one of the most precious elements in their lives and had to be treated with respect. No one was allowed to burn rubbish in its flames, and if that happened by some accident it was believed that a calamity would befall the house. Magsa cited the Tuvan belief that if old onion skins were thrown on the fire, the owner's horses would all go blind. Also the Tuva considered it very bad luck to put a knife near the flames, just as seven centuries earlier Carpini had noted of the Mongols that "there are certain traditional things, invented by them or their ancestors, which they say are sins: for example to stick a knife into the fire or even in any way to touch fire with a knife."

Once a year Magsa's family held a ceremony to relight and bless the central flame in their *ger*. On that day the brazier was smeared with butter, and its legs decorated with red ribbon. Then incense was placed on the coals, and the brazier was carried outside the *ger* so that all the cattle could be led through the smoke in order to purify them and cure them of disease, because fire had the magic property of driving away evil. It was precisely the same purification ritual that Carpini had described, and he himself had been exposed to similar treatment when he arrived at the pavilion of Batu Khan, Genghis's grandson. He was obliged to walk between two fires as he approached the imperial pavilion, and when he asked why it was necessary, the palace guards had told him: "Go without any fear, for we are making you pass between two fires for no other reason than this, if you are planning to do any evil to our lord, or if you happen to be carrying poison, the fire will remove all that is harmful." Carpini's interpreter had been made to leave his weapons outside the imperial tent, and Tuva etiquette as Magsa described it still had a similar suspicion of visitors. It was good manners, he explained, to dismount some distance from the *ger* even when arriving in response to an invitation, and to wait until your host came out to greet you. If the visitor was carrying a rifle he should put it down well away from the door, and if he had a knife in his belt he should remove it and let it dangle where it was clearly visible outside his left boot. He then entered the *ger* from the right side, pushed open the door with his right hand, and was seated on the right-hand side.

Finally I asked Magsa if he knew any shamans, and he took the question as completely normal. It was as if I had asked him to recommend the name of a good doctor or dentist. He knew of two shamans, he replied, and they were both women. But one had recently moved away with her family and gone to live in another *aymag*, and since that time he had not heard anything more about her. However, the other shaman was still living locally and practicing her craft. But she was very old and would not last much longer. Very few people knew her real name. They just called her Samga, "The Old Woman." When she died, the local people would be at a loss, because many Kazakhs and Tuva consulted her about their marriage prospects, financial matters, personal problems and above all to ask her to cure their sickness. Then would she be the last of the local Tuva shamans? I asked. Magsa shrugged and seemed unworried. Perhaps, because there were no young shamans as far as he knew. But shamans nearly always came from the same families, and their mystic power passed down through the same bloodline, so maybe another shaman might be born one day, possibly skipping a generation. If that happened, then the shaman power would reveal itself once again, either in a man or a woman, because gender made no difference to the manifestation of the shaman power.

The Old Woman had not gone up into the mountains with her family as we had been told in Tsengel. In fact she was probably too frail to make the arduous trek to the high ground, and we would find her on the outskirts of the town in the home she used in winter. Before I left, I asked Magsa why the valley was called the Valley of Mirages. Because at certain times when you look down the valley it appears to be filled with a lake covered with lashing waves, he replied with equal composure.

We thanked Magsa and went back down the slope, only to be intercepted by a covey of children running out from the Kazakh yurts lower down the hill. Please would we stop for a moment? Their parents had never laid eyes on a Westerner before and wanted to know what we looked like. A crowd of adult Kazakhs emerged and clustered around the jeep, gazing in. Doc chortled. "They are very disappointed. They say you look just like Russians."

In Genghis Khan's time the shamans had wielded great power and commanded considerable prestige. Besides serving as intermediaries between the ordinary Mongol and the ninety-nine great spirits which ruled the firmament, shamans were also prophets and even political advisers. The most ambitious of them, a head shaman by the name of Teb-tengri, grew so prominent that Genghis Khan feared him as a rival and arranged for him to be assassinated. Teb-tengri was tricked into a wrestling match and had his back broken by three muscular thugs. His corpse was then placed in a small *ger* and the door was wedged shut and guarded. Three nights later, according to *The Secret History of the Mongols*, the body and spirit of Teb-tengri had fled the *ger* through the smoke hole in the roof. When the door was opened, it was found that his corpse had vanished, thereby proving that the shaman even when dead had the power to fly through the air and ascend into the blue eternal heaven to consult with the gods.

Given that shamans had such a picturesque history, I began to have second thoughts about whether I really wanted to find Samga.

Perhaps she would turn out to be a charlatan and a disappointment, and I was naïve to expect that I would find a real shamaness in modern Mongolia. Perhaps such colorful mystique was best left alone, because I knew that I would have to approach the subject with a degree of skepticism.

Our initial contact with Samga increased my doubts. We tracked her down to a cluster of four rather humble yurts a short distance out of Tsengel. A Tuva man about 30 years old, neatly dressed in a suit, came to the door of one of the yurts and told us that he was sorry but Samga was indisposed and unable to see us. That morning she had seen some visitors who had come to consult her. Now she was sleeping off the effects. "Samga is my grandmother," said the man frankly, "and she has a very bad hangover. People bring *arkhi* as a gift for her, and she loves to drink, maybe up to two liters a day. It helps in her work. Normally she needs a full day to recover. It would be better if you came back tomorrow. I will tell my grandmother to expect you, and I will make sure that everything is ready for you."

Odd though it seemed, Samga's alcoholic binge could be explained. Historically shamans employed stimulants or deprivation to induce their trances. They ate hallucinogenic plants, inhaled smoke, exposed themselves to extremes of heat and cold, starved themselves, or took alcohol. Also they repeated chants over and over again, or beat steady rhythms on drums and tambourines to create a self-hypnosis.

The following morning we returned, still not knowing what to expect beyond the fact that our alleged shamaness was very old and very alcoholic. It was one of those insipid days when, although there was not a single cloud, the blue of the sky seemed washed out and pale, and the horizon of the mountains appeared distant and ill-defined. Nor was there anything remarkable about the little group of *gers* where she lived. The felt tents were pitched on bare ground about a mile from the edge of town where a low rise gave a view over Tsengel and its river flowing through a grove of tall trees, providing an unusual block of dark green in that otherwise treeless and muted landscape. Behind the smallest *ger* was a small corral for sheep, but it was empty, and there was no one to be seen except two toddlers and, off to one side, a very ordinary-looking woman in a purple *del* crouching on the ground over a large soot-blackened cooking bowl, which she was giving a vigorous scrubbing. I glanced at her for a moment, wondering if she was the famous shamaness, but dismissed the idea. She did not look old enough and was certainly far too normal, busily getting on with the everyday chores. She gave me a cheerful toothless smile in return and straightened up slowly before hobbling off into a small tatty *ger*.

Doc found the grandson, who was now dressed in a very colorful Tuva national costume. It turned out that he was a high-school teacher who taught both Russian and Tuva, and he would be happy to be our interpreter if we wanted to interview his grandmother, because she spoke only Tuvinian and did not know either Mongol or Kazakh. His offer of help was a great bonus for us as he was well educated, and I had been concerned that my questions for Samga would founder in the translation. I had certainly not expected to find how thoroughly normal everything was. There was no sense of awe or mumbo-jumbo. It was simply that Samga was a shamaness, everybody accepted the fact, and we had come to see her.

Yet I still hesitated. I was uncertain about putting my questions to an old lady who was perhaps being manipulated by her family. Also I feared that my curiosity would be seen as an intrusion, and if I was skeptical it would be taken as an affront. My qualms began to subside as I saw the evident pride and affection the family had for their Old Woman. I had half-anticipated that we would hold an interview in a gloomy tent, suitably mysterious, or huddled privately in a corner. But now Samga's extended family began to emerge from the *gers*. There was her careworn daughter, a pair of great-nephews, and a swarm of giggling children. Most of them had taken the trouble to dress up in their traditional costume as if on a national holiday, and they were obviously delighted that we had come. Excitedly they escorted us to the small *ger*, and we all crammed inside to find that the pot-scrubbing woman was indeed Samga. She was sitting on a bed, hands folded in her lap, and looked at us expectantly while all the children scrambled to find places sitting on the ground in a circle round the edge of the *ger*. They gazed at us in wonder, and it was very obvious that two pale-skinned foreigners were far more exotic than a great-grandmother who was a witch-doctor.

Samga was ancient enough, though she did not look her full 86 years. She was stooped and her face was deeply lined, and she had a wide mouth with a single tooth in the right upper jaw exactly like a witch's fang in an illustrated book of children's stories. A row of empty *arkhi* bottles on the cheap dresser beside her testified to her alcoholism, and there were other signs of someone who drank far too much. Her eyes were rheumy, and her hands shook as she repeatedly took hefty pinches of snuff from a little blue cotton bag. It was clear that when her family talked about getting her ready to meet us, it meant that they had to sober her up and wait for her hangover to subside. She was also very deaf, and her grandson took up his position sitting on the ground beside her, where he could lean against her knee and relay my questions in a loud shout. Conditions could hardly have been less suitable for chicanery, and as Samga talked, regarding me with a quizzical, almost amused expression, I found my misgivings ebbing away.

To put her at ease I began by asking about her family, and like any normal great-grandmother she was pleased to list them and their accomplishments. She had given birth to fifteen children of her own and had adopted a sixteenth. Out of the total, only two had been sons, and seven were still alive. She was very pleased that one of them had been elected a people's deputy of the Hural, Mongolia's parliament, and another had been decorated as a Labor Hero. I found it odd, to say the least, to hear a shamaness with her medieval heritage recounting her children's contribution to modern communism, but then I was in for several more surprises. I asked her how many grandchildren and great-grandchildren she now had. "At least sixty or seventy," she replied with a definite twinkle in her eye, "but I can't keep track."

Turning the subject to her own childhood, I asked her how and when she had first known that she possessed shamanistic powers. It was a key question, because the standard authorities on shamanism state that a shaman's training was normally done by elder shamans who channeled and developed their pupil's natural psychic gifts.

She began by saying that she had been instructed by two great Tuva shamans, and she could give me their names. They were Chengelay and Magnai. These two had taught her, as had her father, Dorj, who was also a shaman but had not played a major part in her training. From Dorj she had inherited the power itself, but it was the other two shamans who had really taught her how to use it. I asked how they had schooled her, but the answer was vague. They had told her the chants and spells and encouraged her, she said. How old had she been when she realized she possessed shaman's powers, and how had she known? "I was thirteen," she answered, and then suddenly she stood up from the bed and gave three or four double hops, shuffling forward, ungainly in her heavy felt boots. Seeing that I was puzzled, she gave a cackling laugh and explained. "It was the energy in my body. I could not stay still as a child. I did not sleep at nights. I had to run. I would be shut up at night in my *ger*, but I would climb out through the smoke hole, and run and run. I loved to run at night, to climb trees, and to imitate the owls. No one could catch me because I ran so quickly, and sometimes they let loose the dogs to hunt me down. But they could not catch me."

A doctor might have said that she was describing a hyperactive childhood, but Samga had—unprompted—offered particulars that authorities on shamanism have long identified as classic elements in shaman behavior and that she could not have been expected to know in such detail. The frantic energy and the urge to climb were typical. Shamanistic initiation ceremonies normally culminated with the new shaman climbing up a pole to symbolize the ability to climb to meet the sky spirits. Entering and leaving the *ger* by the smoke hole in the roof was also very characteristic. According to *The Secret History of the Mongols*, not only had Teb-tengri's ghost fled this way, but one of Genghis Khan's ancestors was the magic child of a beam of yellow light which came down through the *ger* smoke hole and entered the belly of a Mongol woman. Literature was full of tales of shamans who could fly through the air, yet Samga was illiterate and spoke a language that had no script of its own. Possibly she had learned some of the information from conversation with educated Tuva-speaking informants, but that seemed an unlikely source. Her explanation and the way she expressed herself appeared authentic and without guile.

Samga's daughter passed the old lady a small tumbler of *arkhi*, and she took it eagerly and gulped it down. She was beginning to remember more of her childhood and youth. "There was another shaman—Kuzhuk—he also taught me. He saw that I had strange abilities and directed them in the right way. But when I started to 'see,' I did not wish it. There was nothing I could do. I had to fly, and I had to fall from rocks. It was a strange start to life, and very hard." Impatiently she held out her hand for another glass of *arkhi*.

"My father liked me and spoiled me. He had two horses. One was white, the other yellow. How I loved to gallop on those horses. How I loved the speed. No one could stop me once I was on those horses. Then one day an old man came to see my father with two skins of *arkhi* in his saddlebags. He asked me if I would be his daughter-in-law. I ran away, but a mustached man came and took me home anyhow. My husband was a very great hunter. He was a caravan guide, and brought red salt from a faraway sea."

Here Doc whispered to me that Samga was probably referring to the caravans that brought salt out of China across the Tien Shan Mountains. Samga took no notice and continued her monologue until suddenly Doc looked startled and interrupted his running translation to tell me an amazed comment of his own.

"Right in the middle of what she was saying, she changed the subject. She just said to me casually, and in passing, that there is a pair of spectacles at my home, and I don't know who owns them. Then she went straight back into her stories about her childhood."

I knew why Doc was taken aback. Ten days earlier when I had been unpacking our expedition kitbags in his apartment in Ulaan Baatar, I found a pair of spectacles. I handed them to Doc, who always wore glasses. But he gave them back, saying they did not belong to him. Indeed he had thought the glasses must belong to Paul or to me. But they did not, and so the mysterious spectacles had been put to one side. Neither of us had given the matter another thought, though in a country as poor as Mongolia it was very unlikely that someone would not try to recover a pair of lost glasses. It was only a trivial detail, and how Samga had known it was an utter mystery. Of course it proved nothing. It could have been a lucky guess or a trick of the trade. I had deliberately refrained from asking Samga to demonstrate any of her supposed powers, and she herself obviously attached no significance to her remark. She took it for granted that the unclaimed spectacles were there.

Her *ger* was very modest and unpretentious. There was no special paraphernalia for a shaman. It was sparsely furnished, and the roof wheel was held up by a single untrimmed branch stuck in the ground. There was nothing unusual or occult about the place. It was a very plain workaday *ger*, now filled to bursting with wide-eyed Tuva children and Samga's immediate surviving relatives. The teacher grandson wanted to make quite sure that we appreciated Samga's talents. "She sees into the future," he said, as if he were describing the quality of her cooking. "She foretold Brezhnev's death more than ten days before it happened, and she knows when she will have a visitor. She tells us in advance. She can also say in which direction certain events are taking place, and what is happening in those faraway regions even when she herself is right here at home."

"Can you foretell anything about your own family?" I asked her. I avoided asking the obvious question of whether she had foreseen our own visit, as I did not want to risk offending her by too obvious cross-examination.

"No," said Samga. "The only thing that I was able to see ahead was the death of my mother, when and how it would happen."

The *arkhi* was having its effect, and she was growing more talkative, wandering from subject to subject.

"I never wanted to have this ability, and now I would like to leave and die. But people won't let me go. They keep me here. They need me. When anyone is exhausted or weary like a wasted dog, I will fly to them and help them. When my spirit is strong, I can fly through the whole valley and see into everyone, and whether they are worried or in need."

"Is there any time when your power is at the strongest?" I asked.

"On the ninth day of each month* or on the New Year."

Her grandson intervened to ask if we wished to see her conduct the shaman's ceremony before she got too tired. "Only if she wants to," I answered. "If she is too exhausted, it is not necessary. Maybe this is not the right time or a suitable place for her."

But Samga impatiently brushed aside my hesitation. She was happy to show us how she worked. "Only bright light or electricity disturb my work and make it more difficult to concentrate," she said. "But I am sorry that I no longer have all the right equipment. The shaman's tambourine drum which I inherited from my father wore out a long time ago, and I have never replaced it. Also I once had a shaman's special dress but that too fell to rags, and I am too old to need another. I can work without them. All I have left is my cap and flail."

She rose to her feet and her daughter helped her to put on the

*Nine is the Mongol lucky number; seven is unlucky.

headdress of a shamaness. It was a cross between a headscarf and a
closely fitting cowl, with a long flap down the neck and a row of
pearly buttons sewn across the top. Its strange feature was the heavy
coarse black fringe which hung across Samga's forehead like a badly
made wig worn back to front. The effect was to turn the rather homely
Old Woman into a sinister creature like a witch from a Grimms' fairy
tale.

But the Tuva children were not the least frightened. As far as they
were concerned, here was their great-grandmother behaving as she
regularly did. They waited for the seance to begin. Samga began to
mumble and chant rhythmically, swaying back and forth. She shuffled
a few steps to one corner of the *ger*, still chanting, and sank down to
her knees. She knelt with her body rocking back and forth, and her
head turning from side to side. In her hand was a small flail, about a
foot long and topped with short strips of white rag. Among the strips,
attached to the top of the handle, was a round ball of crystal or glass.
As she chanted, Samga flicked the flail back and forth rhythmically.
Occasionally she would stop and rest a while, and draw breath before
taking up the steady chant again. Abruptly she halted. Her daughter
was behind her. Still kneeling, Samga put her hand behind her back,
and her daughter placed in it a lighted pipe. Samga put the pipe to
her mouth, drew a mouthful of smoke, and blew it out toward the
corner of the *ger*. Then, peremptorily, she thrust the pipe behind her
back and it was taken again by her daughter. Painfully and slowly,
the Old Woman climbed to her feet, took a small ladle of milk from
her daughter, and threw its contents up into the air as an offering.
Three more times she repeated the action, praying and making offerings in each corner of the *ger*. Then she sank back on the bed and for
a moment or two began to tremble and shake as if in a trance. Her
tremors could have been caused by tiredness or they may have been
pretense. I could not be sure.

Unexpectedly she stood up again and went to the door, stepping
outside into the bright sunlight, though she had said that bright light
disturbed her concentration. Opposite the door, about five yards
away, was a glowing brazier. Samga knelt before it, crouching down
so her face was almost on her knees, and again took up the crooning
chant, still flicking the flail back and forth. Her daughter came forward and sprinkled incense on the coals and then from a kettle filled

with mare's milk poured out libations into a glass and again threw the drops of milk to the spirits of the sky and hearth fire. Rising, Samga hobbled slowly back to the door of the *ger* and went back inside, followed by her daughter carrying the smoking brazier. Finally Samga made a second circuit of the room, this time stopping in front of each adult, passing the incense under their nose, and shaking her flail before their face. Pulling back the flail she thrust her face into the strips of rag and inhaled with a deep snuffling grunt as if to suck out the air from the flail. Finally she returned to her original position, sank back on the bed, and sat exhausted.

I had seen enough to convince myself that even if Samga was not a fully skilled shamaness, she was no fake and that she had acquired authentic shaman behavior patterns, most likely by imitation or instruction. She had entered and left the *ger* in a manner that was genuine shaman behavior. Both times when she passed through the door, she had turned around and had gone through backward. Yet when I had first seen her by the *ger*, cleaning the cooking pot, she had gone indoors normally, facing forward. When she was in her role as a shamaness, she had reversed the process, just as—to a lesser degree—she had acted in reverse when she insisted on taking the pipe from behind her back instead of accepting it from in front of her. Reversed actions were a mark of shamans down through the centuries. Shamans lived partly in our world and partly in the other-world. When they were in the other-world they communed with the spirits, and everything back on the mortal realm became upside-down, inside-out, or back-to-front in a mirror of reality. Some shamans wore their clothing inside out and their gloves with the fur inside, for example. The stiff hairy fringe sticking out from Samga's headdress, I now realized, could be seen as if her hair were growing in the wrong direction.

I felt there was nothing more that I could reasonably expect of the Old Woman without overstepping the bounds of her family's invitation and risk giving offense. Samga's tale of how she had become a shamaness was certainly plausible. Her lifetime dated back to the days when shamanism was rife in Mongolia, and she could well have been trained by a bygone generation of shamans. Her basic ritual, which she had demonstrated, had shown every appearance of being genuine, and it was only incidental that she had revealed one fact—

the extra pair of spectacles—that she could not have been reasonably expected to know.

Indeed I was to remain completely unaware of another strange facet of our encounter until two months later when I was back at home. Before she began her seance, she had stated that two factors interfered with her shaman's power—bright light and the presence of electricity. While we were packed together with her family in the little *ger*, I had used a miniature camera to film her as she went through the shaman ritual. Although there was a semi-gloom in the tent, I had no portable lights so there was neither bright light nor the electricity to power them, and Samga would not have been disturbed. But the small camera *did* use electricity, and that I had not told Samga. The camera was powered by six AA-size batteries and, unknown to me, it had earlier developed a minor electrical fault. A condenser had failed and the miniature drive motor was transmitting a high-frequency spark that was being recorded on the film soundtrack as a crackle like the sound of frying bacon. When I eventually came to process the film and check the result, I found that this sound of electrical interference occurred consistently in the material that I had filmed before and after my visit to Samga. But in the intervening time, when she was in front of the camera, the sound was noticeably muted. The interference was still there, but it was less pronounced. My immediate conclusion was that either this was another coincidence like the story of the missing spectacles in Doc's apartment, or that in some odd way Samga's shaman powers, which she knew were antipathetic to electricity, conflicted with electrical pulses near her and suppressed them.

But this was later speculation, and I had not visited Samga to make a crude test of her "magical powers." Indeed, I felt it would have been impertinent to do so. Instead I had observed something I found both convincing and central to my quest to the survival of the world of Genghis Khan, and that was the obvious fact that her family and her community accepted the "Old Woman" as a shamaness, without any hint that she was counterfeit or taking advantage of the situation. The ultimate validity of a soothsayer's role is that, in the eyes of the community, he or she is held to possess special powers that can be consulted and trusted. And in the case of Samga there was no doubt that this was the case. Ultimately it was this conviction of the people who knew her that made Samga the guardian of the shaman tradition dating back to the time of Genghis Khan.

The family would not let us go until Paul had taken their photographs. They lined up beaming, with Samga now wearing a Tuva national costume and holding a Tuva baby in swaddling clothes. Paul, who had been as favorably impressed as I had been with Samga's bona fides, asked one final question: What advice would she give the younger generation? She answered without hesitation. "I would tell them, respect nature, which is all about you! Look after the rivers and streams because they supply the water you drink! Look after the sky and the air which gives you heat! And take care of the land because it feeds you!" It occurred to me that the doctrine of a Tuva shamaness was timeless.

16

The Eternal Icon

My main purpose in coming to Mongolia had been to see how much of the traditional way of life survived, and I had not been disappointed. Almost a month had passed since Paul and I had ridden out of the gates of the lamasery of Erdenzu with our Mongol companions and the herd of remounts and had circled around the stone tortoise of Karakorum in honor of the memory of the empire founded by Genghis Khan. In that time we had seen the Hangay massif flourishing in its summer glory in contrast to our earlier experience of the half-frozen Hentei, had met with Kazakh eagle hunters, had talked with a shamaness, had stumbled across the Black Death, and had witnessed the revival of a religion led by 70-year-old lamas who had escaped the great purges of the thirties.

After our interview with Samga, I returned to Ulaan Baatar with Paul and Doc and we tried to find out how Ariunbold, Bayar, and Delger were getting on. But there was no news. No one we spoke to had heard anything, and the riders must still have been toiling across the arid lowlands, because it took them much longer to reach Bayan Olgei than the original forecast. It was not until January the following year that Doc wrote to me to say that the riders had eventually arrived in Bayan Olgei some time in September. He did not know the precise date, because he had seen little of Ariunbold, but he judged that at least three men had shown the tenacity to finish out the season's ride. I agreed with his verdict. It was a fine effort. However, their average speed was only two-thirds of what Ariunbold and Gerel had earlier anticipated, and I hoped that they would take this fact into account if they ever attempted the far more ambitious plan to ride to Western Europe.

Ariunbold himself sent a courtesy card in the New Year, but he made no mention of his experiences or whether the great transcontinental ride would still take place. I gleaned a little more information from a roll of film that Bayar sent. He had shot the film during the ride to Bayan Olgei, and there was a scene showing that they had been obliged to have shoes fitted to their horses. This was against their earlier ideas, and it appeared that the job was done with little finesse. The horses were pinioned to the ground, and the makeshift shoes were hammered on with crude nails by a local man, not a member of the riding team. I judged that the hooves of Mongol horses were tough enough to stand this treatment once or twice, but if it was done repeatedly they would be lamed on a really long-distance ride.

From Doc's letter I also learned that the gift horses had been left in Bayan Olgei for the winter. Presumably the riders had set aside their prejudices about the horse-eating Kazakhs, because it was unlikely they would have found a Mongol herdsman to shelter the animals. Thus it seemed that they had learned one lesson of expedition-making: they should trust the goodwill and cooperation of the people they met. But Doc could provide no information about whether Gerel was prepared to rejoin Ariunbold, and whether the two of them, with Bayar and Delger, would continue the following year across the Altai and enter Kazakhstan on the next stage of the long road to France. Seen from abroad, the prospects looked increasingly doubtful. Civil and economic chaos was spreading across the territories of the Soviet Union, which they would have to cross, and it was difficult to imagine the governments of the various Soviet republics having much time to attend to a small party of Mongol horsemen riding across their territory.

In Mongolia, too, there was much that was undecided and problematical. The nation was facing a chill wind of change. That summer when Paul and I rode over the countryside was the last in which the Mongolian People's Republic basked in the old certainties. The snug days of Soviet coaching and economic assistance had drawn to a close. Troops and munitions were not the only contribution Moscow intended to remove from Mongolian soil. Soviet economic aid was slashed as the government tackled more serious priorities closer to home. Very little aid was available to send to Mongolia, which had once received more Soviet assistance per capita than even Cuba, the most conspicuous and favored godchild of the Eastern Bloc.

To make matters worse for the Mongols, the Soviet government was demanding repayment of huge amounts of earlier aid, which was now classified as loans, not grants, and which Mongolia was patently unable to repay. The immediate penalty was a sudden cutback in the amount of cheap fuel which had been shipped regularly into Mongolia from the USSR, and on which Mongolia depended utterly. The entire transport system of Mongolia fell into paralysis, and the distribution network on which the country—especially the capital—relied, ceased to flow. So an incongruous situation arose: a country that had more head of livestock—whether counted by sheep or cattle or horses or goats—than it had people could not supply the population of its capital with meat. Vegetables of course were not to be had.

Doc wrote me to say that the citizens of Ulaan Baatar had been issued ration cards. By midwinter mutton had vanished from the state food stores, and small portions of camel flesh were being peddled on the black market. Flour had become virtually unobtainable and was being hoarded illegally. Reports appeared in the Western press telling how housewives in Ulaan Baatar were carefully sweeping the stairs of their apartment blocks to wipe out traces of spilled flour that would be telltales of their black-market stockpiles.

Suddenly a country that had previously exported significant quantities of surplus food was facing a real threat of famine. The government sent an appeal to Japan for humanitarian aid and doled out bottles of *arkhi* instead of food. The grim reports of life in the capital emphasized the good sense of our friendly Mr. Gombo, the *somon* official who had been determined to improve the lot of the *arats* locally so that they could stay in the countryside and lead a decent life there rather than having to move to an already overcrowded and overstretched Ulaan Baatar.

Historically, in times of confusion, uncertainty, and stress, the ordinary Mongol has always clung even more staunchly to the memory of Genghis Khan. The rumor Prjevalski heard in the 1870s that Genghis Khan would rise again was a reaction by the people of Inner

Mongolia to centuries of Chinese domination. They believed that
Genghis Khan was physically present, in the flesh, in his tomb in the
Ordos where lay "the figure of a man apparently asleep, although no
mortal can account for this phenomenon." Similarly in 1911, when
the Mongols of Outer Mongolia rebelled against their Chinese overlords, there was the hope that Genghis Khan would come again,
riding to their rescue. Nor has it mattered to the Mongols in times of
turmoil that the memory of Genghis Khan was invoked by foreigners.
When the "Mad Baron" Ungern-Sternberg claimed that he was the
reincarnation of Genghis Khan, even though he was a white-skinned
Balt, he won the support of many of the leading lamas who then ruled
in Urga.

A generation later a historical novel appeared in France with the
title *The Blue Standard of the Blue Mongols*. The book portrayed the
world of Genghis Khan as peopled by knights and ladies where feats
of derring-do were performed by Mongols with superhuman talents.
Though the novel was undiluted romance written by a foreigner, it
was hugely popular when translated into Mongol and distributed
among a people whose fairy stories and folk wisdom still drew heavily
on the alleged sayings and deeds of Genghis Khan.

The glamour of Genghis Khan's memory still appeals to the ordinary *arats* in a way that it was easier for me to appreciate now that I
had spent some time riding with the herdsmen. Their lives were so
exacting that any touch of color would have been welcome, but it
was equally important that they retained the belief that they represented the true Mongol lifestyle. The "real" Mongol, they felt, did
not live in Ulaan Baatar but out in the countryside with the herds.
So whether in the Hentei or in the Hangay, whether among cattle-
herders or among camel-breeders, most of the *arats* we met seemed
to approve of the theory behind our trip—to ride across Mongolia and
evoke the time of Genghis Khan and the medieval courier tradition.

Strangely enough, the same *arats* also gave the impression that they
were less interested in the expedition's aim to travel outside Mongolia
and on to Europe. They were more interested in the route it would
take within Mongolia, how it was to go from one *aymag* to the next,
and how we had got on in the places we had already visited. Their
curiosity made me realize that the *arats*, though they appeared mobile
and semi-nomadic, in fact lived quite restricted lives. They did not

travel widely within Mongolia but tended to stay within the orbit of their *somon* or *aymag*, with an occasional trip to Ulaan Baatar. They scarcely knew their own country at all, with all its great diversity, apart from what they had seen on television in the *somon* centers. The nostalgia for Genghis Khan was perhaps part of their need for a common Mongol identity, a point of contact with fellow Mongols from other areas whom they did not know.

Like the great heroes of other nations Genghis Khan was a Mongol's natural symbol of a glorious past. But his special status, I felt, was reinforced by the tendency to ancestor-worship that has flourished in Mongolia as long as records exist. Rubruck noticed it everywhere he traveled. Ancestor-worship then became interleaved with the belief in reincarnation, the central tenet of lamaism. The possibility of the regeneration of political leaders was taken seriously at least until the beginning of this century. When the eighth Khutukhtu died, the Mongolian People's Revolutionary Party felt obliged to announce that the line of Khutukhtu Reincarnations had finally come to an end. To convince the pious country folk, they concocted a false legend that said an eighth Khutukhtu would be the last.

By contrast, no such finality has ever been applied to the memory of Genghis Khan, rather the reverse. Even when his commemoration as the Great Ancestor was discouraged in Mongolia itself, it was kept alive elsewhere. Of all the nations adjacent to Mongolia, the Chinese had most to rue that he had ever lived. Yet, when it suited them, they adapted their previous policy, which had sought to emasculate the Mongol military threat by turning the Mongols away from their traditional loyalties, and restored the icon of Genghis Khan for their own purposes. In 1939 the Kuomintang government removed his supposed "relics" from their resting place in the Ordos and took them for safety to Kansu Province. Ten years later they moved them farther west for additional security. When the relics eventually fell into the hands of the Chinese communists, the communists publicly put them back into the Genghis Khan sanctuary and promoted the building as a place of pilgrimage for the Mongols of Inner Mongolia. Ironically, it was the Chinese who would not let Genghis Khan rest, and today the notion of allegiance to the memory of the Great Ancestor draws strength from that long, virtually uninterrupted tradition.

Thus the real gauge of Genghis Khan's abiding appeal among the Mongols is that his cult has managed to survive the seventy years of official disapproval under Soviet-inspired communist rule. Propaganda and modernization have failed to expunge his memory or diminish his importance even though the entire social and economic fabric of the country was transformed, not necessarily for the worse. Traveling in Mongolia in search of the people's cultural heritage, I had witnessed that the effects of Soviet tutelage were often noxious. Language, native art, regional diversity, traditional skills, and long-held beliefs had all been eroded. But this was decline in matters that were of particular interest to me, and it was also clear that the achievements of Soviet intervention were remarkable. Soviet advisers, Soviet technology, and Soviet training had redefined the backward, lackluster country that Prjevalski and Beatrix Bulstrode knew. For example, Beatrix Bulstrode came up with the eccentric theory that Mongols seldom washed because they believed that too much association with water in this life meant that they would be born again as fish in the next. But the "dirty Mongols" whose total lack of hygiene revolted her now scarcely exist.

Paul and I had remarked on the daily grubbiness of life—at mealtimes in particular—but seen in the context of our surroundings dirt was unavoidable. It is hard to remain clean when you are handling horses day after day and living rough. Instances of ingrained and lazy squalor were more obvious because they were comparatively rare in the countryside, though the same could not be said of the depressing life in the city. It was noticeable that if ever we made camp near a lake or a running stream, the herdsmen who rode with us headed off with soap and towel to wash when the day's work was done.

Meanwhile, on a far more serious level, the Soviet effort had produced extraordinary results. The raging syphilis, which affected as much as 90 percent of all Mongols at the end of the 19th century, has been virtually eradicated with Soviet medical help, though tuberculosis remains a problem. Literacy has soared. In 1928 only 9 percent of male Mongols could read and write, and less than half of 1 percent of all women. Books, teachers, methods, and materials were imported wholesale from the Soviet Union, and basic adult literacy is to all intents and purposes total. Set against such vast strides in health and education, the impoverishment of a language and the near-loss of a native script seem small penalties if those trends can be reversed with a return to genuine Mongol national independence. In the meantime the Soviet intervention checked the ebb tide of hopelessness and apathy that was draining away Mongolia's very existence and threatening, in the words of the historian Charles Bawden, to reduce the Mongols "to the level of the bushmen of South Africa—mere interesting remnants of a lost civilisation and otherwise of no account."

Most valuable of all is that Soviet protection has been the geographical salvation of "Outer Mongolia." From long before the time of Ch'ang Ch'un, Mongolia's natural overlord was China with its huge, industrious, and expanding population. Beijing is far closer to Ulaan Baatar than Moscow. It was a Chinese army that razed Karakorum, and it was a Chinese-based dynasty, the Manchu, that reduced the Mongolian nobility, the *noyans*, to the state of vassals. Over the past fifty years China would have spilled over Mongolia, as it has into Tibet, but for the Soviet presence there. Ethnically and culturally, it was against all natural laws that Russia rather than China should dominate Mongolia, but that contradiction has meant that Mongolia survived, partially Russified but at least with space to breathe.

By contrast, the Chinese part of the old Mongol world—the misleadingly named Mongolian Autonomous Region, which is essentially the old Inner Mongolia—has little trace of genuine Mongol autonomy. It is estimated that by 1954 Chinese settlers already outnumbered native Mongols three to one, and the Chinese immigration has gone on ever since. Chinese settlers have moved in and occupied any territory that could be made arable and have pushed the Mongol herdsmen to the marginal lands where the Mongol *arats* have become ranchers rather than semi-nomads. Culturally, as Mongols in their own Republic will tell you wistfully, much has survived in Inner Mongolia that has been lost in their own country, particularly language, folklore, and customs. But that survival has largely been the result of neglect by the Chinese authorities, who were not prepared to apply the same amount of resources as the Russians in their sphere of influence.

So the Mongols of Inner Mongolia subsist, living under pressures far greater than their more independent cousins across the border. Understandably, some of them aspire to leave Inner Mongolia and migrate to Mongolia itself. It is precisely the same yearning that

Prjevalski found a century earlier, and still the name of Genghis Khan is invoked as the common link.

The real cost of Soviet patronage in Mongolia itself, however, has been the sterilization of Mongol leadership. Just as the Mongol princes in Manchu times were obliged to travel to Peking to pay tribute and stay at the Chinese court to learn Chinese ways and probably amass a debt to Chinese merchants as well, so the past three generations of Mongol leaders have been supplicants at the Soviet court. In Moscow, and to a lesser extent at the Irkutsk in Siberia where Mongols are encouraged to attend university, the chosen leaders of Mongolia have been reduced to the role of sleepwalkers following the Soviet dream.

There is a conspicuous parallel between the complaints that outsiders aimed at the rule of the lamas in the late nineteenth century and the situation revealed when the first Westerners began to travel in the modern Mongolia of the People's Revolutionary Party. The earlier visitors noted that lamaism was an imported faith—like Soviet communism—and that it had flourished in such isolation that it had lost touch with reality. The lama leadership, like their communist successors, was opposed to the introduction of liberal education or new scientific teaching. Lamas taught that the earth was flat, just as in 1990 the Party theorists in Ulaan Baatar were still preaching the "all-conquering theory of Marx-Leninism," to cite the country's constitution. For thirty years the Chairman of the Mongolian Presidium, with his personality cult and his pretensions to infallibility in political thought, came closer and closer in character and function to the priest-king who also surrounded himself with a vast state hierarchy and spent the people's taxes on monumental works such as the estimated quarter-million rubles lavished on a new temple to give thanks for the healing of his sight, which was itself a fallacy.

Set against such aberrations, the nostalgia for Genghis Khan seems at least harmless, if somewhat contradictory. More sophisticated Mongols appreciate the awkward fact that the hero figure of the Mongols is viewed by the outside world as a symbol of destruction and mayhem. The popular idol of Mongolia is to the rest of the world an arch-villain, and thoughtful Mongols take pains to emphasize Genghis Khan's national role and gloss over his record as the great conqueror. They praise his statesmanship, his vision, the laws he promulgated, and his folk wisdom. Very rarely, if ever, do they refer to any of his deeds outside the present boundaries of Mongolia. But Genghis Khan the warrior is difficult to separate from Genghis Khan the statesman and lawgiver, and had it not been for his military conquests history would have paid little attention to a tribal chief who united the Mongol people but never led them beyond the confines of their Central Asian homeland.

It has been a very long time since the Mongols ranged about the countryside with their flocks and herds to the same extent as in the days of Genghis Khan. First the Manchu authorities ordered the Mongol princes to keep their people in defined areas. Then the lama-series acquired such an onerous proportion of the country's lands and flocks that pure nomadism became impossible even if many of the *arats* had not been tied as serfs to the lamaseries themselves. Yet in the time of Genghis Khan long-distance, large-scale migrations had been exceptional. In the heartland of Mongolia, in the well-favored regions of the Hentei and Hangay, the herdsmen would not have needed to shift their animals between cold-season and hot-season pastures any farther than the modern *arat* now moves between sum-mer and winter grazing according to the directives of the work brigade he serves. He may change the location of his *ger* only twice a year, where his father and grandfather shifted camp four or six times to follow the pasture. But I had seen how the nomadic features remain the same: the lack of a permanent home, the portability and simplicity of possessions, personal wealth however small calculated almost en-tirely in numbers of livestock, a certain attitude toward the values of herding life with its sense of freedom, individual responsibility, and the self-sufficiency of family units scattered widely across the vast land.

Among the *arats* I had found the qualities I had expected: hardiness, endurance, and hospitality. The ordinary Mongol herdsman still lives in a harsh and demanding environment that demands his perseverance and physical stamina and gives little in return. For many years the West's leading expert on Mongolia was the scholar-traveler Owen Lattimore, who coined the neat phrase that "the poor nomad is the pure nomad." His judgment can be applied to the *arats* of modern Mongolia. The country is too poor to have overcome the basic limita-tions of herding life in the Dead Heart of Asia, and the *arat* is the exponent of what is in many ways a medieval lifestyle. He and his family now dress in factory-made boots and clothes, eat off cheap imported crockery, and use plastic products all the time. But the clothes and the crockery are little different from the chinaware and cloth that his forebears purchased from the caravans out of China, and the felt tent he lives in, the saddle he uses day after day, the ropes of rawhide and twisted hair, the crude metal bits he fits into his horses' mouths are homemade and scarcely changed from their medieval patterns. His most prized possessions—the pink-topped snuff bottle of jade, the ornate knife and steel, the fancy brocade jacket— still come from Chinese sources, just as they have always done.

The environment has locked him in a world that is almost unimaginable for most outsiders. Charles Bawden cites the memoirs of a government official, *Tales of an Old Secretary*, published in Ulaan Baatar in 1956, which recount how as a young *arat* he was caught in a *dzud*, the Mongol word for a natural calamity such as the late-season blizzard which freezes to death the emaciated cattle. When the lad was thirteen years old, he had been sent out to watch over the family's horse-herd when it began to snow. Soon the snowflakes were falling so heavily that

> it was just like the depth of night. I groped around as if I were blind, unable to see the head of my mount, let alone the horses I was guarding. . . . Frozen ice tinkled on the body of my mount. He couldn't keep from shivering, and made off neighing in some direction. Snow and ice were clinging to my outer clothing and I couldn't even manage to knock it off. My mouth and nose were stiff with cold, and my hands and feet were nearly dropping off. Though I had on my furry goatskin overcoat I couldn't keep warm. It was all I could do to think of surviving, and I settled down in a sheltered hollow wondering if I would ever outlive the blizzard and see my dear mother again. I shivered and shook. . . .

The young man survived, but he never forgot his childhood sufferings. Neither did Choybalsan, the country's malevolent dictator, whose family was so destitute that his mother placed him as a child in a lamasery where he was so badly treated that he ran away and preferred to live as a waif in the squalid streets of Urga.

I had never doubted that I would still find the horse-handling skills that had made the Mongol cavalry the finest in the medieval world. The *arat* is a master of horsemanship, but in a style that would shock or mystify the Western purist. He has a rough-and-ready way with his horses because he lives with them constantly, drinks their milk, depends on them for his transport. Simply put, the average scrawny Mongol horse is an integral part of his life, and there is no room for sentiment any more than a dairy farmer would cherish his milk cows. Of course the fastest and bravest riding horses are valued. The champion long-distance runners of Naadam are pampered and admired, and even the ordinary entrant in a Naadam race has its tail plaited and its forelock done up in a Mohican topknot that gives it a jaunty and surprised air. A 16th-century Chinese author, Hsiao Ta-heng, wrote that the Mongols

> love good horses more than they love other animals. If they see a good horse they will gladly give three or four other horses for it. If they can obtain it, they will caress it.*

But for the famed Mongol horses time has stood still or, like the culture of the people, has even gone backward. The Naadam champions would not shine in international long-distance competition. Other breeds have long ago been developed for more stamina or speed. Only in their hardiness are the Mongol horses still special. They survive where others would die and, like the Mongol traditions in Inner Mongolia, that quality has persisted from necessity and neglect, not from deliberate policy. When the great horse-herds were privately owned, there was more interest in breeding and improvement. With communal ownership, the sense of striving was lost. Significantly, it is now proposed that each herdsman should be allowed to own more private horses. Seventy-five head of stock per family has been proposed, and a Mongol Horse Society has been founded to improve and promote the breed.

There were two puzzles for which I could find no explanation. How was it, I often wondered, that a people who were so addicted to alcohol should have achieved so much? In the heyday of their success the Mongols were renowned for their drunkenness. Kara-

---

*Cited in C. R. Bawden's *The Modern History of Mongolia*, Kegan Paul International, London and New York 1968, and derived from Henry Serruys *Pei-lou foungsu, Les Coutumes des Esclaves Septentrionaux* in Monumenta Serica, 10 (1945).

korum seemed to swim in an alcoholic haze. After the famous theo-
logical debate between the lamas and the Nestorians, Rubruck
observed that the priests of both persuasions had sat down together
for a heavy drinking session which lasted the rest of the day. And
Rubruck emerged from his final interview with the Great Khan
Möngke suspicious that the supreme ruler of the Mongols had been
drunk throughout the session. Yet despite this constant toping the
medieval Mongol machine continued to function, whereas today it is
all too clear that alcoholism is a major problem among the country
folk and in the city.

The second puzzle was where and when the Mongol character lost
direction. *Margaash*, the Mongol word for tomorrow, has earned
the same connotation as *mañana*. Complaints of margaashism are a
commonplace in Soviet reports of the difficulties of working in modern Mongolia, and yet an outstanding feature of the Mongol empire
was the promptness and efficiency of the Mongols themselves. Their
army went to war on the very day that a military campaign had
been planned six months earlier. A posthorse system with a million
remounts could not have been run unless all the chores had been done
on time.

The only possible answer to these puzzles seems to lie, yet again,
with the extraordinary, domineering figure of Genghis Khan himself.
The character, toughness, and horsemanship of his people are not
enough to explain the phenomenon of the Mongol Empire. Nor can
the success of Mongol arms be ascribed to the weakness of its neighbors. China and the great empire of Khwarazm were formidable
opponents. The brilliance of Genghis Khan is the only explanation
for so much that happened in the imperial heyday, and his genius
goes much further than mere military skill. In many ways he remains
an enigma, despite the invaluable insight from *The Secret History of
the Mongols*. He must have been one of the world's great natural
leaders. He was 42 when he was recognized as the leader of the
"people who live in felt tents." His childhood was so beset with
troubles, and his opportunities for advancement so slight, that it took
him half his adult life to stitch together an alliance of what would
have seemed very insignificant tribes. Yet nearly everything flowed
from the decisions he made as an obscure tribal leader: the men he
picked to serve him, the military system he inaugurated with its

royal bodyguard and professional horse-army, the personal awe he commanded. On that foundation he built a world empire in only 20 years.

His military talent is manifest. Of his campaign against the Khwarazm Shah, Liddell Hart remarked that

> in these harmoniously executed operations we see each of the principles of war—direction, mobility, security, concentration, and surprise— woven into a Nemesis-like web in which are trapped the doomed armies of the Shah.

In civil matters it was Genghis Khan's direct descendants, particularly his sons Ögodei and Möngke, who built up the structures of the huge Mongol world empire. But they took their direction from the principles laid down by their extraordinary father, whose sayings— apocryphal or otherwise—were faithfully combined into a collection of *biligs*, or aphorisms, summarizing the wisdom of the Great Mongol. Those maxims were still being invoked by regimes that endured for 150 years in China, almost that long in Persia, and in one form or another for three centuries on the steppes of Russia. It was a remarkable homage from a small nation to a tribal chief who, it is said, preferred to dress as a simple herdsman all his life.

Genghis Khan was already being treated as a god when Rubruck was in Karakorum. The Franciscan friar thought it a blasphemy that the letter he was told to carry back to King Louis of France from Möngke should begin with the phrase "This is the order of the everlasting God. In Heaven there is only one God; on earth there is only one lord, Genghis Khan. This is the word of the son of God."

Seven and a half centuries later, that divine aura still clings to the memory of the Father of the Nation and illuminates a modern cult worship. In the summer of our Mongolian ride in the Hentei and the Hangay a great conference was called to ponder the subtleties of *The Secret History of the Mongols*. To the learned professors and eminent Mongolists who assembled in Ulaan Baatar from Japan, China, the Soviet Union, the United States, and Europe it was a chance to exchange ideas on the intricacies of language, folklore, provenance, and interpretation. But to many ordinary Mongols it was something more. They saw it as international recognition of their long-neglected hero and his proper reinstatement in history. A feature of the conference ceremonies was a stone pillar that was to be erected at the spot where the unknown scribe who wrote *The Secret History* had penned the final lines. Some of the artists who had ridden with us in the Hentei had been carving the stone shaft that would be unveiled on that day. So excited was the public response to the occasion that the government had to forbid people from traveling to the site without special permission. Thousands evaded the prohibition. The crowds that assembled at the pillar exceeded even those of the Great Birthday Party in Ulaan Baatar. They circled the stone in a hysterical mass, moving clockwise as around a sacred *obo*. Next morning they came singly or in twos and threes to pray openly to the graven image on the column.

So perhaps the real test of Genghis Khan's extraordinary status in the minds of Mongols in the twentieth century has yet to be applied: what will happen if the genuine tomb of Genghis Khan is ever found? How will the Mongols then react? On the one hand there will come the scientific response, based on the principles of Soviet education and Mongolia's desire to seem modern and enlightened to the rest of the world. That response will surely call for a controlled and documented excavation of the grave, followed by detailed and scholarly study of all the contents.

On the other hand, there will be the more mystic reaction, which already obliges the archaeological search by the Japanese–Mongol Three Rivers Expedition to tread delicately. They have promised not to disturb the soil, only to survey the surface. But what if their array of sensors and probes locates the underground chamber which reason tells them holds the corpse of Genghis Khan? Will the Mongols allow a god to be disinterred? If so, it will certainly be only Mongols who will be allowed to disturb the tomb. Or will today's Mongols respect the wishes of the Father of the Nation and let him rest on the slopes of Burkhan Khaldun, the Mountain of the Shaman Spirit, as he had wished? After riding with the *arats* and observing their nostalgic respect for Genghis Khan, I am sure that even if the tomb is found and excavated, the events of the excavation and the inventory of what is found within the grave will only add to the myths and folktales about the man who will always be the Great Ancestor.

Index

233